Consuming
Ancient Egypt

UCL

PRESS

Institute of Archaeology

Encounters with
Ancient
Egypt

Titles in the series

ENCOUNTERS WITH ANCIENT EGYPT

Consuming Ancient Egypt

Edited by

Sally MacDonald and Michael Rice

PRESS
Institute of Archaeology

First published in Great Britain 2003 by UCL Press,
an imprint of Cavendish Publishing Limited, The Glass House,
Wharton Street, London WC1X 9PX, United Kingdom
Telephone: + 44 (0)20 7278 8000   Facsimile: + 44 (0)20 7278 8080
Email: info@uclpress.com
Website: www.uclpress.com

Published in the United States by Cavendish Publishing
c/o International Specialized Book Services,
5824 NE Hassalo Street, Portland,
Oregon 97213-3644, USA

Published in Australia by Cavendish Publishing (Australia) Pty Ltd
45 Beach Street, Coogee, NSW 2034, Australia
Telephone: + 61 (2)9664 0909   Facsimile: + 61 (2)9664 5420

© Institute of Archaeology, University College London   2003

British Library Cataloguing in Publication Data
MacDonald, S.
Consuming Ancient Egypt – (Encounters with ancient Egypt)
1 Egypt – Civilization 2 Egypt – History 3 Egypt – in motion pictures
I Title II Rice, M.
932

Library of Congress Cataloguing in Publication Data
Data available

ISBN 1-84472-003-9

1 3 5 7 9 10 8 6 4 2

Designed and typeset by Style Photosetting, Mayfield, East Sussex
Email: style@pavilion.co.uk

Printed and bound in Great Britain

Cover illustration: View of colossal figures in the interior of the 'Egyptian Hall', Crystal Palace,
at Sydenham (ca. 1854) (Day and Son, Lithographers Company, Christmas 1854: pl. IV).

Series Editor's Foreword

This series of eight books derives from the proceedings of a conference entitled 'Encounters with Ancient Egypt', held at the Institute of Archaeology, University College London (UCL) in December 2000. Since then, many new chapters have been especially commissioned for publication, and those papers originally provided for the conference and now selected for publication have been extensively revised and rewritten.

There are many noteworthy features of the books. One is the overall attempt to move the study of Ancient Egypt into the mainstream of recent advances in archaeological and anthropological practice and interpretation. This is a natural outcome of London University's Institute of Archaeology, one of the largest archaeology departments in the world, being the academic host. Drawing on the Institute's and other related resources within UCL, the volumes in the series reflect an extraordinary degree of collaboration between the series editor, individual volume editors, contributors and colleagues. The wide range of approaches to the study of the past, pursued in such a vibrant scholarly environment as UCL's, has encouraged the scholars writing in these volumes to consider their disciplinary interests from new perspectives. All the chapters presented here have benefited from wide-ranging discussion between experts from diverse academic disciplines, including art history, papyrology, anthropology, archaeology and Egyptology, and subsequent revision.

Egyptology has been rightly criticized for often being insular; the methodologies and conclusions of the discipline have been seen by others as having developed with little awareness of archaeologies elsewhere. The place and role of Ancient Egypt within African history, for example, has rarely been considered jointly by Egyptologists and Africanists. This collaboration provides a stimulating review of key issues and may well influence future ways of studying Egypt. Until now, questions have rarely been asked about the way Egyptians thought of their own past or about non-Egyptian peoples and places. Nor has the discipline of Egyptology explored, in any depth, the nature of its evidence, or the way contemporary cultures regarded Ancient Egypt. The books in this series address such topics.

Another exceptional feature of this series is the way that the books have been designed to interrelate with, inform and illuminate one another. Thus, the evidence of changing appropriations of Ancient Egypt over time, from the classical period to the modern Afrocentrist movement, features in several volumes. One volume explores the actual sources of knowledge about Ancient Egypt before the advent of 'scientific' archaeology, while another explores knowledge of Ancient Egypt after Napoleon Bonaparte's expeditions and the unearthing of Tutankhamun's tomb. The question asked throughout these volumes, however, is how far fascination and knowledge about Ancient Egypt have been based on sources of evidence rather than extraneous political or commercial concerns and interests.

As a result of this series, the study of Ancient Egypt will be significantly enriched and deepened. The importance of the Egypt of several thousands of years ago reaches far beyond the existence of its architectural monuments and extends to its unique role in the history of all human knowledge. Furthermore, the civilization of Ancient Egypt speaks to us with particular force in our own present and has an abiding place in the modern psyche.

As the first paragraph of this Foreword explains, the final stage of this venture began with the receipt and editing of some extensively revised, and in many cases new, chapters – some 95 in all – to be published simultaneously in eight volumes. What it does not mention is the speed with which the venture has been completed: the current UCL Press was officially launched in April 2003. That this series of books has been published to such a high standard of design, professional accuracy and attractiveness only four months later is incredible.

This alone speaks eloquently for the excellence of the staff of UCL Press – from its senior management to its typesetters and designers. Ruth Phillips (Marketing Director) stands out for her youthful and innovative marketing ideas and implementation of them, but most significant of all, at least from the Institute's perspective, is the contribution of Ruth Massey (Editor), who oversaw and supervized all details of the layout and production of the books, and also brought her critical mind to bear on the writing styles, and even the meaning, of their contents.

Individual chapter authors and academic volume editors, both from within UCL and in other institutions, added this demanding project to otherwise full workloads. Although it is somewhat invidious to single out particular individuals, Professor David O'Connor stands out as co-editor of two volumes and contributor of chapters to three despite his being based overseas. He, together with Professor John Tait – also an editor and multiple chapter author in these books – was one of the first to recognize my vision of the original conference as having the potential to inspire a uniquely important publishing project.

Within UCL's Institute of Archaeology, a long list of dedicated staff, academic, administrative and clerical, took over tasks for the Director and Kelly Vincent, his assistant as they wrestled with the preparation of this series. All of these staff, as well as several members of the student body, really deserve individual mention by name, but space does not allow this. However, the books could not have appeared without the particular support of five individuals: Lisa Daniel, who tirelessly secured copyright for over 500 images; Jo Dullaghan, who turned her hand to anything at any time to help out, from re-typing manuscripts to chasing overdue authors; Andrew Gardner, who tracked down obscure and incomplete references, and who took on the complex job of securing and producing correctly scanned images; Stuart Laidlaw, who not only miraculously produced publishable images of a pair of outdoor cats now in Holland and Jamaica, but in a number of cases created light where submitted images revealed only darkness; and Kelly Vincent, who did all of the above twice over, and more – and who is the main reason that publisher and Institute staff remained on excellent terms throughout.

Finally, a personal note, if I may. Never, ever contemplate producing eight complex, highly illustrated books within a four month period. If you *really must*, then make sure you have the above team behind you. Essentially, ensure that you have a partner such as Jane Hubert, who may well consider you to be mad but never questions the essential worth of the undertaking.

Peter Ucko
Institute of Archaeology
University College London
27 July 2003

Contents

Note: No attempt has been made to impose a standard chronology on authors; all dates before 712 BC are approximate. However, names of places, and royal and private names have been standardized.

Contributors

Okasha El Daly has been teaching Egyptology at Birkbeck College, University of London for the past 10 years. After studying Egyptology at Cairo University and undertaking a season of excavation on the Giza Plateau, he worked as a guide and guest lecturer in the tourist industry. He has translated several books on Ancient Egypt into Arabic and has contributed to and co-edited *Desert Travellers from Herodotus to T. E. Lawrence*. He has recently submitted a doctorate at the Institute of Archaeology, University College London, on the contributions of medieval Arab writers to the study of Egyptology.

Fayza Haikal is Professor of Egyptology at the American University in Cairo. In addition to her dissertation on religious papyri from the British Museum, her publications include an analysis of religious and literary documents. Her current research focuses on cultural and linguistic analogies between ancient and modern Egypt through a fresh approach to ancient texts. She received her D Phil from the University of Oxford.

Fekri A. Hassan is Petrie Professor of Archaeology at the Institute of Archaeology, University College London. He is the editor of the *African Archaeological Review*. His current research interests focus on the cultural dynamics of Ancient Egypt, and the strategies of cultural heritage management. His current fieldwork includes an investigation (with B. Barich) of the archaeology of Farafra Oasis and he is the principal investigator at Kafr Hassan Dawood in the eastern Delta. His recent publications include *Droughts, Food and Culture* (2002), *Alexandria's Greco-Roman Museum* (2002) and *Strategic Approaches to Egyptian Cultural Heritage* (2001). He received his PhD from the Southern Methodist University, Dallas, USA.

Jean-Marcel Humbert is Conservateur Général du patrimoine and Deputy Director of the National Maritime Museum in Paris. Alongside his professional work, which has included positions in several museums such as the Louvre, the Musée de l'Armée and the Musée du Légion d'honneur, he has continued his research on 'Egyptomania', both within the Centre National de la Recherche Scientifique, as well as in many universities and museums around the world. Among his many publications are *L'Egyptomanie dans l'art occidental* (1984), *Egyptomania* (1994, with Michael Pantazzi and Christiane Ziegler) and *L'Egyptomanie à l'épreuve de l'archéologie* (ed., 1996). Apart from his many interests, ranging from Egyptology to 'Egyptomania', from museology to museography, from the military to the nautical, as well as the history of art and the history of opera, he has also been responsible for several exhibitions of 'Egyptomania'. He has a Doctorat d'Etat des lettres et sciences humaines and a Doctorat en histoire (Egyptology) from the University of Paris-Sorbonne.

Carter Lupton is Curator of Ancient History at the Milwaukee Public Museum. He has carried out archaeological fieldwork in the US, Europe, Syria and Egypt, the latter with the Hierakonpolis excavation, for which he edited *Nekhen News*. Since 1986 he has been involved with research into mummies through CT-scanning, endoscopy and other approaches. Among his publications are 'Contribution of CT to the Understanding of Egyptian Mummification Technique' (*Proceedings of the First World Congress on Mummy Studies*, 1992) and 'An Historical Study of Two Egyptian

Mummies in the Milwaukee Public Museum' (*Human Remains: conservation, retrieval and analysis,* 2001). He has an MSc in Anthropology from the University of Wisconsin, Milwaukee.

Sally MacDonald is Manager of the Petrie Museum of Egyptian Archaeology, Institute of Archaeology, University College London, and a lecturer on its Museum Studies course. She has worked in archaeology, social history and decorative arts museums. At Croydon she established and ran a museum service that won a number of awards for the innovative use of new technology and marketing. She has also worked at the Geffrye Museum, London, and at Manchester City Art Galleries, and has been responsible for curating several major decorative arts exhibitions. She has published on museum audience development and marketing.

Genny Morris recently completed her MA in Public Archaeology at the Institute of Archaeology, University College London. Her research focused on the portrayal of Ancient Egypt in the media.

Lynn Picknett is a former teacher, journalist, magazine editor and television presenter, and is now a full-time author. She has worked with Clive Prince since 1989 and together they have published several books, including *Turin Shroud – In Whose Image* (1994), *The Templar Revelation* (1997) and *The Stargate Conspiracy* (1999). She is also the author of *Mary Magdalene: Christianity's Hidden Goddess* (2003), which traces Jesus' female companion back to the goddess-worshipping tradition of Egypt. She graduated from the University of Wales.

Clive Prince is a full-time writer, researcher and lecturer on the occult and historical and religious mysteries, with a particular interest in belief systems and the way they shape both conventional and 'alternative' views of the past. He is the co-author, with Lynn Picknett, of *The Stargate Conspiracy* (1999), a study of esoteric, New Age and 'fringe' beliefs centred on Ancient Egypt.

Michael Rice has worked extensively in the Middle East, particularly in the Arabian peninsular states, to several of which he has acted as an Adviser. He has been particularly identified with Bahrain and with Saudi Arabia and has been responsible for the creation, design and installation of museums in both countries, all with important archaeological components; he and his colleagues have produced 13 museums in all. He has also been involved in the organization of Departments of Antiquities in the region and in the planning and publication of two learned journals. He is the author of *An Introduction to the Archaeology of the Arabian Gulf* (1994), *The Power of the Bull* (1997) and three books on Ancient Egypt: *Egypt's Making: the origins of Ancient Egypt 5000–2000 BC* (1990), *Egypt's Legacy: the archetypes of western civilization 3000–300 BC* (1997), and *Who's Who in Ancient Egypt* (1999). He was appointed a Companion of the Order of St Michael and St George (CMG) in the New Year Honours List, 2002.

Tim Schadla-Hall is Reader in Public Archaeology at the Institute of Archaeology, University College London. His interests lie mainly in public involvement in archaeology, including the role played by the media in archaeology today, the economics of archaeology, and 'alternative' archaeology. He edited an issue of the *Journal of European Archaeology* (1998) devoted to the subject of Public Archaeology, and has also published *Authenticity and Reconstruction in Archaeology* (1998). His forthcoming publications include an edited volume with Paul Lane on the excavations of early Mesolithic sites in the Vale of Pickering, North Yorkshire. He received his MA from the University of Cambridge.

Bernadette Schnitzler is Curator of the Archaeological Museum, Strasbourg. She has been responsible for more than 20 archaeological exhibitions, focusing on two main themes: 'Recent Excavations', and 'A Further Perspective on Archaeology'. Within the latter context, she has examined the use of antiquity in commercial advertising, in fiction and in the history of archaeological research. Her current research is on the history of archaeological research in Alsace during World War II. She is currently studying for a doctorate in national antiquities at the Strasbourg University of Human Sciences.

Sam Serafy is an independent filmmaker and film researcher. He has researched and edited the audiovisual component of many Library of Congress exhibitions, including 'Sigmund Freud: conflict and culture' and 'John Bull and Uncle Sam: four centuries of British American relations'. His short films have been screened at various film festivals and on the Independent Film Channel. He received a BA in Fine Art (painting) from Canterbury College of Art, UK, and an MA in Film and Video from The American University, Washington, DC.

Covadonga Sevilla Cueva is Professor of Egyptology and Ancient History, and co-director of the Centro Superior de Estudios de Asiriologia y Egiptologia, in the Autonoma University of Madrid. She has participated in archaeological fieldwork in Egypt (Herakleopolis Magna) and was a member of the organizing committee of the 1998 first conference of Egyptology in Spain. She is co-editor of *Trabajos de Egiptología* and her main interests and publications have focused on the role of the wives of Amun in the Third Intermediate and Late Periods, and the topography, archaeology and history of Egyptian Naucratis (Per Meryt). She gained her doctorate from the Autonoma University of Madrid, Spain.

Julian Walker is an artist and researcher whose work centres on the nature of objects and sites, particularly in terms of the sense of presence projected onto them. This has led him to work with objects such as the Rosetta Stone, King John's teeth at Worcester Museum, and Piltdown Man, using video, live art, photography, sculpture and installation. Much of his work is site-specific, and has included constructing a glass pathway over a collection of birds' eggs in a natural history museum in Nottingham, running his hands over the entire surface of an 18th century family portrait in Wolverhampton Art Gallery, and living with his family for a week under the gaze of surveillance cameras in Kettle's Yard, Cambridge. He has exhibited extensively in the UK, the US and Europe, and is currently working with two medical institutions in Berlin and London on the perception of contagion as applied to historical objects.

Andrew Wheatcroft is Director of the Centre for Publishing Studies, University of Stirling. He is Consultant to the publisher, Routledge, Taylor and Francis and, prior to taking up his post at Stirling, was the editor responsible for their archaeology, Egyptology and history publishing. He continues to act as an adviser in these fields and is also Routledge's Editor in Chief of The Heritage: care-preservation-management Publishing Programme. He lectures on museum and heritage publishing at the Museum of Texas Tech, Lubbock, USA, where he is also a Research

Associate. His most recent books include *Infidels: the conflict between Christendom and Islam 638–2002* (2003), *The Habsburgs: embodying empire* (1996), and *The Ottomans: dissolving images* (1993).

List of Figures

COLOUR SECTION

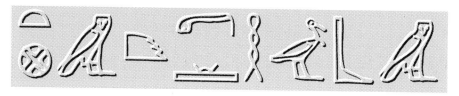

CHAPTER 1

INTRODUCTION – TEA WITH A MUMMY: THE CONSUMER'S VIEW OF EGYPT'S IMMEMORIAL APPEAL

Michael Rice and Sally MacDonald

The series of volumes of which *Consuming Ancient Egypt* is one sets out to express something of the catholicity of engagement that exists between Egypt in antiquity and the world of today, by focusing on the idea of 'Encounters with Ancient Egypt'. To encounter a civilization of the distant past in the variety of guises and contexts revealed here represents a range of experiences far beyond what might be expected in the interface between a subject of academic study and the world outside. It is a resounding tribute to the power and vitality that Egypt's past still commands, extending from the time of the foundation of the Egyptian state, 5,000 years ago, to the present day.

No other ancient society evokes so many responses, at so many different levels, as Ancient Egypt. Such responses range from the measured studies of the scholar's library and the scientist's laboratory to the meticulous excavation of ancient sites and the careful recording of their contents by the archaeologist, as much as to the enthusiasm for Egypt displayed by a multitude of people who, for an immense variety of reasons, are excited by its unique and complex past. The whole cavalcade of scholars, archaeologists, artists, writers, film makers, all manner of specialists and a significant percentage of the world's literate population, is swept along by a tidal wave of books, films, television documentaries, architecture of Egyptian inspiration – some august, some bizarre – and a medley of works of art of the widest spectrum of quality. They are supported by an uncounted mass of products, designs, services, buildings, entertainment and communications media which, one way or another, for good or ill, are inspired by the physical remains of the ancient Egyptian civilization.

What other academic discipline concerned with the ancient world would be represented by an explicit linkage with 'consumerism' as in the title of this volume, a concept which was not even thought of when the first serious studies of Egypt's past began to be formulated? Of course, there is none. It is this very direct relationship between Egypt, the scholars who study the evidence of its past and the lay public that produces this singular conjunction: sometimes, 'confrontation' may seem a better word.

That it is indeed a confrontation is evidenced by the assertive way in which parts of Egyptology's constituency make their views and apprehensions known to those professionally engaged in the discipline; it is singular because no other academic discipline is obliged to maintain such a degree of dialogue with the lay public. What should be the scholar's response to this public invasion of his or her domain? Indifference, dismissal, cautious acceptance? Perhaps, more perceptively, a degree of recognition is called for, if only because of the validity of the interest and enthusiasm expressed by members of society who have no professional involvement or responsibility, for in a variety of ways they contribute to the economic viability of the study of the past. We live in an age when the survival of scholarship in all its aspects is increasingly determined by society's readiness, or lack of it, to commit public funds to the support of its activities. The degree of support forthcoming is often determined by the decisions of elected assemblies whose abiding priorities will assuredly be far from those of the Egyptologist; there can be little doubt where the answer lies. In such a context, recognizing the role of the 'consumer' becomes a means of recognizing the essential partnership of the academy and society at large.

This volume presents a view of the present state of Egyptology in all its aspects from the viewpoint of the market place, that locus of popular political myth. It accepts that the perception of Ancient Egypt is very complex: scholarly, aesthetic, morbid, sensational, occult, dotty. All these perceptions contribute to the prevailing image of the exceptional culture that evolved in the north-eastern quadrant of Africa in antiquity and, indeed, it is this matter of perception that really determines the nature of this volume. While it sometimes may invoke a shudder in the breast of the Egyptological purist, the commitment is real and, this volume contends, should be acknowledged and, if at all possible, respected.

Having said this, it is proper to acknowledge also the very particular nature of an academic discipline which touches the lives of so many and which engages a particular set of perceptions amongst those who follow its progress and occasional triumphs. Brain surgery does not attract alternative theorists, let alone practitioners; nuclear physicists are generally allowed to follow their path in peace. But for some perhaps arcane reason the history and the mystery of Egypt, real or perceived, are regarded as part of the inalienable heritage of the western world.

This volume, then, acknowledges the validity of this often fractious concern and the inevitable impact of the consumer society on the future welfare of the study of Egypt's antiquity. As human society gropes its way uncertainly towards what may be a better understanding of its nature, its origins and perhaps its destiny, Egypt's contribution to the history of the world in which we live becomes ever more pertinent. *Consuming Ancient Egypt* recognizes that the enthusiasm which so many diverse people demonstrate is itself often directly generated by the dynamics of the consumer society and especially by the immense impact of modern communications. The consumer – the hero(ine) of this volume – is the focus of those who are concerned to study and conserve, on the one hand, and of those who seek to popularize, on the other, the extraordinary heritage of Egypt.

But it is not the influence of mass communications alone which has produced this powerful, if sometimes fraught, alliance between professional and non-professional interests; nor is it a phenomenon peculiar to our day (Ucko and Champion 2003). In the Renaissance, Egyptian themes inspired legions of architects and artists; in the 18th century writers joined the party and began to explore 'the mystery of Egypt'. By the early 19th century Ancient Egypt had already entered the public domain with vigour in Europe and America, with exhibitions, lectures by charismatic explorers and the public demonstrations of its wonders attracting mass audiences. Important public collections (and many private ones too) of Egyptian antiquities began to be assembled, which brought the experience of the glories of ancient Egyptian craftsmanship to the people, most of whom would never in their lifetimes reach the banks of the Nile. The acquisition of Egyptian artefacts became one of the defining marks of the emergent nationalisms in the 19th century, an ironic fate perhaps for the products of the first nation-state in the history of the world.

Geographical and historical factors are significant in assessing the extent and nature of the impact of Ancient Egypt on the modern world. There is patently a degree of bias that tilts much of the presentation, if not the study, of Egypt's past onto a western axis. Medieval Arab writers documented the monuments of Ancient Egypt, and wrote extensively about its culture (El Daly 2003). Mummies and parts of mummies were being sold to consumers as early as the 12th century AD (El Daly, Chapter 10: 140). But from the late 18th century, and even earlier if the studies of Renaissance scholars are included, the discovery, promotion and exploitation of Ancient Egypt has been largely a eurocentric phenomenon (Jeffreys 2003: 4–9).

'Eurocentric' is used here in a cultural, not a geographical sense. There is no judgmental consideration involved; it is simply the way that it is. Although scholars from every quarter of the world now study Egypt's history and culture, the fact remains that in its earliest manifestations scholars, artists, travellers and collectors trained in European traditions laid down many of the paradigms which still determine the study of its past in the present day. It is the dynamic of the response to that past which these paradigms evoke.

It may be that this consideration will become nugatory or at least less relevant in time. Egyptian Egyptology is well established, and Egyptological studies are to be found in Asia, the Central Asian Republics, Latin America and other regions far from the western matrix (Jeffreys 2003: 15). The western bias that can be detected arose from the wider educational opportunities, increased access to printed information and the growth of museum collections of Egyptological exhibits in western societies, making Ancient Egypt suddenly a reality in the lives of people who before had probably never given it a second thought.

Archetypal Egypt

It is suggested here that one reason that Ancient Egypt, once known, was so readily absorbed into the culture of the western world, is because of the archetypal character of so many of its forms. C. G. Jung, the father of analytical psychology, who was responsible for the articulation of the concept of the archetypes in his analyses of the individual psyche and of the unconscious, said: "The archetype is essentially an unconscious content that is altered by becoming conscious and by being perceived, and it takes its colour from the individual consciousness in which it happens to appear" (Jung 1959: 6).

Jung derived his concept of the archetypes from the earlier terminology, attributed to Jakob Burckhardt (1818–1897), of the "primordial image" (Burckhardt

1855 quoted in Jung 1956/1967: 45 n. 45), a term which is perhaps rather more explicit in its meaning. Jung saw the archetypes as unconscious, pre-existent forms, which are part of the universal inherited structure of the human psyche. Because they are part of the common neuropsychological inheritance of all people at all times, the archetypes can manifest themselves anywhere, at any time. Once recognized, the archetypes become part of the common vocabulary of human experience.

According to Jung, the archetypes and the impact of their recognition are the products of the collective unconscious, a phenomenon of which he wrote: "The hypothesis of a collective unconscious belongs to the class of ideas that people at first find strange but soon come to possess and to use as familiar conceptions" (Jung 1959: 195). Like the archetypes which arise from it, the collective unconscious is a faculty of all humans, in all societies, at all times; it is the product of those common neuropsychological mechanisms which all humans share. It can be argued that the Egyptians of the earliest dynasties and of the cultures that immediately preceded them were simply the first to give expression to the archetypes, in many cases in a three-dimensional, hence a particularly enduring, form. This may explain why later ages have reacted to them with something like instant recognition.

The archetypes in Egypt express themselves in the constellation of peculiarly satisfying forms and images developed by artists and architects, to employ modern terms to suggest the function involved rather than to define specific avocations, who transmitted the demands of the unconscious into concrete terms. The pyramid, the temple interior rich in columns, the multiplicity of symbolisms associated with kingship, the gods, especially the animal and animal-headed divinities later in Egypt's history, are all archetypes which came to light in Egypt.

Of these, the pyramid, that miracle of petrified sunlight, is one of the most enduring and satisfying of all forms (Humbert 2003), which appears in many human societies, though Egypt seems to have priority in its expression. In Egypt it is a peculiarly forceful example of the archetypes at work, as it lay deep in the collective unconscious of the people of the Nile Valley, waiting to be recognized and called into existence; it can be seen in the lines of the little triangular hills painted on Naqada II pottery and in the terraced mound which lay in the heart of many first Dynasty mastabas. This ultimately erupted into the Step Pyramid at Saqqarah and so led on to the fourth Dynasty and later pyramids in their most familiar form.

Similarly, the figure of Horus, the Young Prince, as the falcon flying in the upper air, is the perfect metaphor for kingship. Tutankhamun is another example of this archetype which, apart from the sumptuous contents of his tomb, has guaranteed his posthumous celebrity; more will be said of him below. The Egyptian temple, dark and invested with a potently numinous quality, is a metaphor for the forest and hence, and by extension, for the human mind as it is in the Jungian canon.

The most revealing of all Egyptian archetypes is represented in the person and office of the king. Egypt was the first land, anywhere in the world, to grasp the idea of elevating one man above all others to personify the nation-state, its nature and essential individuality, around whom all the processes and paraphernalia of the state would constellate. It was an audacious concept, made still more penetrating by adding the dimension of divinity to the holder of the office, thus neatly securing all aspects of the management of the society in the person of one transcendental human being. It is hardly an exaggeration to observe that the creation of kingship in Egypt and the consequent recognition of its archetypal character was the single most important political decision of the last five millennia.

Like all good ideas, once the archetype of Egyptian kingship was released it swept across the ancient world as an ideal method of managing an emerging complex society, powered by the commitment of a powerful and pervasive elite to undertake the creation of the nation-state and all its departments. (This is not, of course, to argue that other examples of kingship were derived from Egypt directly, merely that the similar historical circumstances of evolving complex societies demanded the adoption of similar or comparable solutions to each society's needs.) The role of the elite in early Egyptian society is crucial, both to the process of creating the state and in ensuring its ultimate viability. Attended by his close coadjutors, the king of Egypt is the first example in history of an archetypal psychological figure, 'the Great Individual', examples of which were to emerge throughout history (Neumann 1954: 421–435).

The fascination of Ancient Egypt can be explained by the fact that so many of its most powerful images are archetypes, in the literal sense that they are primordial, the first patent and identifiable representation of an enduring form. It was in Egypt that the archetypes of many of what have tended to be dominant cultures of the last five millennia were recognized and named as such for the first time in human history. This is in no sense an occult or mystery-laden phenomenon, for the archetypes, though their influence and mechanisms may seem mysterious, are entirely grounded in the human psyche. The generally occluded nature of the archetypes that well up from the collective unconscious – in this case of the early inhabitants of the Nile Valley – is the consequence of their relatively late identification and definition, over little more than the past century, the outcome of the science of the mind probing the deeper levels of the psyche and the unconscious.

This excursion to the margins of analytical psychology is only relevant here in so far as it may help to explain why people of all times respond so powerfully to Egyptian forms, and why these forms so often return in various shapes in many of the societies that have emerged since Egypt began the process. It is because the essential character of Egypt in its pristine guise was determined by the workings of the collective unconscious of the early Egyptian people and was manifested in ways that were peculiarly right for the stage of development that this first of all complex societies was undergoing, that it still continues to be wholly relevant today.

Ancient Egypt mass-produced

Ancient Egypt's acceptance by the western world in the early 19th century was heralded by the expedition that Napoleon Bonaparte led to Egypt in 1798. This was of profound importance in bringing the 'reality' of Ancient Egypt to the academic world and to the public, releasing a mass of literally monumental forms into the consciousness of dilettanti and the expanding literate classes alike (Jeffreys 2003) (e.g. Figure 1:1, a painting dating from the same year as the expedition). These monumental forms first took hold of the public consciousness with the appearance of

Figure 1:1   'Girls dancing around an obelisk' by Hubert Robert, 1798 (Montreal Museum of Fine Arts 1964: 1464).

Vivant Denon's (1802) handsome and superbly illustrated *Voyage dans la Basse et Haut Égypte*, which provided the first generally available conspectus of the antiquities of the Nile Valley. The interest which Denon aroused was accelerated when the *Description de l'Égypte* was published in its 10 superb folio volumes in the 1820s (*Description* 1809–1828) which, like its forerunner, inaugurated a tradition of sumptuous book production in the service of Ancient Egypt that continues to this day (Wheatcroft, Chapter 11).

The subsequent decipherment of hieroglyphs by Champollion and his successors opened a doorway into an entirely new world: complex, magical, vastly distant from the 19th century, oddly reassuring yet disturbingly familiar. These are the conflicting characteristics that the public reaction to Ancient Egypt still demonstrates, and which would later be identified as archetypal phenomena.

The early 19th century was a time of radical change and of political and social turmoil, during which many of the old values were overturned and new matrices were developed for the type of society which was to develop in Britain, Europe, later the United States and later still across much of the world. The Egypt that was presented to the 19th century world was immediately recognizable to the society of the day. In an era of flux Egypt was seen as providing a point of stability, its antiquity equating with certainty, its monuments and monumentality contrasting with dissolution (Figure 1:2 col. pl).

Ancient Egypt was seen to be hierarchic, oligarchic, centrally governed; the state personified by a crowned king, with the power and authority of the state expressed in monumental buildings and the lavish creation of public works of high quality. In the eyes of the contemporary world, Egyptian monumental sculpture, architecture, tomb reliefs, paintings and the lavish appurtenances of an elite aristocracy were recognized as being of high artistic merit, indeed the first great artistic tradition known to history. At a time when western colonial empires were being established and consolidated these concepts were particularly powerful. Ancient Egypt was attractive territory for appropriation.

Among the first appropriators were the artists and designers who assimilated ancient Egyptian forms or recorded the monuments that survived. In the early 19th century the work of itinerant artists in Egypt did much to familiarize the growing bourgeoisie in Europe and the United States with the splendours of the Nile Valley and, in doing so, contributed immeasurably to the formulation of the taste of the increasingly important consumer.

Events such as the Great Exhibition of 1851 in an England whose influence in political and economic affairs reached across the world, did much to secure the introduction of Ancient Egypt into the 19th century parlour, the country house library, the industrial complex and the market place, not only in Britain and throughout the British Empire, but in Europe, the United States and Imperial Russia. Egypt came triumphantly into its own when the Exhibition moved from Hyde Park, an elegant district of west London, to Sydenham in the southern suburbs of the rapidly expanding capital city. Here the Exhibition had its permanent home until it was destroyed by fire in the 1930s; in its new location it was visited by millions over the years (Werner 2003: 95).

The principal displays at Sydenham were set into a number of 'courts', each designed to present a major historical period; of these the most spectacular was The Egyptian Court "with huge pillars, sphinxes, mummies and enormous statues", designed by Owen Jones and Joseph Bonomi (Auerbach 1999: 200–202, pl. 65; Werner 2003: 95–100; see cover illustration). In this court were concentrated many of the most powerful images which were thereafter to be associated with Ancient Egypt, incorporating the gigantic, the expression of power, kingship and superlative craftsmanship, even though everything that gave the court its character and impact, including the great statues which dominated it, were replicas – another factor in the ancient Egyptian engagement with the consumer which receives further attention here (Walker, Chapter 7). The dominating qualities of this design were to be repeated countless times over the coming years. Already the 'Land of the Pharaohs' was acquiring what may properly be called its archetypal character in the public imagination. As a consequence of the Great Exhibition and other similar events there was ample evidence of commercial 'spin-off' in domestic articles, textiles and furnishings and architecture with a 'pharaonic' inspiration (Humbert and Price 2003).

Egyptianizing shapes and motifs remain popular today, as demonstrated by the legions of sphinxes, recumbent lions, obelisks and supposedly pharaonic figurines and statues produced for the benefit of interior decorators and their clients. In the 1920s and 1930s Egyptianizing forms were adopted in quite modest contexts: the cinema, the department store, bars, on shipboard, in the suburban house (Figure 1:3 col. pl.). Today Egypt is the source of inspiration for more grandiose interiors, swimming pools, dining rooms and bedrooms, suggesting a regression to the popularity of Ancient Egypt amongst the newly rich of the mid-19th century. That these artefacts still exercise a notable appeal may be seen in the auction rooms today. Often the Egyptianizing influences are second-hand, derived from the meretricious and often comically inaccurate interpretations of film, theatre and opera directors, thus piling fantasy upon illusion. This process of consumption and re-consumption, with images and products feeding off one another to produce increasingly complex forms and sets of references, can only take place in an era of mass communication. This explains the considerable increase in the number of Egyptianizing products from the mid-19th century onwards, and the surges in interest apparent in response to widespread reporting of particular events, particularly the discovery of Tutankhamun's tomb in 1922 (Schnitzler, Chapter 12) and the pre-millennial fever of the late 1990s (Picknett and Prince, Chapter 13).

Schnitzler (Chapter 12) chronicles the growth of commercial advertising from the mid-19th century onwards, the frequent naiveté of the exploitation of Ancient Egypt and the readiness with which its enduring symbols can be employed for something less than the highest purposes. It is significant that in this context the use of Egypt is not infrequently accompanied by an attempt at humour, though admittedly of a generally simple-minded sort, and often involving mummies (Lupton, Chapter 2). But Egypt has far more frequently been used to associate products with ideas of luxury, wisdom and eternity; testimony to the power that it is assumed to have to move and, mysteriously, to induce confidence (Figure 1:4).

One of the editors of this volume has some experience of the power thought to be inherent in Egyptian images in the commercial sector, in that he was introduced to the celebrated Black Cat cigarette factory, more properly Carreras Limited, Arcadia Works, at Mornington Crescent in North London, when it was still operational (Elliott et al. 2003). It was built for the manufacture of Craven 'A' cigarettes in the 1920s, in the after-glow of the opening of the tomb of Tutankhamun. The proprietors of the factory apprehended early on that an association with the king and with things Egyptian would, in some magical way, enhance the sales of their product. They were not mistaken, as was demonstrated by the successful presence of The Black Cat, the

Figure 1:4   Perfume bottle with pharaonic head stopper, produced by the Baccarat glass factory for the Bichara company, 1913. The features of the pharaonic head resemble those of Mr Bichara (Cristalleries de Baccarat, Paris).

Egyptian symbol selected to identify Craven 'A', which throughout its career served to epitomize one of the most popular cigarette brands in Britain in the pre-war period.

Sadly, the two colossal black cats (Figure 1:5; Elliott *et al.* 2003: Figures 6:2–6:4), which sat on each side of the main entrance to the factory, were separated when the factory was sold in the late 1950s (Price and Humbert 2003: Figures 1:8, 1:9). Years later, this editor came upon a film crew working in the Valley of the Kings in the middle of the day, late in July, producing a commercial for television extolling the virtues of one of the brands of cigarette made by the company that had bought the Black Cat factory. The magic of Egypt was still at work, serving as an enviable recreation destination for the smarter set, who were presumed to smoke the brand of cigarettes concerned. In this case Egypt's magic was expected to defy Egypt's summer

Figure 1:5
Sculptures of two
black cats in front of
the Craven 'A'
cigarette factory,
Carreras Ltd, Arcadia
Works, Mornington
Crescent, London.

heat; unless it was the curse of the displaced Black Cats being vented on the hapless camera crew, filming in the unshaded valley in temperatures approaching 150 degrees.

The authors of all the chapters in this volume recognize the special attitudes which possess many of the visitors to Egypt and which, broadly, can be expressed as a preparedness to enthuse about what they have seen or are about to see. This acquires particular force in the discussion about the definitions that may be applied, on the one hand, to the enthusiasm for and admiration of ancient Egyptian culture and material remains and, on the other, to the exploitation of Egyptian forms, symbols and design elements, in objects or contexts never remotely contemplated when they were created.

Humbert (1994; Humbert and Price 2003) has identified 'Egyptomania', 'Egyptophilia', 'Egyptianizing', 'Egyptian Revival', 'Nile Style', 'Pharaonism' as some of the terms that have been employed to define this elusive concept. He gives a respectable status to 'Egyptomania', divesting it of its often pejorative applications, which tend to emphasize the manic elements, rather than the Egyptian.

'Egyptomania' is interpreted in this book (Haikal, Chapter 9) as the manifestation of the Egyptians' own enthusiasm for their past. This may be fair, but given that 'Egyptomania' is frequently employed in an ambivalent sense, with something more than a hint of patronization about it, it is perhaps less aptly applied to the more thoughtful and responsible exploitation of Egyptian forms and concepts in contemporary applications, especially in the arts. For an Egyptian artist, craftsman or architect to return to ancient Egyptian themes is surely more properly to be seen as a return to an autochthonous inspiration. Egyptomania has often come (*pace* Humbert) to mean the adaptation of Egyptian forms, symbols and designs to purposes far removed from their original domain. Sometimes the subjects of such applications are entirely happy, if still exiled from their original home; the word 'kitsch' does however frequently come to mind. There is also a manic element which, not infrequently, can be seen in popular architecture, furniture design, fashion, the decoration of a funerary monument, cinema or railway terminus with aspirations above its proper station.

Borrowings of all kinds demonstrate the extent to which ancient symbols may take on different meanings for different cultures. This is not simply a matter of geography: in other contexts, modern Egypt has embraced her ancient past (Haikal, Chapter 9). While it has been argued that a Jungian approach may help to explain the enthusiastic reception of Ancient Egypt in a world of mass marketing and mass consumption, individual consumers and consumer groups will always adapt such forms to suit their needs.

Mythical Egypt

Another reason why Jung's views are pertinent to the study of Ancient Egypt is to be found in his intense and protracted examination of myth. In this he was very much in the tradition of European scholars of the earlier years of the 19th century, but he gave its study a particular force by conflating the idea of the unconscious and the archetypes with the power of myth. Jung demonstrated the universality of the great mythic cycles and their essential autonomy. Like the archetypes, myths emerged at many different times and places but always in a form whereby their common psychic matrix could be recognized. Jung saw myth as an essential part of the psyche's inheritance and he insisted upon the valuable creative and liberating role that it can discharge. It is in this sense also that Jungian analysis may be thought to be applicable to the emergence of the historic Egyptian personality.

It is no coincidence that two of the authors in this book (Lupton, Chapter 2, and Serafy, Chapter 5) deal with the influence that Egypt has wielded on the most important of modern art forms, the cinema. Of course, film is a particularly apt medium for the perpetuation of archetypes and of myth. In the case of the latter, Egypt was always to be relied upon by hard-pressed producers to produce arresting spectacles, from the original flickering images of the silent movies to the blockbusters of the 1950s, and on to their more circumscribed successors of the present day. These rely more on technology than spectacle to delight an audience still hungry for sensation (Schadla-Hall and Morris, Chapter 14). Film works so well in both creating and transmitting myth by virtue of its approximation to the dream; the powerful element of mystery associated in the popular mind with Egypt contributes to this approximation. It is clearly a forlorn hope that films with an Egyptianizing theme will invariably advance the cause of responsible scholarship. Rather it is apparent that sensation will usually tend to outweigh rigorous scholarly discipline.

The films considered by Serafy (Chapter 5) raise interesting questions about the attitude of modern mythographers to Egypt. Despite the acknowledged grandeur of *Land of the Pharaohs*, Egypt in film has customarily been portrayed as repressive and superstition-ridden, its people downtrodden and brutalized, in contrast to the more enlightened proponents of beliefs ancestral to Christianity and western democracy. The redactors of the 'historical' books of the Old Testament have much to answer for.

It is not difficult to accept that the monumental scale of Egyptian public buildings would appeal to movie-makers, but it is less clear why the essentially positive characteristics of Egyptian society – its extraordinary achievements, its humanity, the often elevated character of its ideologies – are generally suppressed. The particular agendas of contemporary politics have played their part in representing a view of Egypt which is little influenced by the realities of its history or the achievements of its people, but it is nonetheless strange that such positive elements, reflecting a profoundly significant phase of human experience, have so generally and firmly been disregarded. It is the depressing ability of stereotypes to resist correction, but it is remarkable that the cinema still repeats the time-worn clichés of malignant mummies, corrupt rulers and wicked princesses. Such stereotypes did not originate in celluloid. Artists such as Sir Edward John Poynter (Figure 1:2 col. pl.) and Alma Tadema (Werner 2003: Figure 5:11) were inspired by the marketing possibilities of large-scale paintings on supposedly biblical themes, the myth of the building of the pyramids for example having been the work of whip-lashed slaves; images derived from such productions were adopted enthusiastically by the makers of sundry Hollywood spectaculars (Serafy, Chapter 5) and have been profoundly influential in our time.

Other media likewise tend to perpetuate the mythical view of Egypt. Humbert (Chapter 3) alludes to the element of fantasy behind the popularity of increasingly grand scale operatic performances, while Lupton (Chapter 2) cites the dream-like, erotic element of much early mummy literature. The workings and re-workings of such fictions, particularly in Hollywood, have pervaded supposedly evidence-based presentations in museums (MacDonald, Chapter 6). Computer games use Egypt as a fantastic backdrop and develop Egypt's associations with mystery and hidden danger as challenges for modern treasure hunters and tomb raiders (Schadla-Hall and Morris, Chapter 14).

In the context of film-making and its relevance to the theme of consumer acceptance it is encouraging to observe that the most critically acclaimed film celebrating an episode in Egypt's history is not the work of Hollywood or of a European director, but of an Egyptian (Haikal, Chapter 9). Shadi Abdel Salam's *Night of the Counting of the Years* (its title on its English release) is an entirely serious and thoughtful production, with not a reincarnated mummy in sight, though true mummies abound at the heart of the film, which tells the story of the discovery of the great cache of royal mummies at Deir el-Bahri in the 1880s. This perhaps suggests a more committed approach by one who was Egyptian-born to the realities of his nation's history, compared with the subjective, not to say downright sensationalized, response of foreign producers whose principal interest is predictably the box office rather than the integrity of the Mansions of Millions of Years.

In the opera house, Egypt has fared rather better than in the cinema, reflecting perhaps a class difference in the perceived response between the audience of popular cinema and that of the more rarefied theatrical or operatic performance. In the case of opera productions, Egypt has certainly been treated more respectfully, though hardly more accurately in Egyptological detail. Mozart, perhaps influenced by his Masonic associations and the imagination of his librettist, Emanuel Schikaneder, portrayed a mystical Egypt in *Die Zauberflöte*, dominated by a powerful 'magus' figure, Sarastro,

Pistrucci dis. et inc.

colorite da Balelli e Fanf.

Figure 1:6 Costume design by Filippo Pistrucci for Sarastro in Mozart's *The Magic Flute*, performed at La Scala, Milan in 1816 (Museo Teatrale alla Scala, Milan).

in whom a conflation of Sesostris I-Sesostris III and Ramesses II was concealed (Figure 1:6) (and see Hamill and Mollier 2003: 209). But his genius did suggest something of the nobility of the temple ceremonies and their ambiance, despite the very un-Egyptian presence of the Queen of the Night, though an early appearance by her was responsible for one of the most evocative of pseudo-Egyptian stage settings.

Verdi's *Aida* is the Egyptian operatic oeuvre *par excellence* (Humbert, Chapter 3), but it has come to express the Egypt of monumentality and of imperialism. Whilst Radames is sympathetic, the pharaoh is a cut-out; Amneris, though powerfully realized, is a villainess (the archetypal wicked princess); the Egyptians provide the chorus and only the Ethiopians are noble. The Egyptology, despite its distinguished origins, hardly bears consideration; productions have become increasingly extravagant and spectacular affairs combining elements from many periods. In our own day Philip Glass's *Akhnaten* shows how the genre still flourishes; this work at least has the merit of having introduced the Pyramid Texts to the operatic stage

Figure 1:7   Philip Glass'
Akhnaten (© Arena Images).

(Figure 1:7). And an opera on Egyptian themes is being written by Egyptians and performed in Egypt today (Haikal, Chapter 9).

Mythical Egyptian stage and film sets have served as the fictional backdrop for powerful social and political messages. Serafy (Chapter 5) examines the contemporary subtext of three American films of the 1950s, one of which, *The Ten Commandments*, retains its popularity 50 years on. Sevilla Cueva (Chapter 4) describes an engaging Spanish operetta of 1910, attributing its huge popularity to its topical and satirical treatment of the Spanish government and the Catholic Church, safely distanced by its spectacular biblical/Egyptian setting.

Several authors in this volume chart the rich but largely unexplored hinterland between documentary and fiction, alternative and orthodox. Picknett and Prince (Chapter 13) trace the long history of what are now deemed 'alternative' theories, some of them ancient by comparison with academic Egyptology, a 19th century science, and suggest reasons for their contemporary resonance. Several theories suggest for instance that the Ancient Egyptians, through possession of hidden knowledge or contact with extra-terrestrials, could foretell future events. These theories found particular pre-millennial support in the last years of the 20th century (Figure 1:8 col. pl.).

The modern age is as alert to the transcendental as was the newly liberated Renaissance. The comparison between the two periods is revealing: the 15th and 16th centuries were times of social and religious turmoil in Europe following the successful challenging of the supremacy of established religion and its vice-like bonds with the state. The Reformation provided a vision of an alternative way; its early decades were marked by the appearance of all manner of cults and of popular expressions of the search for an understanding of the relationship between humankind (specifically, European humankind) and the Divine.

Some Renaissance intellectuals, generally branded as humanists, turned to and began to rediscover Ancient Egypt. The 20th century went through a similar, even more traumatic disturbance of accepted strategies for spiritual survival. In a way that is peculiarly satisfying to those who see a pattern of repetition in historical experience, the same thing occurred in modern times. The importance of this aspect of alternative Egypt may be gauged on the one hand by the enthusiasm with which the media, possibly cynically, receive each new theory, and on the other by the innocent consumer who frequently demonstrates a touching readiness to believe. No other great ancient culture has been invested with the quality of awe that attends the cults (to the extent that they can be apprehended at all), the temples, the tombs and the accumulated mythology of Egypt. The Greeks specifically fostered mystery cults, bursting with magic and skillfully staged dramas; even Eleusis however has not delivered a fraction of the long-standing wonder that surrounds this aspect of Egypt in antiquity.

'Alternative Egypt' is essentially consumer-driven. Writers, film makers, television producers, even the charismatic leaders of peripheral religious cults, are responding to consumers' need for entertainment, excitement and, in an age when orthodox religion is much under stress, enlightenment. Egypt exercises a strange appeal to those people who, fascinated by ancient cultures and the past of mankind generally, find orthodox explanations for the objects of their enthusiasms unsatisfactory. Though many will strike the Egyptologist as perverse, they remain part of Ancient Egypt's constituency and hence consumers of its culture, history, mystery and magic. 'Alternative Egyptology', like Egyptophilia and the rest, is one of the pillars of a remarkably broad Temple.

The unwillingness of orthodox Egyptologists to engage with popular debate must be partly to blame for the formation of opposing camps: academics on the one hand, 'forbidden' archaeologists on the other. It is not difficult to understand the exasperation with which professionals in the field regard attempts to teach them their business, their critics frequently accusing them of wilful obfuscation and the suppression of evidence, urging them to discard their training and experience and to accept the one true faith – whatever, for the occasion, it happens to be. It is less easy to understand why Egyptology does not face the challenge that these contentions, maverick or manic though they may be, offer to the accepted canons of the discipline.

This becomes the more pertinent when the relative ease of countering the arguments advanced by the alternative Egyptologists is examined. Thus, the much publicized claims relating to the age of the pyramids and the sphinx have been comprehensively answered by at least two apparently well-researched books, neither of them written by an Egyptologist. At some point Egyptology will probably find itself having to address this matter. The ultimate justification for doing so must be that some members of Egyptology's responsible constituency to a greater or lesser degree take such ideas seriously. There are anomalies in Ancient Egypt that require serious study; the architecture of parts of the Giza Plateau is one obvious instance (Picknett and Prince, Chapter 13).

The dramatic appeal of this rather unhelpful polarization between orthodoxy and heresy has been increasingly exploited by documentary television (Schadla-Hall and Morris, Chapter 14). At the same time, TV producers and publishers realize that their growth markets lie in this middle ground, where science and archaeology meet speculation, and are desperately seeking academic Egyptologists capable of presenting their subjects in a popular way (Wheatcroft, Chapter 11).

Since the late 19th century, books on Egyptian themes have served to familiarize the public in all literate societies with the physical presence of Egypt. Thus, Edwards (1877: xvii) ends the first edition of her book with an illustration (Figure 1:9) and these words:

> Mr Vedder has permitted me to enrich this book with an engraving from his picture. It tells its own tale; or rather it tells us much of its own tale as the artist chooses. [And, finally,] [e]ach must interpret for himself The Secret of The Sphinx.

The reading consumer's demand for books on Egyptian themes seems insatiable. The magical, mystical, this-week's-wonder 'alternative' Egypt always supplies the latest publishing sensation – the age of the sphinx and pyramids, a new chronology, a lost civilization, a hidden chamber. Equally books of serious intent and impeccable scholarship are piled high in bookshops everywhere (Wheatcroft, Chapter 11). Egypt is unmatched by any other archaeological discipline in the variety, extent and sheer quantity of books devoted to it. The publishing of books on Egyptological subjects, scholarly and sensational, has for long been virtually a specialized sector of the industry.

Each must interpret for himself
The Secret of The Sphinx

AMELIA B. EDWARDS.

Westbury-on-Trym,
Gloucestershire.
Dec. 1877.

Figure 1:9   Engraved by S. Pearson after a painting (1863) by Elihu Vedder, illustrated in Amelia Edwards (1877: xvii).

In parallel with the book publishing industry's evident commitment to Ancient Egypt, newspapers and magazines are clearly very powerful and serve to reinforce the messages of other forms of mass persuasion. News coverage of Egyptian excavations and 'discoveries' (of one sort and another) has become a staple of popular printed journalism. One British tabloid regularly allocates as many as six of its costly pages to reports of archaeological import, usually from an Egyptian point of origin. In this, Egypt has today assumed the place that biblical lands enjoyed in the 19th century as the principal source of popular archaeological speculation.

Television shares this journalistic hunger, and as a result its choice of material has a disturbing tendency to return time and again to the speculative and suspect. But it is significant that, for the first 30 years or so in the life of a medium that was becoming more and more important in the lives of people around the world, the documentary on archaeological or historical themes played a major part in fixing the character of television in the developed world (Schadla-Hall and Morris, Chapter 14). Egypt, by reason of its majesty, the splendour of its monuments and its archetypal power, was one of the defining images of the new medium's pursuit of social and intellectual respectability.

The real Egypt?

The involvement of Egyptians with the excavation, conservation and study of the past of their country has a substantial and honourable pedigree (Haikal, Chapter 9). Considerations of language and access to international media have sometimes militated against the work of Egyptian scholars, writers and artists receiving the same degree of recognition as that of their foreign peers. An important section of this volume deals specifically with the consumption of Ancient Egypt within modern Egypt, and viewed from an Egyptian perspective (El Daly, Chapter 10; Haikal, Chapter 9; Hassan, Chapter 8). This includes the tourists and the visitors to Egypt for whatever reason, who may encounter and respond to aspects of her past. These contributions raise important issues, such as the promotion of the trade (much of it illicit) in ancient Egyptian artefacts and the security and preservation of archaeological and historic sites.

In Egypt these problems are compounded by the startling changes in the environment of the Nile Valley, which has already put the fabric of many of the monuments at risk. International tourism, though it lives on the archaeological treasures of others, does little or nothing to protect even the most vulnerable sites. Anyone who has had the privilege of knowing Egypt over a lifetime will have seen what dramatic depredation can occur over only a few years. Thus, in the Pyramid of Unas at Saqqarah, in which the earliest recension of the Pyramid Texts was discovered, the walls of the chambers on which the texts were inscribed in exquisite hieroglyphs were blazoned with a wonderful blue paste, which had miraculously been preserved from the last quarter of the third millennium BC. Ten years ago the paste had disappeared, simply due to crowds of tourists breathing in and out and perspiring gently.

Another problem is that tourists have been encouraged to believe that they have the right to virtually untrammelled access to even the most environmentally or archaeologically sensitive remains. They have no such rights, other than those conferred on them by the erstwhile custodians of the antiquities. Egypt, in common with other archaeological nations, has tried earnestly to protect its heritage. But much more will need to be done, particularly in persuading tourists to respect the sites they visit and their extreme vulnerability. In this the promoters of tourism have a particular responsibility, though it may not be cheerfully embraced. El Daly (Chapter 10) and MacDonald (Chapter 6) highlight the implications of what tourists and museum visitors do not see: modern Islamic Egypt in particular is repeatedly ignored in favour of the pharaohs and pyramids of popular stereotype.

The politics of souvenir purchase is an important factor in the relationship between Egypt, tourists and museum visitors. Walker (Chapter 7) asks the important questions: what, for example, is a 'genuine replica', a term which is not unknown in the vocabulary of the purveyors of such *simulacra*? Is a museum-made replica somehow more genuine than one produced by a more commercial manufacturer, no matter how worthy? Why *do* museums manufacture and sell replicas, except to create revenue, if not also to meet a demand from their visitors? And what is it that the visitor believes he or she is getting when a replica is bought? The quality of souvenirs is perhaps largely irrelevant if they serve their primary purpose: to aid memory. But the acquisition of products with however slight a resemblance to authentic ancient Egyptian artefacts will draw the attention of some to 'the real thing'. A disturbing factor here is the appearance of individuals, tourist organizations and media which, though not infrequently attempting to clothe themselves in academic respectability, nonetheless promote and encourage the sale of genuine antiquities (Hassan, Chapter 8).

Laser-produced replicas in materials identical to those used in the original can now be fabricated, virtually indistinguishable from the original object. The development of such techniques is also likely to make the work of excavators more challenging, if such replicas find their way into unexcavated strata of a site, a device not entirely unknown in excavations in the past.

The sale of souvenirs and replicas is not, therefore, a trivial matter; it has profound implications for the future knowledge and understanding of Ancient Egypt, as well as for modern Egypt's trade, creative and traditional skills. Hassan (Chapter 8) points to the need for a more mature and constructive relationship between modern Egypt and the huge international heritage industry that feeds off Egypt's past.

Museums play a key role in this industry. Museums had their origins in storehouses for collections of objects ('the cabinet of curiosities'), excavated, looted, gifted and otherwise acquired. Though some have still earlier credentials, from the 18th century onwards in Europe and America museums became an essential part of the cultural economy of any self-respecting state. For a long time museums flourished as the domain of scholars; intervention by the public was, to put no finer point on it, frequently not encouraged. Several factors here combined to alter this situation drastically. First, in the case of those museums with archaeological collections, increased awareness of the ancient world focused attention on the origins and history of states known previously only from the Bible or schoolbooks. Then, the growth of communications, the recording of excavations, the discovery of new or otherwise unknown cultures and survivals, and the opportunities for dramatic photography, brought the content and purpose of museums more and more to the public attention. Museums often led the way in the scientific exploration of ancient sites and their diligence was rewarded with material, in the early days often of the highest quality, from the sites that they dug.

The latter part of the 20th century saw this situation begin to change. Two factors were particularly important: public funding failed to keep up with the demands of the conservation and preservation of the collections and demand grew for improved access to the museum itself. The Egyptian collection reflects the glory of Ancient Egypt in its most immediate and compelling form. It owes its paramountcy to the sheer abundance of the material that it has to hand and available for exhibition. But museums are not infrequently criticized for the large quantity of artefacts, provenanced and unprovenanced, which they hold in their storerooms or, more acceptably perhaps, as study collections.

In many major international museums the Egyptian collection is one of the most compelling attractions (MacDonald, Chapter 6). This inevitably gives rise to the consideration of the Egyptian collection as a marketing tool. It also prompts thoughts about the role and nature of museums today, the challenge of the theme park and the function of the museum in promoting excavations and enlarging its often already gargantuan collections. It is questionable whether western museums should continue to finance large-scale expeditions to major archaeological loci, the guardians of which are themselves not unreasonably disposed to maximize the revenue, often sorely needed, which 'their' sites can produce. It is all very well to talk piously about the responsibility of the countries involved acting as the custodians of the world's heritage, but this argument becomes less convincing when unalloyed poverty is the lot of such nations.

Tourists are of course consumers and may change the meanings of their purchases in the way they use them. Walker (Chapter 7) examines the encounter between Ancient Egypt and museum visitors through their choice of backdrop for photographs of themselves, *in situ*. This is an important issue because it must have a bearing on the relative popularity of certain objects and their locations, prompting the question whether these should be made specially accessible, in the marketing strategies of museums and archaeological sites.

Consuming Ancient Egypt examines the extraordinary spread and depth of the public's engagement with Egypt over the last two centuries and considers the continuing vigour of its existence today. It is a very singular phenomenon and the review of some of its characteristics prompts the thought that, quite apart from the explanations suggested here, there is one special quality about Ancient Egypt and the heritage it has passed on to the world that succeeded it – a quality which evokes a degree of engagement like no other. It is possible to put forward some tentative explanations as to what may be happening; it is quite another matter to propose that they are in any sense definitive. It will be clear that they cannot be, for they are faced with an enigma that has perplexed all who have given thought to the majesty of Ancient Egypt.

Beyond the confines of the land of Egypt, still resting secure in the north-eastern quadrant of Africa after five tumultuous millennia, and beyond the physical, topographical Egypt, there is another, supra-Egypt. This is not the Egypt of the mystologues and the fanciers of explanations, which deny logic or probability; it is the Egypt which spews out mythical phenomena like no other land. In part this is the consequence of its unique material culture, the huge monuments, the most commanding of which stood unparalleled for centuries, their power unchallenged. In part it is the consequence of the streams of divine entities who crowded the banks of the Nile and who conveyed a particular vision of the transcendental which still induces awe. In part it is the consequence of the flood of artefacts, ranging from the exquisite to the monumental, which poured out of the workshops of artists, sculptors, painters, metalworkers, makers of pottery, the carvers in wood, all the largely nameless craftsmen who represent the true inheritance of Egypt. Again, the products of their creative genius are seen to be all the more exceptional in that they appear to have been so vastly in advance of all others of their kind on earth, for so very long.

Egypt's power, reaching out from the earliest centres of the first of all nation-states to every corner of the world today, in all the products and influences, some of which *Consuming Ancient Egypt* records, may be gauged by the survival of some of its historic figures who, when they have been recognized as the archetypes that they have become, acquire an enduring and universal existence. Three such individuals jostle for recognition: Nefertiti, Tutankhamun and Cleopatra, whose names are familiar now in virtually every land on earth. Nefertiti is the archetype of the mysterious, feminine beauty, elegant, remote, with her empty eye adding a startling factor of the bizarre to her otherwise transcendental loveliness. To Hitler, Nefertiti was the archetype of the purest Aryan stock (Rice 1997: 216–217 n. 8), a judgment for which the poor queen could not be held responsible. She remains, breathtaking and peerless, her celebrity doing nothing to diminish her power to move.

Tutankhamun, the boy-king, the Lost Prince, the wonder-child surrounded by his golden toys, though forgotten for 3,000 years, burst into the world like a whirl-wind, instantly becoming one of the most powerful icons of the 20th century. Apart from his youth and, to judge from his images, his exceptional beauty (real or conventional) he lay in his small tomb surrounded by his astonishing treasure, the last, effete survivor of a line of conquerors. The magic of his name is in part the reason for his renewal of life: Tutankhamun is unlike any of the familiar names of Egyptian kings. Had he been Amenophis V his immortality might never have been so ensured. In the world into which he was reborn his throne-name could be abbreviated to an affectionate diminutive, the ultimate accolade of public acceptance.

The third of this trio of the definitely un-dead, Cleopatra, has enjoyed the longest resurrection though she is the youngest in historical terms. If Nefertiti is the unattainable queen, Cleopatra is all too evidently the siren, serpent, enchantress, *lamia*. She stands at the threshold of the modern world and the fact that she is Greek matters little for she was undoubted Queen of Egypt, that paradox in the popular mind, a female pharaoh.

These three are shadows of exceptional substance. They are not alone, for all periods of Egypt's history have produced larger than life figures that have seized the imaginations of later times. Imhotep deified, 'Senwosret', Sesostris to the Greeks and Sarastro to Schikaneder and Mozart, Tuthmosis III, Ramesses II: the list is long. There is some particular quality that made these men and women live on in the memory of later generations, like no others from any other great historical culture, not even the gods and heroes of the Greeks, the putative cultural ancestors of the west. These Egyptian 'Great Ones' belong to this strange, supra-Egypt, an Egypt of myth certainly but not of fantasy, for their lives are known and their roles are clear. The extra-dimensional Egypt they inhabit is still pouring out myth like a sustained lava-flow. They contribute profoundly to the perception of Ancient Egypt that the worlds which came after them have sustained.

This volume seeks, in a way seldom attempted in the past, to assess the impact of public interest in and preconceptions of Egyptology on the public fancy. It has shown that the discipline touches the community from which it emerged and on which it lives to an exceptional extent and on a remarkable variety of occasions. The significance of this interconnection is plain to see. Egyptology has an opportunity to engage itself with the society on which it depends for its support to an extent exceptional when compared with other academic disciplines. To recognize this prospect is also to prepare itself for a beneficial relationship, avoiding any diminution of its academic status and authority. It needs also to recognize the needs of the public that sustains so notable an interest in its affairs. This interest not infrequently is manifested in a special, perhaps unwontedly affectionate, response from those who regard the activities of Egyptologists as providing sources of excitement and delight, inspiration and a rich vein of opportunity for their own endeavours or avocations. But then that is what makes the study of Ancient Egypt unique and so significant a part of contemporary human experience.

That the wonder still prevails is amply demonstrated by *Consuming Ancient Egypt*. The excitement and anticipation which a first exposure to Ancient Egypt can generate is exemplified by the experiences of a group of children aged 9 to 10, whose engaging, often penetrating, always highly enthusiastic if occasionally off-course comments enliven the report (Fisher 2000) cited in this volume (MacDonald, Chapter 6). One of these delightful, if inevitably unfulfilled aspirations provides the title for this introduction. Perhaps a visit to the British Museum will trigger a lifetime of Egyptological delight.

For one of the editors of this volume the following anecdote has a curious sense of time collapsing, of showing how close the archetypes still are to Egypt and how powerful the experience of them can be. As a child he heard the now celebrated archival BBC broadcast of the sounding of the 'War Trumpets' of Tutankhamun from the Egyptian Museum, Cairo. The original broadcast occurred in 1938, and, predictably, the sounding of one of the trumpets was later blamed for the outbreak of World War II the following year. For that small boy, also a 'Child 9–10', the sound of the bronze trumpet, high, clarion clear and really rather unearthly, was like a call from another world. It is one which is still redolent of wonder and which requires no further impress of magic.

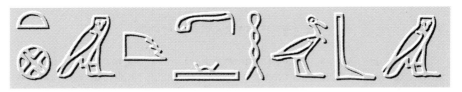

CHAPTER 2

'MUMMYMANIA' FOR THE MASSES – IS EGYPTOLOGY CURSED BY THE MUMMY'S CURSE?

Carter Lupton

The popular fascination with the physical and intellectual manifestations of Ancient Egypt has long been recognized by the term 'Egyptomania', a phenomenon stretching back at least 500 years (Curl 1994; Humbert 1989). A major wave of 'Egyptomania' followed the appearance of the *Description de l'Égypte* (*Description* 1809–1828; Gillespie and Dewachter 1987), begun under Napoleon and completed in the 1820s, concurrently with the translation of hieroglyphs by Champollion. The discovery of Tutankhamun's tomb just a century later ushered in a distinct aspect of 'Egyptomania' labelled 'Tutmania' (Frayling 1992). Though it concerned all things Tut, so to speak, many of the more exotic elements of 'Tutmania' were concerned with the alleged curse from the tomb (Figure 2:1). This in turn became a factor in Hollywood horror films, notably Universal Studios' *The Mummy* (1932), thus sparking a subgenre of 'Egyptomania' which can be called 'Mummymania'. The far-flung incarnations of 'Mummymania', especially those aspects dealing with living mummies and curses, might be seen as a curse itself, a potential threat to an appreciation of legitimate Egyptology by a broad public (but see Schadla-Hall and Morris Chapter 14, this volume).

The use of Egyptian mummies in fiction did not originate with Boris Karloff's portrayal in 1932, but goes back over a century earlier. Rooted heavily in literature and film, and reflected in popular culture items such as toys, action figures, role-playing games and Hallowe'en decorations, to name a few, 'Mummymania' has been little more than a footnote in standard works on 'Egyptomania' which deal primarily with architectural, decorative and fine arts. Though it has been covered extensively in specialized literary and cinematic histories (Glut 1978; Halliwell 1986), only recently have Egyptological works begun to deal somewhat seriously with aspects of popular 'Mummymania' (Addy 1998; Brier 1994, 1998; Green 1992). Yet much of the lay person's 'familiarity' with Egypt and its mummies derives from popular fiction and film, which are often at odds with standard Egyptological interpretations. The study of 'Mummymania', its genesis and evolution, can provide a better appreciation of some of the most drastic and diverse ways in which the cultures of Ancient Egypt have been refigured (Schadla-Hall and Morris Chapter 14, this volume).

Figure 2:1 *The Mummy's Hand* (1940), clearly representing the curse from the tomb (Universal Studios).

The literary legacy of the mummy

In 1931, Universal Studios produced two films based on literary classics: *Dracula* and *Frankenstein*. The latter starred Boris Karloff as the man-made 'monster'. Wishing to cash in on their latest horror star, Universal executives began searching for a new storyline. It has often been stated that the opening of Tutankhamun's tomb a decade earlier and its associated curse was the inspiration for doing a film about an Egyptian mummy (Brunas *et al.* 1990: 50; Glut 1978: 164). However, as will be shown later in looking at the actual history of the script development, a much more complex picture emerges. Since the 1932 version of *The Mummy* (Figure 2:2) is generally believed to be the patriarch of mummy films, a close look at its origins reveals much about the general tenor of mummy fiction and how this genre has diverged from scholarly Egyptology. King Tut's tomb, along with the 'curse' surrounding it, is only the initial and most obvious source of inspiration for the Karloff film. Though it had no single obvious literary origin, unlike *Dracula* and *Frankenstein*, film historians have proposed a number of fictional works as likely or definite sources. To trace the ultimate origins of *The Mummy* we must examine a literary tradition that began over a century before the film was produced.

The earliest literary work thus far identified as dealing with revived mummies is Jane Webb Loudon's *The Mummy – A Tale of the 22nd Century*. Published in 1827, this long novel is set 300 years later, in 2126/7. The society depicted, though technologically

Figure 2:2   Boris Karloff in *The Mummy*, following his turn as Frankenstein (Universal Studios).

quite advanced, still has its share of problems, in particular moral degeneracy. The author, a woman not yet 20, was projecting the trends of her own post-Regency era – scientific and technological advancement alongside political and moral decline – into the future (Rauch 1994: ix–xxxiv). Her protagonists revive the mummy of 'Kheops', builder of the Great Pyramid, who becomes the central figure in critiquing the future society, basing his judgments on the very failures he had shown as a leader in pharaonic Egypt. Of course, Kheops' despotic nature in the novel is derived from the unflattering portrayal of him by Herodotus, the only source that would have been available to Loudon in the 1820s. Her work shared several attributes with *Frankenstein*, published the previous decade by another young woman, Mary Wollstonecraft Shelley (1818). Both novels used revitalization of deceased humans as a mechanism to explore the potential dangers of scientific/technological progress unfettered by moral boundaries. It is not surprising that Loudon should select an Egyptian mummy in the immediate wake of the completion of the *Description de l'Égypte,* the exploits of Belzoni, and the achievements of Champollion.

In 1833 a mummy appeared in a farce play by W. Bayle Bernard entitled *The Mummy*. This work set a trend to be followed by nearly all subsequent theatrical approaches to the mummy theme – broad farce (Madison 1980: 64).[1]

An anonymously published *Letter From a Revived Mummy* in 1832 may have inspired efforts by 'named' authors. In 1840 the French writer Theophile Gautier published a short story titled *The Mummy's Foot*. This whimsical fantasy concerns a man who buys, from a curiosity shop, the beautifully preserved foot of a female mummy to use as a paperweight. Falling asleep at home while musing over this oddity, he is awakened by the sound of the foot jumping about on his desk. Next he hears a woman hopping on one foot. She has come to reclaim her other foot, taken from her mummy by tomb robbers. With her foot returned, she 'flies' the young man to Egypt for a gathering of all the mummied royalty of past times, where he is considered too young to marry a princess 4,000 years old. Awaking the next morning at home and assuming all to have been a dream, he finds the foot replaced by a charm the princess had worn around her neck. Gautier later wrote a novel entitled *Romance of a Mummy* (1856), essentially a love story set in ancient times but with an extended prologue detailing the excavation of the mummy's tomb and the discovery of the papyrus which forms the narrative of the body of the novel. Gautier later became involved with mummies for real when he observed the unrolling of a mummy at the Paris Universal Exhibition.

The episode of *The Mummy's Foot* concerning the hopping noise made by the princess recalls the tapping on the window in Edgar Allan Poe's *The Raven*, and it may be no coincidence that Poe wrote his own mummy story shortly after Gautier's, in 1845. *Some Words With a Mummy* centres around a group of men who revive a mummy by galvanic (electrical) stimulation; Gautier, five years earlier, had described his animated foot as if it were "in contact with a voltaic battery". Unlike so much of his work, Poe's mummy story is not a tale of horror, but of lighthearted social satire. After reviving the mummy, whose name is Allamistakeo, the learned gentlemen of 1845 Baltimore enter into a discussion lionizing modern society and technology, only to find the mummy able and willing to counter their claims in favour of Ancient Egypt. The entire episode turns out to be the narrator's dream caused by overeating, reminiscent of Scrooge's initial explanation for seeing Marley's ghost. This story is very subtly referred to in Hammer's 1959 film *The Mummy* when the sceptical police inspector, upon hearing that the archaeologist believes that a living mummy exists, remarks that this is reality, "not some fantasy out of Edgar Allan Poe".

Louisa May Alcott, best known for *Little Women*, has recently been identified as the earliest writer to actually utilize a mummy's curse plot (Montserrat 1998: 70–75), though a tale from 1699 of a near shipwreck thought to be caused by mummies aboard may have foreshadowed the folklore surrounding a British Museum mummy often incorrectly claimed to have been aboard the *Titanic* (Green 1992: 35). Alcott's 1869 story, *Lost in a Pyramid; or the Mummy's Curse*, puts a feminine, if not feminist, slant on things as both the mummy and the victim are female.

The next mummy story, Grant Allen's *My New Year's Eve Among the Mummies* from 1880, takes place primarily in a pyramid, as had Alcott's tale. Happening upon a conclave of mummies that awake for just 24 hours once every thousand years, a young man falls in love with a princess and agrees to undergo mummification so he may live eternally with her, but loses consciousness just as the chest incision is made. Allen was obviously lampooning Gautier's tale of the foot as well as poking fun at Egyptian dynasties by referring to Hatasou (Hatshepsut), the princess, as daughter of Tuthmosis XXVII!

H. Rider Haggard's *She*, first published in serial form in 1887, is a classic romance/adventure novel. Ayesha, feared by her followers as 'She Who Must Be Obeyed', is a 2,000 year old woman who is seemingly ageless, the result of immersion in an eternal flame. She has waited centuries for the return, through reincarnation, of her ancient lover Kallikrates. When he appears in her lost African kingdom in the form of Leo Vincey, she destroys Kallikrates' perfectly preserved mummy. Hoping to entice Leo into the flame so they may share immortality, she enters it again, only to find the initial effects reversed as she rapidly ages and crumbles to dust. This tale would have a deep impact on many future writers.

In 1890, the young creator of the detective Sherlock Holmes, Arthur Conan Doyle, published the first of two mummy stories. *The Ring of Thoth* concerns Sosra, a man who has lived since ancient Egyptian times, rendered virtually immortal by an elixir he developed. When Sosra's beloved princess hesitates to take the injection and then dies, he must live alone through the centuries until finally her mummy is excavated and placed in a museum. He is weary of life and finally acquires the ring, that of the story's title, containing an antidote to his elixir, developed by an ancient associate, that will allow him to join her in death. Some writers have seen traces of Haggard's *She* in this tale (Cox 1985: 207), and certainly the scene of the female mummy's beautiful face deteriorating when unwrapped recalls the end of Ayesha. There is an inversion of theme, however. In Doyle's story, Sosra has lived through the centuries only to seek reunion in death when his beloved's mummy becomes accessible to him. In Haggard, Ayesha, who often refers to herself as "She Who Waits", has spent the centuries pining for her lost love with the plan of uniting with him in a shared immortality. Perhaps they are two sides of the same coin, but dramatically different in their impact. Doyle's final scene of Sosra's body found embracing the shrivelled mummy hauntingly evokes the entwined remains of Quasimodo and Esmeralda in Hugo's (1831) *Notre Dame*.

Conan Doyle's second mummy tale, *Lot No. 249*, centres on an Oxford student who, having purchased a mummy at auction, restores it to life through a combination of reading an ancient papyrus and burning certain leaves. He then proceeds to send it out on missions of mayhem to threaten the lives of people he feels have wronged him. Though living mummy stories had been around for more than half a century when this tale appeared in 1892, Doyle was the first to use a physically active mummy as a tool of vengeance motivated by another's will (Figure 2:3).

Conan Doyle's mummy stories were followed by Julian (son of Nathaniel) Hawthorne's 1893 *The Unseen Man's Story*, part of an anthology of unrelated stories held together by a framing sequence. This is more of a ghost/love story than a mummy tale, with elements recalling Gautier's and Grant Allen's eternal afterlife of mummies and the theme of reincarnation, perhaps derived from Haggard. *Iras, A Mystery* by H. D. Everett, published in 1896, is not really a mystery, but a romance involving a female mummy reawakened to life. She marries the modern hero but gradually fades away under repeated magical attacks by an ancient priest who wants her for himself, until the hero is left with just a mummy again.

Bram Stoker, most famous as the author of *Dracula* (1897), published the less well-known *The Jewel of Seven Stars* in 1903 (Figure 2:4). This rather slow-moving novel concerns the attempts by the spirit of an ancient Egyptian queen, Tera, to possess the body of her modern twin, who happens to be the daughter of the archaeologist who discovered the queen's tomb and mummy. Originally ending with Tera dominating the modern woman, a new edition with a rewritten climax in which her evil spirit is vanquished appeared in 1912, the year Stoker died, though it is unclear if he or his

Figure 2:3   An active mummy, used as a tool of vengeance, from Conan Doyle's *Lot No. 249* (Harper Magazine).

wife was responsible for the change. This novel essentially brought the fictional mummy story into the 20th century, attempting to meld notions of mysticism, attached to Egypt by occult writers since medieval times (see El Daly 2003), with the progressiveness of modern science. One Stoker admirer has suggested that it is the "defining" work of the mummy horror story (Leatherdale 1996: 9), but it is neither wholly original nor iconic. Stoker seems at least partially indebted to Haggard;

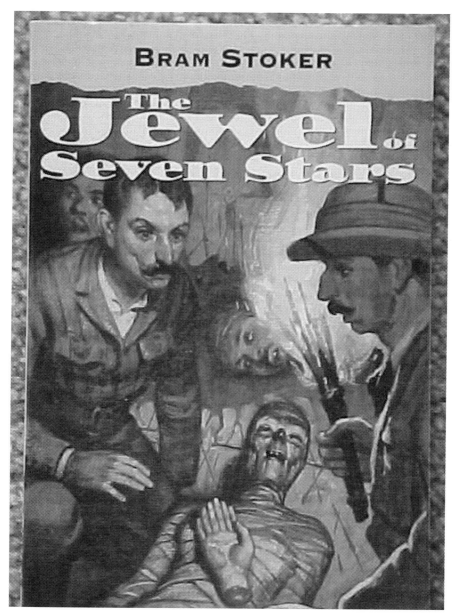

Figure 2:4   Mysticism and science (Stoker 1903 [1966]) in *The Jewel of Seven Stars* (artist: Paul Slater).

Ayesha has been interpreted as the direct inspiration for Queen Tera (Glover 1996: 85). And without an actual living mummy, the book remains atypical of the mummy subgenre as a whole.

Guy Boothby's *Professor of Egyptology* from 1894 is actually an evil Egyptian who has been cursed to live forever. He develops a hypnotic power over a young woman and, in the Cairo Museum, before his original mummy, she relives her past life in Egypt as the object of his love. Later, in 1898, Boothby wrote *Pharos the Egyptian*, a novel about an evil mummy also cursed to live forever. *Pharos* was certainly influenced by Stoker's *Dracula* of the previous year, culminating in a similar worldwide plague spread by the evil creature through a mentally controlled acolyte. George Griffith's *The Mummy and Miss Nitocris* (1906) combines reincarnation with the notion of time as the fourth dimension, an idea popularized by H. G. Wells in the previous decade.

Written early in Haggard's career, *She* was not his only foray into the mystical world of the pharaohs. Haggard was fascinated by Egypt throughout his life, visiting on four separate occasions and becoming good friends with prominent Egyptologists, most notably Wallis Budge. His first trip in 1887 came shortly after the royal mummies had been placed in the Cairo Museum and in 1904 he was among the first to see the newly discovered tomb of Nefertari (Addy 1998). Following the success of *She*, Haggard had been offered a mummy story plot by Rudyard Kipling in about 1889 but he never developed it (Cohen 1965: 28–29). He was opposed to the excavation and public display of mummies (Haggard 1904) and wrote the story *Smith and the Pharaohs* in 1912–1913 as a plea on behalf of the long-deceased Egyptians to be left in peace. Perhaps his message took precedence over artistic creativity, as this story, concerned as it is with a man locked in a museum overnight who comes face to face with the spirits of all the dead royalty, seems tediously repetitive of Gautier, Allen, Doyle and Hawthorne.

One writer has argued that much of the mummy fiction from the Victorian and Edwardian periods, including many of the stories summarized above, can be viewed as a reflection of the economic and political changes occurring in the British Empire at that time (Daly 1994). He believes the mummies in these stories, objectified commodities sought after for their exotic nature, are usually turned into subjects – living creatures or phantasms. Interestingly, most of these tales have an erotic element as well, involving resurrection, reincarnation or a dreamlike fantasy encounter between a modern man and an ancient Egyptian woman. Daly ends his survey with Haggard's *Smith and the Pharaohs*, suggesting that after the opening of Tutankhamun's tomb, the curse stories associated with vengeful living mummies came to be dominant in mummy fiction. However, the mummy romance story continued to evolve throughout the 20th century, with novels ranging from the subtle supernaturalism of E. Temple Thurston's *Mr Bottleby Does Something* in 1926 to the more explicit occultism of Sax Rohmer's (1928) *She Who Sleeps* just two years later.

Rohmer, like Haggard, was a writer heavily immersed in Ancient Egypt. His most famous creation, the Chinese criminal mastermind Fu Manchu, is regularly described as having features nearly identical to those of the well-preserved mummy of Seti I. Many of the Fu Manchu novels contain Egyptian settings or elements and one in particular, *The Daughter of Fu Manchu* (Rohmer 1931), involves a man found inside a coffin in a tomb but brought back from supposed death. Rohmer also wrote numerous other stories and novels throughout his long career exploring various occult aspects of Ancient Egypt: *The Leopard-Couch* in 1904, a story reminiscent of both Gautier and Haggard; a series of stories featuring the psychic "dream detective" Moris Klaw, most notably *The Headless Mummies* (Rohmer 1913) about a series of mummy beheadings in search of a magical papyrus by a villain named Pettigrew (presumably inspired by Thomas Joseph Pettigrew, author of the 1834 *History of Egyptian Mummies*); and *The Green Eyes of Bast* (Rohmer 1920) about a woman who may or may not be an incarnation of the Egyptian cat goddess.[2] Much of Rohmer's output dealing with mummies contains no supernatural element. One example is *The Mummy That Walked* (1938, re-published in 1939 as *The Mummy of Cleopatra*), involving a magician using a swathed lady friend to stand-in for a mummy in a museum while he switches a real coffin/mummy for a forgery; this is a reworking of elements from his first published story in 1903, *The Mysterious Mummy*. Another non-supernatural mummy tale, *She Who Sleeps* (1928), alluded to earlier, begins as a seemingly occult tale and is in fact evocative of Haggard, whose own title character, 'She Who Must Be Obeyed', often refers to herself as "She Who Waits". Rohmer's story details the discovery and clandestine excavation of the tomb of a woman not truly mummified but preserved alive since the time of Seti I. The hero believes that he may be a reincarnation of her ancient lover. Thus far the novel is quite similar to Haggard's. However, the resurrection episode at the end is much more reminiscent of the climax of Stoker's *Jewel of Seven Stars*. In the end, the entire tomb/mummy/resurrection turns out to be a hoax perpetrated by the modern woman's foster father, a former stage magician.

Brood of the Witch Queen, first appearing in 1914, is one of Rohmer's few unequivocally supernatural Egyptian stories. A child mummy is re-animated by translating the Book of Thoth, and he grows up to be an evil entity who makes sorcerous attempts on others' lives, ultimately raising a fire-demon which causes his own demise.

Other occult novelists are not as well remembered as Rohmer, though they have produced some interesting variations on the theme. Early examples are Ambrose Pratt's *The Living Mummy* from 1910, which introduces invisibility for the mummy; Burton Stevenson's *A King in Babylon* (1917) concerning the making of a film about a reincarnated mummy in which the star turns out to be a true reincarnation while an actual vengeful mummy is excavated as well; and Jack Mann's *The Ninth Life* (1939) which further develops the theme of human incarnation of a cat goddess already seen in Rohmer's *Green Eyes of Bast*.

King Tut's Curse, Karloff's Mummy, etc.

The cinematic story of *The Mummy* (1932) was developed within a particular cultural/historical context, the aftermath of the discovery of Tut's tomb and the attendant sensationalism surrounding an alleged curse. However, it was also developed within the context of the literary tradition of mummy fiction discussed above. This seminal film in many ways set the stage for much of the mummy cinema and literature to come.

The steps leading to the tomb of Tutankhamun were discovered on 4 November 1922, a date still celebrated annually in Luxor. Just four months later, in early March 1923, Lord Carnarvon, the sponsor and official excavator, took ill from an infected insect bite, eventually dying on 5 April, precisely five months after exposure of the tomb's entrance. The notion of a curse connected with the tomb had already begun to appear during Carnarvon's illness, fuelled by occultists including Marie Corelli

(Frayling 1992: 43–44). Following his death, the curse story was expanded by journalists seeking original stories to break from the exclusive excavation coverage granted to *The Times*. Prominent fiction writers were queried in an attempt to appeal to the general public. H. Rider Haggard had a devoted amateur's knowledge of Egyptology (Addy 1998) but felt that anyone such as he expressing an opinion on the "efficacy of magical curses against despoilers [of] ancient mummies" would "make a public fool of himself" (Higgins 1980: 256). Nevertheless, an even more influential writer, Arthur Conan Doyle, famous in the 1920s (or infamous to many) as the acknowledged champion of Spiritualism, made vague comments about "elementals" in the tomb (Frayling 1992: 46–47; Reeves 1990: 63).

Most professional Egyptologists dismissed the notion of a curse, but Arthur Weigall, Egyptologist turned journalist, fanned the flames enough to help keep the idea viable (Frayling 1992: 53–54). In his various writings at the time of the Tut discovery, Weigall, like most others, denied a curse associated with the tomb, yet teasingly recounted seemingly supernatural occurrences, only to dismiss his personal belief in them (Weigall 1923). In this way he not only fostered interest in the curse but ultimately gave it some measure of credence (Winstone 1991: 261–263). A case has been made that Weigall may have had a grudge of sorts with Howard Carter (James 1992: 252) but a new biography of Weigall suggests that the problem was from Carter's side (Hankey 2001). Aged only 53 when he died in 1934, Weigall is often listed as one of the 'victims' of the curse he may have helped to create.

Today the curse is still with us, though in greater or lesser amounts, depending upon the context. *The Complete Tutankhamun,* a book with a seemingly all-encompassing title, dismisses the curse in a minor sidebar, little more than an extended footnote (Reeves 1990: 62–63). Recent biographies of Howard Carter, the excavator, detail the curse in varying degrees (James 1992: 370–372; Winstone 1991: 261–266). *The Face of Tutankhamun*, dealing as much with 'Tutmania' as with Tut, allots considerable space to this issue (Frayling 1992), and of course there exist entire volumes devoted exclusively to this curse and its offshoots (Naud 1977; Vandenberg 1975).

The details of the alleged curse are less relevant here than its 'existence'. The curse may not be real, but the idea of the curse is. Tomb curses are known of course, but seldom from royal burials and seldom of the vague sort – "Death on swift wings ..." (Silverman 1997: 146). No actual curse as claimed has been proven for Tut's tomb, yet a curse story was planted, took root and grew. Numerous victims, in addition to Lord Carnarvon, have been listed, but with little or no compelling suggestion that they died mysteriously (Silverman 1987). Scientific explanations, such as fungus from the tomb walls, have been proposed to explain the curse's victims, but if no curse actually exists, and no truly inexplicable deaths can be cited, what need is there of explanations, scientific or otherwise? The events surrounding the Tut discovery offered great dramatic possibilities for use outside Egyptology proper, but how direct and significant was their role in solidifying the modern folklore of mummies' curses as exemplified in the Karloff film which appeared just as the Tut excavations were completed?

The Times newspaper for 2 February 1932 reported briefly that Howard Carter, after a decade's work in Tutankhamun's tomb, had finally finished (Frayling 1992: 60). Supposedly that same week writer Nina Wilcox Putnam completed the story which was eventually to develop into the screenplay for *The Mummy* (Jensen 1996: 6). If this timing was more than mere coincidence, at most the Putnam story, *Cagliostro*, could owe little to the Tut episode other than its designation of the lead character as Egyptian. *Cagliostro* was revised over the next week or so by Richard Schayer, of Universal's scenario department, but that version reportedly has little if any additional Egyptian flavour (Jensen 1996: 6–7). The title character, whose name is actually derived from an Italian alchemist, is an ancient Egyptian magician who developed an elixir of nitrates which, through regular injections, has kept him alive since antiquity. The plot concerns his attempts to kill various women resembling one who wronged him long ago. It is difficult to believe that this scenario resulted from studio heads at Universal commissioning a film plot around Tut's curse, as has often been claimed (Brunas *et al.* 1990: 50–51), since the story treatment in fact did not involve mummies or curses. A short story version of *The Mummy* by James Whitlatch, published concurrently with the film's release in late 1933 (reprinted in Riley 1989: 41–50), is stated to be based on the 'film drama' by Putnam and Schayer. While far from identical to the finished film, this story is nevertheless far closer to the published script than to the original *Cagliostro*. It seems likely that this published short story was actually based on an early version of the screenplay, developed through several revisions by John Balderston, though he is not credited in the Whitlatch version.

Balderston had been called in by Universal to develop a full screenplay from *Cagliostro* after his adaptations of *Dracula* and *Frankenstein,* which they had filmed the previous year, became box office successes. The final shooting script, dated 12 September 1932 and titled Im-Ho-Tep (reprinted in Riley 1989) is close, but again not identical to the released film. Paul Jensen, in a detailed study of the sources for the film plot, attributes all of the presumably Tut-derived elements – the Egyptian setting, the intact royal tomb and especially the curse – to Balderston's hand (Jensen 1996: 8). Certainly Balderston had the right background, having been a reporter covering the Tut discovery. He probably never met Arthur Weigall, as the latter reported on the Tut excavations in 1923, while Balderston seems to have done so a couple of years later (Rubincam 2001), but he was familiar with the writings of the one-time Egyptologist, as his final script includes notes recommending one of Weigall's books as a source for costume designs (Mank 1989: 22). One of Weigall's essays published in his 1923 book on Tutankhamun detailed the story of a mummified cat whose spirit may have broken forth from its bandages and clawed his hand before escaping into the night, though he leaves the verdict to the reader. Was this the inspiration for Balderston's inclusion in the Karloff film of an apparently demonic cat which actually kills a large dog, or is this simply the writer turning Bastet (or Sekhmet) into a familiar for his villain? Contrarily, the 1999 'remake' of *The Mummy* turned this around and made a white cat Imhotep's nemesis.

The original version of *The Mummy* (summarized by Brunas *et al.* 1990: 48–59) concerns an expedition which finds the tomb of Imhotep (not the famous third Dynasty sage) recovering not only his mummy but a box containing the Scroll of Thoth, which when read aloud restores life to the uneviscerated mummy. This notion is clearly derived from the story of Setne Khamwas, one of the few ancient Egyptian tales concerning actual revivification of mummies (Lichtheim 1980: 125–138), and is indicative of Balderston's familiarity with some aspects of Egyptology.

The curse, promising death to anyone who opens the box containing the scroll, is actually a bit of a gimmick in the film, apparently inserted simply to play off the Tut's curse phenomenon. In the film, the curse is not directly responsible for any deaths. The young man who unwittingly restores Imhotep to life goes mad at the sight of the living mummy, and we are told later that he died shortly after, but this is pure circumstance, with no attempt by the mummy to harm him; all Imhotep wants is the scroll. All later victims in the film are people who attempt to thwart his use of the scroll. In fact, contrary to almost all later mummy films, in which the mummy is bent on the destruction of anyone remotely connected with desecrating a royal tomb, Imhotep, after divesting himself of his mummy wrappings to masquerade as a modern day Egyptian, actually manipulates the archaeologists to excavate a new tomb, that of Princess Anck-es-en-amon, daughter of Amenophis. We of course know that the historic Ankhesenamen was the wife of Tutankhamun, and her name was used, as was the curse, to relate to audience familiarity. (More detailed historical background detailing her life as the third daughter of Akhenaten was retroactively added to the story in a 1976 paperback novelization of the film by Ramsey Campbell, writing under the name Carl Dreadstone.)

Imhotep's goal in pointing the way to the discovery of the princess's tomb is recovery of her mummy which he plans to revive with the scroll. Before this is accomplished, however, he comes into contact with Helen Grosvenor, a half-Egyptian woman who, he comes to realize, is the reincarnation of his lost love. A major element edited out of the finished film concerns Anck-es-en-amon/Helen's rebirth in many lives throughout history. Why would Balderston, apparently quite familiar with certain aspects of Egyptian belief, introduce a theme of reincarnation, a clearly un-Egyptian concept?

While still developing this screenplay, Balderston was commissioned by Universal to do another based on Haggard's *She*, and worked simultaneously on both throughout the summer of 1932 (Jensen 1996: 9). All of the elements from *She* – eternal life, love across the ages, reincarnation – are found in *The Mummy*, though with the genders reversed. Ayesha, the title character of *She*, is Imhotep and Kallikrates/Leo is Anck-es-en-amon/Helen. Though Balderston's version of *She* was never produced, his work on it seems to have significantly affected the final overall structure of *The Mummy*. (RKO released the first sound version of Haggard's oft-filmed tale in 1935, from a script by Ruth Rose, who had written *King Kong*.)

Many commentators have noted that *The Mummy* bears striking structural resemblances to Universal's 1931 *Dracula* (Brunas *et al.* 1990: 52–54; Glut 1978: 164; Jensen 1996: 10–11; Skal 1993: 168); hardly surprising since the latter film was also based on a Balderston adaptation. This underscores, however, that the truly Egyptian elements of the film are only trappings for a plot with themes and characters that can apply to a variety of situations. There is nothing truly Egyptian about the film itself. Bram Stoker's most famous novel had been followed by his own mummy story, *The Jewel of Seven Stars*, which itself has been compared to his earlier vampire classic (Leatherdale 1996: 9–11). Despite these suggested influences and derivations, it is important to note that *The Jewel of Seven Stars* is essentially a story of hate wherein evil triumphs (at least in the original edition), whereas *The Mummy* is a story of eternal love in which evil is vanquished.

A more controversial source for the Karloff film is Conan Doyle. Film historian Leslie Halliwell proclaims *The Mummy* to be directly inspired by, indeed nearly plagiarized from, *The Ring of Thoth* (Halliwell 1986: 203), though several Doyle biographers had noted the similarities first (Cox 1985: 207; Higham 1976: 309). Halliwell believes that the similarities between Doyle's story and the Karloff film are overwhelming, "except that the ring … [of Thoth] has become a scroll [of Thoth]" (Halliwell 1986: 212–213). But the ring brings death, the scroll life. As noted above, Doyle's story concerns union in death; *The Mummy*, much more like *She*, concerns union in eternal life. A more convincing parallel involves Sosra's injection of an elixir to confer immortality in the Doyle story, a feature virtually duplicated in the original film story by Putnam and Schayer in which Cagliostro has remained alive since pharaonic times through injection of nitrates.

Is *The Ring of Thoth*, a 40 year old story in the early 1930s, to be considered a possible source for *The Mummy*? Doyle's well-known pronouncements concerning Lord Carnarvon's death would likely be familiar to people working on a mummy's curse scenario. Conan Doyle himself died in 1930 and that same year a collected edition of his works appeared, including both of his mummy stories. His name and work thus had a currency just prior to the development of this film. In fact, this seems obvious from a story by pulp writer Arlton Eadie which appeared in the magazine *Weird Tales* in the spring of 1932, just as Balderston was adapting *Cagliostro* into *The Mummy*. The *Nameless Mummy* is Eadie's bald-faced rip-off of *The Ring of Thoth*, exchanging the genders and adding big-name mummies, so that Cleopatra seeks out the mummy of Marc Antony to get, from his ring, the antidote to the elixir that has kept her alive for 2,000 years. If anyone 'plagiarized' Doyle, it was Eadie far more than the screenwriters from Universal, but maybe they were copying from him!

A stronger candidate than Doyle, but thus far overlooked as an influence on *The Mummy*, is Guy Boothby. The hypnotic influence that his 'Professor of History' exercises over a young woman is strikingly evocative of the relationship between Imhotep and Helen in the film. The encounter in the museum before a mummy case and her 'remembrance' of her past life in Egypt mirror entire scenes from the Balderston screenplay, though not all appear in the final film. Without studying the script, many of these parallels are lost, which may partially explain why this story does not seem to have been proposed as a source. Another factor is that today Boothby is a more obscure author than Haggard, Doyle, Stoker or Rohmer, but he was probably more widely read in the 1930s, so he is likely to have been more familiar to Balderston's generation than today.

Another possible source for themes utilized in *The Mummy* is Sax Rohmer's *Brood of the Witch Queen*, first published in 1914 but re-issued as *It Came Out of Egypt* in 1923, just after the Tut discovery, and serialized yet again as *The Witch's Son* in 1933, perhaps in an attempt to cash in on the film's release. If Balderston did not convert Doyle's 'Ring of Thoth' to the film's 'Scroll of Thoth,' which seems unlikely, he may have renamed Rohmer's 'Book of Thoth', though again it is quite possible that he was relying on his own familiarity with matters Egyptian. Also in the Rohmer novel, the evil 'mummy' is eventually struck down by occult forces – fire-demons – just as Karloff's Imhotep is shattered by the power of the goddess Isis before he can commit the blasphemy of killing Helen, mummifying her, and then resurrecting her into immortality by reading the scroll. Rohmer's *Daughter of Fu Manchu*, already noted for its pseudo-mummy resurrection scene, was also released in book form in 1931, just prior to the film's development.

Obviously, the Karloff film seems to utilize elements from a number of sources, both literary and historical. The Tutankhamun curse may or may not have been the initial spark for conceiving the film's plot, but it certainly came to occupy a role in developing the theme of the script. The actual plot shares elements with numerous earlier mummy stories and novels, many of which themselves show cross-influences and borrowings. This brings us back to Daly's thesis of early mummy fiction sharing elements reflective of Victorian commodity culture, in particular some form of either physical or spiritual revivification of Egypt's ancient dead, with erotic overtones. The Universal film unquestionably falls into this pattern. As entertaining and enlightening as a search for *the* source for the film in specific authors or stories can be, in the end scholars might better see *The Mummy* as a legacy of all that has gone before, a mélange of elements from literature, popular culture and historical reality, much as *Star Wars* has re-mixed Flash Gordon, space opera, B-westerns, and Saturday afternoon serials into something new.

Viewed this way, it is not surprising that relatively little of authentic Egyptian flavour is apparent in *The Mummy*. Each of the authors cited above enjoyed varying degrees of familiarity with Egyptology, and some material in these works is simply wrong. But even those with fairly extensive knowledge, such as Rider Haggard, were writing at a very early period in the development of Egyptology as a discipline, and much of their understanding is now outdated. More important, however, is that strictly factual Egyptology was irrelevant. These writers were not attempting to recreate Ancient Egypt in their stories, but to provide a rough milieu in which to tell a particular story. Had someone other than John Balderston, someone without his basic familiarity with Egypt, been assigned the screenwriting for *The Mummy*, the film would likely feel even less 'Egyptian' than it does, and neither the Universal executives nor the public would have minded, as long as it was a good story. And it was a good story, enough so that it eventually inspired pseudo-sequels, rip-offs and remakes that have further solidified the modern popular, almost folkloric, understanding of Egyptian mummies, tombs and curses.

More mummies in the movies

The Mummy was not the first film to deal with the subject of its title. An interesting case has been made that early cinema, as well as its technological predecessors – the phantasmagorias and lantern slide shows – shared a unique relationship with Ancient Egypt "bound to discourses on death, on preservation, on silence, and on light projection, all resonant with pharaonic import via recent Victorian excavation and exhibition" (Lant 1992: 98). Early movie theatres could be seen as evocative of pharaoh's tombs. Egyptian "dynastic dramas … provided a rich seam of possibilities for narratives" (Lant 1992: 109). Over 40 films utilizing a mummy theme appeared in just a quarter of a century (Kinnard 1995), from two 1899 one-minute films by Georges Melies, *Cleopatra* (or *Cleopatra's Tomb*) and *The Column of Fire* (the earliest film version of Haggard's *She*), to the first feature length production, 1912's *The Vengeance of Egypt,* to the final silent short in 1926, *Mummy Love*. Many of these films were short fantasies and/or comedies, some derived from theatrical plays, but a few dealt with supposed curses, perhaps most notably the 1918 German film *Eyes of the Mummy*. Universal's 1932 Karloff vehicle, however, was the first sound mummy film and the horror classic that spawned a genre.

If *The Mummy* was the culmination of one tradition, primarily literary, the mummy romance emphasizing love through the ages, it was at the same time the lead-in to a new tradition, the mummy's curse emphasizing death for tomb despoilers. Karloff's Imhotep was utterly destroyed by the power of Isis in 1932, but Universal revived the mummy as a horror star for the 1940s. This new mummy, Kharis, ambled through four films from 1940–1944 (summarized in Brunas *et al.* 1990), escaping death from bullets, fire and drowning, to remain constantly in a living state by drinking the fluid of *tana* leaves (grown around Lake Tana, source of the Blue Nile?). At first attempting to kill everyone involved in opening his beloved Princess Ananka's tomb, Kharis later concentrated on keeping the lustful priests of their cult from mating with her modern reincarnation rather than returning her to the tomb where she belonged. This theme of vengeance on tomb defilers is in direct opposition to the plot of the Karloff film and much closer to the so-called curse of King Tut.

The Mummy, as has been seen, potentially owes some inspiration to *The Ring of Thoth*, but the Kharis cycle seems almost certainly derivative of Doyle's second mummy tale. *Lot No. 249* provides the precise *modus operandi* of the Kharis film series – a mute mummy is revived by reading an incantation while burning "dried palmate leaves, the sacred plant", and is then dispatched on missions of vengeance. Doyle's story was televised by the BBC in 1967 and updated, with more gore, as one of three short pieces comprising the 1990 anthology film *Tales From the Darkside*.

Ananka is presumably a simplified form of Anck-es-en-amon, but where did the amazingly un-Egyptian name of Kharis come from? Could the scriptwriters, in attempting to develop a new non-Karloff mummy, have subconsciously (or consciously) inverted and combined the middle two syllables of the actor associated with the role, Boris Karloff? A similar transposition occurred later in the series when the priests of the god Karnak from the first two films suddenly became priests of Arkam in the third. Had the scriptwriters been advised that Karnak was a place rather than a deity and hastily recombined the sounds to something that remained vaguely familiar? These films obviously made little attempt to maintain Egyptian authenticity, as low budgets and short schedules demanded re-use of sets and scenes from earlier films (and see Schadla-Hall and Morris Chapter 14, this volume), most notably the South American temple interior from 1940s *Green Hell* appearing as the tomb chamber in *The Mummy's Hand*, complete with giant llama heads – Egyptianized by adding some hastily painted hieroglyphs around the base (Figure 2:1, above).

The Universal Kharis films are simpler, less logical and more action-oriented than their predecessor; in short, they are aimed at a clearly more juvenile, or at least less sophisticated, audience. Whether this was the result of Universal's belief that audiences in general had changed by the 1940s or simply a conscious production of movies for youngsters, the overall effect was to diminish the stature of the mummy movie from a complex, moody and dark love story to a fast-paced but fairly light-weight horror film.

Universal dropped their horror films altogether by 1945, only to revive them later in a series of Abbott and Costello comedies, with varying success. It is telling that *Abbott & Costello Meet the Mummy* from 1955, their last but hardly their best horror spoof, is not as funny as *The Mummy's Curse,* the 1944 finale of the Kharis series, whose plot and action were yawningly repetitive but filled with supposedly serious scenes which are unintentionally hilarious in retrospect. Earlier comedy teams had attempted to treat the mummy theme with varying success: Wheeler and Woolsey in *Mummy's Boys* from 1936 are pretty stale, at least by modern standards, while the 'Three Stooges' hold up fairly well in the 1939 short *We Want Our Mummy* and to a lesser extent in *Mummy's Dummies* from 1948.

Just as Universal built its reputation in early sound films with classic horror stories in the early 1930s, Hammer films of England, in the late 1950s, produced new adaptations of these same stories as period pieces filmed in colour. In 1959 they released their version of *The Mummy* (summarized by Del Vecchio and Johnson 1992: 121–127), which, because of the title and Hammer's association with Universal monster characters, is often considered a remake of the Karloff film. In fact, this film is a creative mélange of elements derived from all five of the Universal mummy films, combined with several original elements of both plot and milieu. Had it retained the working title, *Terror of the Mummy,* it might command more respect as the original film that it is.

From an Egyptological perspective, Hammer's *The Mummy* exhibits a confusing blend of accurate and misleading references. As in the earlier Universal Kharis films, the priest who revives *this* Kharis again worships the misnamed god Karnak, but here it is depicted not as a giant llama, as in *The Mummy's Hand,* but in an Egyptian style, mummiform with the head of a mongoose (?). Meanwhile, completely appropriate Egyptian deities like Osiris, Anubis and Shu are mentioned virtually in the same breath. The Scroll of Life used to re-animate the mummy is translated with fairly accurate references to '*ka,* the double', '*ba,* the soul' and '*ab,* the heart', although the funeral cortege inaccurately includes a 'casket containing the heart'. Objects found in the tomb are accurate replicas of items from Tutankhamun's burial, yet the tomb structure itself, with hinged double doors, is totally unlike Tut's. The mummy of Kharis, never embalmed, has become grey and ragged over the centuries and has apparently lost its head bandages, despite being locked away in a presumably dust-free niche, whereas the body of Ananka, fully embalmed with all the arts of Ancient Egypt (having lain "for 70 days in her bath of natron"), is swathed with what at first appears to be a gilded funerary mask, until the eyelids flutter just before her revival is cut short, indicating that this is her actual flesh. Unlike the Universal films, this movie does not espouse reincarnation, though it does rely on the strong physical resemblance between Ananka and a modern woman to manipulate Kharis. Despite its frustrating lack of consistency regarding Egyptological issues, Hammer's *The Mummy* is nevertheless an atmospheric film that raised mummy cinema up from the abyss of juvenile horror/comedy into which it had sunk.

Other mummy films followed from Hammer in the following decade: *Curse of the Mummy's Tomb* in 1964 and *The Mummy's Shroud* in 1967. Each is an original story, unconnected to previous mummy films, and each opts for yet another mechanism for reviving the mummy; in the former a medallion of immortality is used and in the latter the text on the shroud must be read aloud. One wonders why the means of reviving these destructive mummies is universally buried with them. Both films are also interesting because each mummy consciously destroys itself. In the earlier film, the mummy kills himself and his long-lived evil brother, the real villain of the piece, by pulling a sewer roof down. In *The Mummy's Shroud*, the mummy Prem crushes his own skull between his hands.

Prem is also unique for his authentic look. Many commentators have observed that Lon Chaney and others have depicted rather well-fed mummies, not much resembling the desiccated bodies found in museums. Nevertheless, it has been claimed that Jack Pierce, Universal's make-up artist, based Imhotep on an actual royal mummy, though a reading of claimed sources is rather confusing. The original of Karloff has been cited as Seti I (Glut 1978: 165), Seti II (Brier 1994: 309) and Tuthmosis III (El Mahdy 1989: 174), the last actually a mistakenly labelled photo of Ramesses III. Ramesses III himself has been cited as the model for Universal's Kharis, but that caption actually accompanies a photo of Karloff's Imhotep (Brier 1994: 313)! No such confusion surrounds Prem, a duplicate in every detail of an unnamed Greco-Roman mummy still on exhibit at the British Museum.

Hammer's final mummy film, from 1972, has the most lurid title of all: *Blood from the Mummy's Tomb*, yet is noteworthy because no living mummy features. Based on Stoker's *Jewel of Seven Stars*, the film ends with the audience unsure if the modern woman or the evil queen Tera has survived. As noted above, the novel resolved the plot each way in separate editions. Later films of Stoker's story, *The Awakening* in 1980 and *Bram Stoker's The Mummy* in 1997, both ended with the queen's evil spirit clearly controlling the daughter. Yet a fourth film of this tale, actually the earliest produced, was presented on British television in 1971 as *Curse of the Mummy* but has not been widely seen or appreciated (Halliwell 1986: 240).

Mummy films continued to be made throughout the 1970s, 1980s and 1990s, frequently for Spanish, French or Italian markets.[3] America primarily produced made-for-TV movies.[4] Low-budget films had limited release or were brought out directly on video: *The Mummy & the Curse of the Jackals* was filmed in 1969 but only released, on video, in 1985.[5] Imagine the plot of the unproduced early 1990s script, *Revenge of the Hollywood Mummies*! Films that *did* get produced included *The Mummy Lives* from 1993 which featured former Hollywood idol Tony Curtis as both high priest and mummy, and the pornographic *Mummy Dearest* trilogy from 1990–1992, in which semen revives the mummy in an ironically Min-like fashion.

Myriad mummies

The Karloff film began a process of transferring the centre of mummy fiction to the screen, but mummies did not disappear from literature. The early 20th century saw the rise of pulp magazines, cheaply produced periodicals featuring genre fiction. Dozens, if not hundreds, of mummy stories were featured in many of these pulps, particularly those dedicated to fantasy, science fiction, mystery and the occult. While many pulp authors are virtually unknown today, some have gained a certain level of lasting fame. Those who produced mummy stories include E. Hoffman Price,

Maxwell Grant, Seabury Quinn, Kenneth Robeson, Robert Bloch, and even Tennessee Williams at the very beginning of his career. Modern paperback books have continued the trends of the pulps with anthologies of mummy stories collecting both older and newly written tales (Ghidalia 1971; Greenberg 1990; Haining 1988; Pronzini 1980; Stephens 2001).

A sub-genre of mummy mystery stories became increasingly popular in the first third of the 20th century. Often such stories involve a mummy's curse as a red herring to mask a non-supernatural crime, or simply use a mummy case as a convenient means of hiding corpses.[6] Romantic suspense novels involving mummies include *Curse of the Kings* by Victoria Holt (1973) and Robin Cook's *Sphinx* (1979).[7]

Occult, fantasy or science fictional mummy tales continue to appear in new variations, ranging from *The Third Grave* by David Case (1981), which combines mummies with Haitian voodoo, to *SUM VII* by T. W. Hard (1979), in which an excavated mummy turns out to be an alien stranded on earth in antiquity, an idea used later in the 1982 television movie *Time Walker*. More traditional horror stories thrive as well, like Charles L. Grant's 1986 *The Long Night of the Grave* and Michael Paine's *Cities of the Dead* (1988), in which a pre-Tut Howard Carter uncovers a sorcerous plot to mummify (and potentially revive) modern Egyptian children. The most recent mummy novel by a major writer is Anne Rice's *The Mummy, or Ramses the Damned* (1989) which includes the resurrection, again by elixir, of both Ramesses the Great *and* Cleopatra! The Khamwas tale involving the Scroll of Thoth was used by Pauline Gedge for her 1990 novel *The Scroll of Saqqara* (also known as *Mirage*). A manuscript announced on the internet in 1999, but apparently still unpublished, *Juniper's Dynasty* by Peter Blinn, was to focus on a mummy cloned in modern times.

In the late 1950s two related phenomena helped spawn a major wave of 'Mummymania' aimed at juveniles, as one facet of a larger 'monstermania'. Universal Pictures released many of its 1930s and 1940s horror films to television as a Shock Theatre package, and the magazine *Famous Monsters of Filmland* was born. Immediately a new generation of young people, primarily boys, became familiar with these 'classic' monsters and the merchandising boom was close behind. Sir Thomas Browne had written 300 years earlier, concerning powdered mummy as medicine, that "Mummie is become Merchandise ..." (Wortham 1971b: 11). How true this would become in a context quite distinct from Browne's original meaning.

Beginning in the early 1960s, monster toys and models began to appear, either based directly on the Universal monsters or some thinly disguised take-off. The mummy was among this group. Games, puzzles, clothes, trading cards, jewellery, costumes and other collectibles followed (Schadla-Hall and Morris Chapter 14, this volume). As this market expanded, companies without licenses from Universal developed alternate lines of merchandise and the variety of mummy action figures and other toys expanded significantly. Today there is a wide range of resin model kits, latex masks, role-playing games and other items based on both licensed mummy characters and original designs. Mummies have come to be part of a group of 'standard' monsters, including man-made monsters, vampires and werewolves, that are now as common in Hallowe'en merchandising as the more traditional ghosts and witches. Mummies have even become Christmas tree ornaments, ranging from those emulating real coffins, to film mummies, to totally whimsical originals.

Even before the Universal films reached the small screen, radio had provided a new venue for fictional mummies. A radio dramatization of *The Ring of Thoth* was presented on the CBS programme *Escape* in 1947, while Gautier's *The Mummy's Foot* was adapted for TV as early as 1949. Since then, mummies have figured in the plots of numerous television programmes.[8]

Mummies have appeared in cartoons since at least 1926, when Mutt and Jeff starred in *Mummy O'Mine*. The earliest sound cartoon with a mummy may be 1933's *Magic Mummy*. An early Superman cartoon from 1943, *The Mummy Strikes*, was followed by Heckle and Jeckle in *King Tut's Tomb* (1950). Numerous television cartoons have featured mummies, ranging from Jonny Quest, the Fantastic Four and Superman to the Three Stooges, Laurel and Hardy and Abbott and Costello.[9] The long-lived Scooby-Doo has encountered mummies from the 1960s through the 1980s. A mummy was a regular on *The Groovie Goolies* in the 1970s, *Thundercats* in the 1980s and *Monster Force* in the 1990s. In 1997 a complete series starring reborn mummies, titled appropriately *Mummies Alive!*, ran for 42 episodes. Many of these shows spun off their own lines of action figures, toys and other merchandise.

Books aimed at the juvenile market have always been popular, often series of adventures with recurring characters. Early examples are *Jerry Todd and the Whispering Mummy* by Leo Edwards (1923) and *The Three Investigators and the Mystery of the Whispering Mummy* by Robert Arthur (1965), in both of which the presumed mummies turn out not to be supernatural. Nearly 30 books for children or juveniles appeared in the 1980s, including entries in 'The Hardy Boys' and 'The Bobbsey Twins' series, not to mention Indiana Jones spin-offs. In the 1990s the 'Goosebumps' series spawned a new interest in horror books for youngsters, resulting in over 75 juvenile-audience mummy books appearing in the last decade, more than one every other month, featuring everyone from Garfield to Scooby-Doo and Carmen Sandiego to Sabrina, the Teenage Witch.

Comic books have been around since the 1930s and mummies have appeared in them for nearly their entire history. In addition to the numerous adaptations of films and novels, comics have presented mummies in stories of cartoon characters ranging through Donald Duck, Bugs Bunny, Heckle and Jeckle, Fritzi Ritz, Tintin, Casper the Ghost, Rocky and Bullwinkle, Richie Rich, Scooby-Doo, Archie, Teenage Mutant Ninja Turtles, Pinky and the Brain and more. A series about the mummy and ba of a cat, *Sheba,* appeared in 1996 (based on a strip originating in 1992). The comic *Little Gloomy* appeared in 1999, featuring a mummy whose word balloons contain hieroglyphs, and *Monster High School*, from 2001, includes Cleo, a teenage girl mummy, among its students. Superheroes have encountered mummies in the comics too, from forgotten 1940s characters like Flash Lightning, Miss Masque and Cat-Man to more familiar names.[10] Comics based on film or TV celebrities or characters that have encountered mummies include Jerry Lewis, Laurel and Hardy, the Three Stooges, 1950s pin-up queen Bettie Page and Xena, Warrior Princess.

There were dozens of gruesome mummy tales in the pre-comics code era of the early 1950s, the best coming from EC's *Haunt of Fear* and *Tales From the Crypt*. Gothic yet ghastly tales of mummies frequently appeared in the large-format black and white comics of the 1970s such as *Eerie, Creepy, Vampirella, Devilina, Tales From the Tomb* and *Terror Tales*. Entire series devoted to a single mummy include *The Living Mummy*

(N'Kantu and Dr Scarab, 1973–1975), *The Occult Files of Dr Spektor* (Ra-Ka-Tep, 1973–1976) and the crossover double-story series *The Mummy Walks/Curse of the Werewolf* (1973–1976). Newspaper comics have produced nothing funnier than Gary Larson's *The Far Side*, primarily from the 1980s, and his more than a dozen one-frame mummy cartoons are among his best, usually dealing with curses in offbeat and comical ways but also making fun of other aspects of life as a mummy.

Music and song with mummy themes date at least to the 1904 musical farce, *The Maid and the Mummy*. After World War I, such songs as 'Mummy Mine' (1918), 'At the Mummies' Ball' (1921) and 'I'm a Mummy' (1930s) appeared. Poet Rod McKuen, in his early days, collaborated to produce the late 1950s album 'Songs Our Mummy Taught Us', featuring the hit single 'The Mummy' and 'Son of the Mummy'. Other gimmick songs were 'My Mummy' (1959) by Mel Cavin and the Kokonuts, 'Mummy Walk' by the Contrails (1966), 'Me and My Mummy' (1962) by Bobby 'Boris' Pickett of *Monster Mash* fame, and 'Rockin' Teenage Mummies' by Ray Stevens (1965). In 1993, Australian Colin Buchanan produced the CD album 'I Want My Mummy' with several mummy songs. Over the years there have also been various instrumentals with mummy themes. Rock groups such as The Rolling Stones, Metallica, Iron Maiden, and Steely Dan have utilized mummies in their product and promotional art, while recent music videos by the Backstreet Boys and Daft Punk have featured mummies. The Mummies, a punk rock group from the early 1990s, performed in bandages, while another group, The Ululating Mummies, wrote and sang mummy-themed music. There was even a Mummy record label in Jamaica.

With all this exposure to mummies in all facets of entertainment, it is no surprise that they have frequently been used to promote products. Mummies have advertised, through magazines, television and point-of-purchase displays, everything from alcohol and cigarettes to milk and sweets: Palmolive soap (World War I era), Scotch tape (1948), Twinkies (1975), Virginia Slims (1984), Bud Light (1985), Carlsberg (1989), Old Milwaukee (1993), Bud Dry (1994), Pepsi (1992), Schweppes Lemonade (1998), Absolut Vodka (1998), Tombstone Pizza (1999), Milk ('Got Milk?' TV spot 1999), and Hershey's candies (1999/2000). Mummies have sold both Koss headphones ('Wrap Music') and Cabot Corp. earplugs ('Your Hearing is Worth Preserving').

Hallowe'en of 2000 saw the release of Blasted Froot Loops cereal with marshmallow mummies, though a complete product, Fruity Yummy Mummy cereal, had appeared as early as 1987. Other mummy edibles have included numerous sweets called Yummy Mummies (1991), Munchy Mummies (ca. 1980), Gummy Mummies (at least two different products, from Fleer in the 1980s and Brach's in 1999) and Mummies and Deadies (1990s). Nabisco released Monster Cookies in 1998 featuring Universal mummies and Pandora's Confections recently offered a chocolate pyramid with chocolate mummies inside.

Millennial 'mummymania'

Today the passion for mummies is stronger than ever, with 'Mummymania' peaking at the turn of the millennium. The latest literary mummies are found in *The Eye of Horus* by Carol Thurston (2000), which develops a double mystery, one ancient, one modern, based on the radiological/forensic study of the actual mummy of Lady Tashat, transplanted from its real home at the Minneapolis Institute of Arts (Notman 1986: 252) to a fictional Denver museum, and in C. E. Albertson's *The Mummy's Curse* (2000) dealing with lost Nazi gold. Juvenile books continue to appear with great regularity.

Recent films include the already mentioned latest Bram Stoker adaptation from 1997; *For Love or Mummy*, a 1998 retro Laurel and Hardy film; and the 1999 video release of Russell Mulcahy's *Tale of the Mummy* (released to European and Asian theatres the previous year as *Talos the Mummy*). A film about a revived Druid witch, *The Eternal* (1999), was subtitled *Kiss of the Mummy* to cash in on the flurry of publicity surrounding mummy films, and the direct-to-video cheapie *Ancient Evil: Scream of the Mummy* (2001), although dealing with an 'Aztec' mummy, was marketed in Europe as *Bram Stoker's The Mummy 2!* The true blockbuster, however, whose production helped to drive much of the lesser competition, was Universal's 1999 'remake' of *The Mummy* (Figure 2:5).

Figure 2:5
Universal Studios'
(1998) remake of
The Mummy.

The Universal film had by far the largest budget and was the most anticipated due to its connection with the Karloff classic. However, rather than produce a true remake, the film's writer/director Stephen Sommers chose to base only the skeleton of his story on the earlier film. The mummy revived in modern times is still named Imhotep, and his goal is still to raise from the dead his beloved Anck-su-namun (an 'updated' spelling), but there the similarities end. Rather than a macabre horror/love story, the new version of *The Mummy* is a grand adventure tinged with both horror and comedy. Various scenes or situations recall a host of diverse films.[11] Just as the Karloff film incorporated elements from a variety of literary sources, this new film took inspiration from a rich tradition of action/adventure/epic cinema.

Some situations suggest the Tut connection, such as the heroine's surname of Carnahan echoing Carnarvon. Many elements introduce Egyptological realities, but again in a frustratingly inaccurate way. Major elements like the City of Hamunaptra and the Curse of Hom-Dai are complete cinematic inventions. The Book of the Dead, the collection of spells for overcoming the challenges of the afterlife, is depicted as an actual bound book (but see Quirke 2003) that can be used to raise the dead. Canopic jars play a crucial role in the mummy's full resurrection, yet they are not the four known from Egyptian tombs, but five, the extra one containing the heart, an organ never purposely removed from a real mummy. Normally, this divergence from fact should be acceptable if it improves or drives the story. In this case it is particularly glaring, as the apocryphal lion-headed heart jar is the one found smashed upon discovery, yet the entire episode detailing this was edited out of the completed film. Few patrons seem to have been bothered by these omissions, probably because the breakneck speed of the film allows little time for serious reflection on such subtle points. Nevertheless, this film breathed new life into the age-old mummy, spawning dozens of action figures, books and other spin-offs.

A sequel released in May of 2001, *The Mummy Returns*, has again taken its own direction, further widening the gap with actual Egyptology. With a bigger budget (the first $100 million mummy movie), it boasts even more action than the first, such that it is actually difficult to assimilate the plot. However, it also made more money than the first and has spawned a major franchise which includes adult and juvenile novelizations of the film, a juvenile book series, more action figures, electronic games, an elaborate trading card set, Hallowe'en costumes, a comic book mini-series, and a weekly animated television show. *The Scorpion King*, released in spring 2002, is nominally based on the predynastic ruler from Hierakonpolis but has virtually nothing to do with mummies, or even Egypt. *Mummy Raider*, a direct-to-video adult film capitalizing on both the Universal film and *Tomb Raider*, the other archaeology action picture of 2001, was released at the end of the year, and it is reported that Ann Rice's mummy novel is being developed into a film. Clearly 2001 was the Year of the Mummy!

The subtitle of this chapter asked, '*Is* Egyptology cursed by the mummy's curse?'. In other words, does this proliferation of mummies into new forms and new media trivialize, juvenilize and even jeopardize a more serious, authentic appreciation of mummies and their archaeological and historical contexts? At first one might be concerned that this is so. But newer analyses of mummy fiction, such as literary studies like Daly's (1994) or cinematic ones like Lant's (1992), suggest that a scholarly interest in mummy fiction is broadening beyond the purview of film or horror *aficionados*. The Karloff film has recently been described as a psycho-sexual feminist tale with Oedipal overtones (Johnson 1991). While intriguing, this interpretation is very personal and open to considerable question, as the author perceives the released film, which is all she seems to have examined, as the product of a female writer, which has been shown to be only a small part of the whole story. From the perspective of semiotics, the study of the relations of signs and symbols in language, Haggard and Stoker have been subjected to psycho-technological analysis (Rickels 1992). Obviously not all such studies have any direct relevance to Egyptology, but they do indicate a growing interest in Egyptian-themed subject matter. And the stories and films that such studies examine are themselves an indicator of a general public interest in Egyptological themes. Indeed, the recent massive wave of 'Mummymania' is not restricted to movie blockbusters and their offshoots.

New archaeological finds and cutting-edge scientific analyses like CT-scanning and DNA research have made mummies one of the premier topics on documentary television for the past decade. Programmes have ranged from *The Curse of Tutankhamen* and *The Curse of the Egyptian Mummies* to *The Curse of the Cocaine Mummies* and have included *The Forgotten Mummies, Magic of the Mummies* and *Secrets of the Mummy*. Howard Carter was featured on a recent episode of A & E's *Biography*. A 1999 television programme, broadcast live from Egypt, showed Zahi Hawass (Picknett and Prince Chapter 13, this volume) 'discovering' mummies as viewers watched; this was followed in 2000 by a live TV visit to open the Tombs of the Golden Mummies. When the new version of *The Mummy* premiered in 1999, its star, Brendan Fraser, hosted a TV event called 'Mummified' which included Fraser's own narration of 'Mummies: The Real Story'. Another recent show, *The Lost Mummy of Imhotep*, deals with the search for the tomb of the third Dynasty sage who is credited with designing the Step Pyramid, but leads into the subject by referencing the title character of the recent Universal films. There are dozens more shows on other aspects of Egyptology, from pyramids to pharaohs' lives. And of course popular books are yet another medium. Recent publications have covered updates on the Manchester Mummy Project (David and Archbold 2000), new finds in Bahriya Oasis (Hawass 2000) and even a detailed look at the researchers who study mummies around the world and report their findings at the World Mummy Congresses (Pringle 2001).

Clearly the fictional portrayal of Egyptian mummies, no matter how questionable historically, can and does engender interest in legitimate Egyptology. But it can also be argued that the strong presence of Egyptology in the popular press and documentary television over the last decade has played no small part in the current revival of fictional mummies. In a symbiotic relationship, each area, factual and fictional, both feeds upon and feeds the other (see Johnson and Cowie 2001).

One cinematic theorist suggested that early films and Egypt shared a mummy complex, a primal attempt to preserve life beyond death (Bazin, quoted in Lant 1992). Perhaps that is the ultimate fascination of mummies – the promise of eternal life, and its link to a fascinating exotic civilization. The realities of that civilization, however, are frequently twisted and perverted, or often simply ignored, in the fictional treatment of mummies. For some professional Egyptologists, such films and stories were doubtless an early source of interest in Ancient Egypt. Perhaps, in some instances, they have remained, or have subsequently become, a guilty pleasure, enjoyed on a certain level but ultimately seen as 'fluff'. Others may simply deplore them for their lack of historical accuracy or cultural authenticity. Obviously, of the manifold incarnations of the fictional mummy in every imaginable medium, some are better than others, as in any genre. However, if accepted and appreciated for what they are, rather than condemned or dismissed for what they are not, fictions of the mummy need not be feared as a threat to serious Egyptology. Who knows, they may even spark the interest of some of the Egyptologists of tomorrow.

Notes

1   The farcical musicals and comedies have ranged from the 1904 musical *The Maid and the Mummy*, through *The Mummy and the Mumps* (1925) and *The Mummy Bride* (1928) to more modern works like Ken Hill's *The Mummy's Tomb* (1980), Charles Ludlam's *The Mystery of Irma Vep* (1984), *The Mummy's Claw* and *The Mummy Musical*, both from 1992. Intriguingly, the two most recent mummy plays, both of which appeared in 1994, one in England and one in America, while authored separately and having distinct plots, share identical titles – *Sherlock Holmes & the Curse of the Mummy's Tomb*.

2   Several Rohmer stories were associated with actual Egyptian sites including *In the Valley of the Sorceress* (1916, Deir el-Bahri), *Death-Ring of Sneferu* (1917, Meidum), *The Whispering Mummy* (1918, Philae), *The Treasure of Taia* (1925, Medinet Habu). Rohmer's last Egyptian story was *The Mark of Maat* in 1944.

3   E.g. *The Mummy's Revenge*, Spain 1973; *Secret of the Mummy*, Brazil 1982.

4   E.g. *The Cat Creature* (1973), *Cruise into Terror* (1978) and *The Curse of King Tut's Tomb* (1980).

5   Other low grade films were *Dawn of the Mummy* (1981), possibly the only mummy movie ever filmed entirely in Egypt, *The Tomb* (1985), *Mummy a Gore Gore* (1986), *Bloodsucking Pharaohs in Pittsburgh* (1991), and *I Was a Teenage Mummy* (1992, distinct from an amateur 1962 film of the same name).

6   Prime examples include Fergus Hume's *The Green Mummy* (1908, though actually concerning a Peruvian mummy), R. Austin Freeman's *The Eye of Osiris* (1911), Mary Gaunt's *The Mummy Moves* (1925), S. S. Van Dine's *The Scarab Murder Case* (1930), and Dermot Morrah's *The Mummy Case* (1933). Mystery/crime movies got into the act with 1935's *Charlie Chan in Egypt* and the 1940 serial *Drums of Fu Manchu*. More recent mummy mysteries include the first three Amelia Peabody books by Elizabeth Peters (1975–1985), *Murder in a Mummy Case* by K. K. Beck (1986), *Dead Men's Hearts* by Aaron Elkins (1994), *The Egyptian Coffin* by Jane Jakeman (1997) and *Little Knell* by Catherine Aird (2000). A 1999 mystery by Carole Nelson Douglas, *The Mummy Case*, features the mummy of a cat!

7   Recent examples with period settings include Dawn Aldridge Poore's *The Mummy's Mirror* (1995) and Bess Willingham's *The Lady's Mummy* (1997).

8   E.g. *Space Patrol*, *Sherlock Holmes*, *Captain Midnight*, and *Topper* in the 1950s; *Route 66*, *The Munsters*, *The Monkees*, *Batman*, *Get Smart*, *Voyage to the Bottom of the Sea*, and *Dark Shadows* in the 1960s; *Dr Who*, *The Ghost Busters*, *The Tomorrow People*, *The Hardy Boys*, and *Fantasy Island* in the 1970s; *Quincy*, *Buck Rogers*, *Amazing Stories*, *Tales from the Darkside*, *Friday the 13th*, and *The Munsters Today* in the 1980s; *Tales from the Crypt*, *Father Dowling Mysteries*, *Eerie, IN*, *Quantum Leap*, *Swamp Thing*, *Ray Bradbury Theater*, *Poirot*, *Highlander*, *Goosebumps*, *Bone Chillers*, *Hercules*, *Sliders*, *Night Man*, and *The Lost World* in the 1990s. Made-for-television movies aimed at a teenage audience include *Young Indiana Jones & the Curse of the Jackal*, a series pilot in 1992, and *Legend of the Lost Tomb* and *Under Wraps*, both from 1997.

9   Animated shows with mummy appearances have included *Inspector Gadget*, *The Original Ghostbusters*, *Alvin & the Chipmunks*, *Duck Tales*, *Beetlejuice*, *Super Mario Bros*, *Cow & Chicken*, and *Timon and Pumbaa*.

10 E.g. *Superman*, *Batman*, *Captain Marvel*, *Wonder Woman*, *Captain America*, *Martian Manhunter*, *Blue Beetle*, *The Phantom*, *Hawkman*, *Catwoman*, and *The Flash*.

11 E.g. *Indiana Jones*, *Aliens*, *Flight of the Phoenix*, *The Egyptian*, *Sphinx*, *Son of Dracula*, *The Ten Commandments*, *Land of the Pharaohs*, *Valley of the Kings*, *The Mummy's Hand*, *Twister*, *Lawrence of Arabia*, *Jason and the Argonauts*, *The Egyptian*, *The Awakening*, *The Four Feathers*, *Beau Geste*, and *Hang 'Em High*.

CHAPTER 3

HOW TO STAGE *AIDA*

Jean-Marcel Humbert
(translated by Daniel Antoine and Lawrence Stewart Owens)

To copy reality can be a good thing,
But to *create reality* is better, much better …

(Giuseppe Verdi)

Aida is an opera built around four principal characters (Aida, Radames, Amneris and Amonasro) and was originally devised for the relatively small stage of the Cairo Opera (Figure 3:1). Nevertheless, it is increasingly performed on huge stages. What are the reasons behind this? Are such decisions economically, rather than artistically, driven? Is there not a risk that this affects the essence of the opera?

As chance would have it, in 2001 – the centenary of Verdi's death – two very different productions of *Aida* were staged almost simultaneously: one directed by Petrika Ionesco at the gigantic Stade de France (capacity 78,000), the other by Franco Zeffirelli at the very small Busseto Theatre (capacity 350).[1]

Franco Zeffirelli's 'chamber' version, which was recently brought out on DVD,[2] reveals many interesting elements. The result of a Carlo Bergonzi master-class and a lyrical laboratory bringing together several young singers, it reveals a more intimate interpretation of Verdi's work that is virtually unknown today. Even though the Triumphal March – which Verdi wanted to be spectacular – is here replaced by chorus-singers seen shaking palm-leaves with their backs to the audience, the integrity of the work as a whole is remarkable. Several factors explain why there is always a tendency to make productions of *Aida* larger and more spectacular.

An atypical work, full of contrasts

Aida is primarily an intimate, small-scale opera. Indeed, apart from the scene of Radames' Triumph (Figure 3:2 col. pl.), the number of characters present on the stage at any one time is always limited. Similarly, the original orchestration – recreated at the Montpellier Festival on 13 July 1992 – surprises audiences with its perfectly balanced sonority: there is no huge, uncontrolled orchestral involvement and (apart from the flourish of trumpets) no triumphal section.

In addition, the exotic nature of the period – Egyptian antiquity – makes *Aida* a visually spectacular opera in terms of characters, stage decoration and costumes. The

Figure 3:1   Performance of *Aida* in Cairo, 24 December 1871: stage design for the first scene of Act 1, by Philippe-Marie Chaperon (Paris, Bibliothèque-musée de l'Opéra).

question of labelling it an 'archaeological opera' never arose at the time of its creation, as Auguste Mariette had based *Aida*'s dialogue and staging (Humbert 1976: 229–255) on archaeological themes. Verdi himself, despite what some people think, never imagined making his characters adapt to any other environment. The message was clear: he had been required to produce an opera that drew its theme, characters and decors from pharaonic antiquity.

Nevertheless, as noted by Chapaz (1990: 83):

> … the action in *Aida* could be taking place anywhere in the world and the characters' psychology is hardly linked to a particular place. In this sense, the scenario imagined by Mariette is universal and could occur in any place where there is a conflict between love, power and homeland. As an author, Mariette is capable of forgetting Egypt when necessary.

The visual spectacle of the opera tends to eclipse any such conflicts, as can be seen in Clemente Fracasi's (1953) film adaptation. Starring Sophia Loren, the film posters for its American premiere highlight the "Exotic splendour! Gorgeous dance! Unforgettable Love!" (*Aida* 1998: 98). This is the contradiction of *Aida*: on the one hand, the visually engaging nature of the opera ensured its success, whereas on the other, this aspect led to it being labelled as an operatic spectacular. Indeed, its Egyptian theme can result in scenery which is an overly extravagant combination of exoticism and gigantism, although this is specifically true only of Radames' famous triumphal scene.

This scene – which was in fact a last minute addition – was supposed to be the 'star attraction' of the spectacle and – like the unavoidable ballets – was a compromise intended to satisfy regular opera-goers. This led to somewhat overstated behaviour by the performers, wildly extravagant accessories and the use of exotic animals.

A shift in stage settings

While there is a world of difference in size between the Cairo Opera stage and that of La Scala Milan or the Paris Opéra, Italian-style theatres have self-imposed limits which serve to restrict the flamboyant imaginations of set-designers and directors.

The true turning point in the history of the staging of *Aida* actually occurred in 1913 when, to celebrate the centenary of Verdi's birth, it was decided that the opera should be performed within the gargantuan setting of the Verona amphitheatre. Its success was such that it sparked the beginning of a festival that exists to this day, and allows the attendance of some 18,000 spectators at evening performances. More than 400 performances of *Aida* have already been given there, not counting numerous revivals and guest performances that have taken place abroad. This represented a real revolution for *Aida*, and consigns it to a new dimension – that of the pharaonic spectacular.

From the very beginning, Ettore Fagiuoli – whose stage sets were used from 1913 to 1936 – was inspired to completely integrate the amphitheatre into the opera's scenery. His creations were later re-used from 1982 to 1986 (in 1982 with Mariette's costumes) and from 1989 to 1998 (Figure 3:3) with the same effect and to critical acclaim. Complementary decorative elements (porticos, solid masses, obelisks, colonnades, etc.) were only employed to emphasize the monumentality of the setting (Figure 3:4). Later, the steps of the amphitheatre were even more seamlessly incorporated into the set, being used to channel the masses of extras, who could either enter directly from the top, facing the audience – a setting which was first used in 1954 under the direction of Herbert Graf and reused by Vittorio Rossi – or parade down meandering side ramps, in the 1966 Graf production (Venturi 1995: 50–52). 'Pharaonic' monumentality, of which this show was to become an enduring standard, was thus reached for the first time. Several other designers tested themselves in Verona, including Nicolas Benois, Franco Lolli, Pietro Zuffi, Pino Casarini, Attilio Colonnello, Luciano Damiani, Giulio Coltellacci, Remo Brindisi and Pier Luigi Pizzi (Figure 3:5 col. pl.) (Vespa 2001). Their interpretations were always successful, using a range of different means including props such as a gigantic sphinx head or a pyramid, and devices such as dramatic stage props (Figure 3:6).

Aida appears to be very much 'at home' in the Verona amphitheatre, where it is performed almost every year and attracts sizeable crowds. The association is so strong that one cannot imagine the amphitheatre at Verona without its favourite opera, as noted in Pasquale Festa Campanile's screenplay for his film *Il Merlo maschio* (1972). In this film of the 1971–1972 *Aida* production, the performance abruptly loses its way for three comical minutes when a chorus-singer undresses on

Figure 3:3   Stage for the first scene of Act 1 for the 1994 production of *Aida* in Verona (stage settings by Ettore Fagiuoli, adapted by Rinaldo Olivieri) (© Jean-Marcel Humbert).

Figure 3:4   1994 production of *Aida* in Verona, emphasizing monumentality with the use of obelisks, etc. (directed by Gianfranco di Bosio with stage settings by Ettore Fagiuoli, adapted by Rinaldo Olivieri) (© Jean-Marcel Humbert).

Figure 3:6 *Aida* in Verona, 2002 (direction and stage settings by Franco Zeffirelli) (© Jean-Marcel Humbert).

stage under the flabbergasted gaze of the musicians, who begin to lose their composure one after the other, resulting in a cacophony that is amplified by the vastness of the surroundings.

Its incredible success (to date, more than 7 million spectators have seen *Aida* in Verona) has resulted in numerous successors wanting to produce open-air performances, following the Verona example. Similarly disproportionate productions have been performed all over the world, and particularly in Egypt.[3] For example, the now-abandoned stage of the Caracalla thermal baths was 1,500 m² (measuring 32 m at the front, 50 m at the back, 32 m in depth and with a 1/10 slope). In Paris, the stage of the Palais Omnisport de Bercy was 3,600 m² (78 m wide, 46 m deep and with a working height of 24 m) (Figure 3:7). The Shanghai Stadium stage was 5,000 m² and included a 30 metre-high sphinx, providing a backdrop to the elephants, tigers and lions, which were accompanied by 1,900 soldiers from the Chinese popular army playing the part of Egyptian soldiers. The Stade de France stage measured 9,000 m², and was equivalent in size to the Place de la Concorde (approximately 119 x 75 m).

Many problems result from the scale of such productions, including scenic misrepresentation (the tendency to turn intimate moments, such as those that occur in Amneris' apartments, into spectacular events), technical tensions (the balance and synchronization of large orchestras and choirs), as well as vocal and acoustical challenges. Only exceptionally powerful voices can conquer such spaces, often to the

Figure 3:7   *Aida* in the Palais Omnisport de Bercy, Paris, in 1984 (direction and stage settings by Vittorio Rossi) (© Jean-Marcel Humbert).

detriment of the piece's subtlety and musical quality, and some deterioration in sound quality – in terms of both power and tone – is to be expected. It is only with regard to ticket sales that the results are truly convincing: the budget for the Stade de France production (€2.3 million) was covered by the sale of only half of the tickets, which were completely sold out more than four months in advance.

Consequently, all excesses are rendered possible and producers do not hesitate to combine spectacular props (such as elephants, camels and pythons) with the latest technology, including virtual reality and other special effects such as the use of lasers, projected images, sound amplification or – memorably – an enormous luminous sphinx. A similar approach was adopted by a travelling production (which recently toured Japan, Canada, Australia, Northern Europe and Spain). The 1996 Madrid production employed more than 1,200 artists on stage. As director Giuseppe Raffa (*Corriere della Sera* 1996) explained, the production team was clearly unconcerned at popularizing the opera in this way:

> We are at the beginning of the 21st century, and what we are doing is the best way to bring the general public into contact with lyrical art. It is ridiculous to remain bound by the limitations of theatres, and to give up multi-media technology.

However, the general public's evident appetite for such productions remains surprising. It resembles a pilgrimage more than a taste for grand opera, and has more in common with a sense of unity achieved through events which – as in football or rugby matches – require to be as large and spectacular as possible. Jean-Christophe Giletta (Roux 2001: 34), the Stade de France large-events director, admits to being confounded at the speed of ticket sales: "We are witnessing the birth of a public representing a very unusual sector of the population. Indeed, apart from members of the business sector, it is primarily supermarket customers who buy the tickets, despite the seats costing an average of 50 euros." To open up opera to a new audience is admirable, but a fundamental question remains: how far should we go in order to make the opera appeal to the general public?

The diversity of producing *Aida*: from the intimate to the gigantic

In addition to theatre styles, stage dimensions, settings (whether outdoors or indoors) or the country in question, many approaches can be taken to the staging of *Aida*. Whatever the style of the production, it should not be viewed in terms of respect for tradition, nor artistic heresy: even if directors make choices that are not necessarily intellectually honest, their approach is always respectful, usually shrewd, and sometimes even amusing. One can distinguish four different approaches.

Imitating Egypt, or the art of returning to antiquity

For more than a century, imitating Ancient Egypt has been the most popular of approaches. It stems from the 'archaeological' style favoured by Auguste Mariette (see pp. 47–48 above; Delamaire 2003; Haikal Chapter 9, this volume; Jeffreys 2003: 10) in the opera's early days, and indulges the public taste for the exotic and spectacular.

It was Mariette's dearest wish to accurately imitate Ancient Egypt on stage. Consequently, and being aware of potential stylistic problems, he decided to take a hand himself in the creation of the scenery and costumes in order to be sure of their quality and historical accuracy. He approached this new work with a rigour and seriousness that was unknown in the theatre of the time. While taking precautions to avoid his name appearing – which may smack more of anxiety than of modesty – Mariette was determined to do everything he could to make his creation as accurate as possible. It is truly astonishing to learn that he spent more than six months in Upper Egypt, recording archaeological details and making sketches of temples and tombs, in order to provide precise guidelines for the craftsmen and painters entrusted with the scenery (Chaperon, Rubé, Lavastre and Despléchin),[4] the furnishings and the props (Maspero 1904: clxxix). In the museum that he created at Bulaq, he commissioned copies of a series of ancient monuments and statues.

He had very precise ideas for the scenery. For 'his' opera, he wanted features which were both accurate and spectacular, and here again he encountered difficulties:

> I found that these artists were extremely skilful in making highly fanciful Egyptian architecture. But this was not what I required and, once more, as I had done by designing the costumes myself, I also provided patterns for the decorations.

> (Abdoun 1971: 12)

Mariette became involved in every aspect of the production, personally solving the problem created by the scene in the crypt in the last act, and was finally satisfied with his creation: "The decorations … are really splendid, as well as being exact imitations of the Upper-Egypt temples" (Abdoun 1971: 83).

As he became increasingly involved, Mariette resumed painting and produced some astonishing watercolours of the costumes (Abdoun 1971: pls. 16–39; Corteggiani 1990: 243–245). His major concern was to be as faithful as possible to the archaeological models: the scenery was a scrupulously exact reproduction of the real thing, as were the costumes. His relentlessness in this area made a great contribution to the success of his creation – in effect, the spectators were transported to the 'Land of the Pharaohs'. Before them they had landmarks and points of reference; they would surely have been confused by a poorer production. The results reflected the effort that had been expended, and the show was a complete success. The quality of the scenery and costumes, in particular, was lauded by all: "Never in any theatre has one seen such a rich production, so beautiful and so scrupulously exact thanks to the devoted efforts of Mr Mariette Bey" (Abdoun 1971: 104).

At its production at La Scala, the principles defended by Mariette were already almost forgotten (Viale Ferrero 1996: 531–550), and even more so during its Paris staging at the Théâtre des Italiens (*Aida* 1976: 10; *Aida* 1993: 9, 13). It was only in the 1881 Paris Opéra production that decorations and costumes were again based upon archaeological research (Wild 1996: 507–529). After this, costumes tended to reflect contemporary fashions (Humbert 1994: nos. 297–302, 442–446) paraded in front of often mediocre stage sets. Recently, quality revivals (such as the La Scala of Milan production (1975–1976), with Lila de Nobili decorations and costumes which were inspired by strict adherence to the original staging, and the Verona amphitheatre productions, have afforded the possibility of appreciating the very distinctive atmosphere in *Aida*'s earliest stagings. However, until the 1960s almost all repeat performances were content to use decorations and costumes from old productions, with the exception of occasional innovations in costume. Such 'creative stagnation' lasted for almost a century.

Even today, productions of this kind are not unknown – such as that presented at the San Francisco Opera in 1981 (using Douglas Schmidt's decor), and Florence's Teatro Comunale production of 1996 (decor by Raffaele del Savio, produced by Lorenzo Mariani): "The staging was a traditional one, with the desert, the palms, the Sphinx, the feluccas on the Nile, a frame with hieroglyphics around the stage" (Ferrante 2001).

In May 1998, the reopening of Palermo's Teatro Massimo after 24 years presented the public with long-awaited scenic splendour:

> Nicolas Joël's production, in monumental sets by Ezio Frigerio, stressed the epic aspect, with columns, hieroglyphic-covered walls and even pyramids for the Nile Scene. Radames made his return on a massive barge. The costume designer – Franca Squarciapino – generously gave almost everyone golden headdresses, irrespective of rank. All overlooked the fact that *Aida* is also an intimate drama.
>
> (Allison 1998)

Even more recently – in December 1998 – the San Carlo amphitheatre of Naples presented a production by Gianfranco De Bosio, using decorations designed by Aldo De Lorenzo which were worthy of *Aida*'s first production. The stage was a pure historical reconstruction from which nothing was missing. Major pieces included oblique views of the temples' interiors, a triumphal procession, the felucca on the Nile and the crypt dug under the temple in the last scene. The result, in spite of this shift in emphasis – or perhaps because of it – is very surprising.

In addition to these historical reconstructions, contemporary Egyptological discoveries have also influenced productions of *Aida*. In the 1927 production, for example, Sigrid Onegin wore a replica of Nefertiti's crown, which had been discovered only 15 years earlier (*Aida* 1976: 115). Similarly, in the 1976 New York Metropolitan Opera production, the guards wore Tutankhamun masks, just at the time that the famous exhibition was monopolizing the news. Productions have also been known to use exact copies of archaeological artefacts. This practice was employed by the English National Opera's 1979 London production, in which many artefacts were copied from – or inspired by – British Museum collections. The question remains as to whether one can conclude that – as noted by Jean-Luc Chapaz (1990: 86):

> Egyptian archaeology's contribution to *Aida's* achievements remains, from an Egyptologist's point of view, incredibly poor. The decorators' attention tends to focus on the more commonplace elements of the pharaonic civilization … The directors' and decorators' imagination appears to be limited to a short catalogue comprising Egyptian clichés distributed by popular magazines and crude adaptations.

It should not be forgotten that such 'commonplace' elements are in fact components of 'Egyptomania's' stylistic grammar, and that – as potent as they are – their salience in productions remains relatively low. Furthermore, such symbols are what the spectators have come to expect, and these potent symbols have become – in opera as much as in 'Egyptomania' in general – Ancient Egypt's trademark signature.

Egypt recreated, or the art of aesthetics

As already discussed, Verona was, and continues to be, the best 'melting pot' for the decorative reinterpretation of Ancient Egypt: the stage sets alternate between – and combine – pyramids, obelisks, blocks of masonry, porticos, sphinxes and colossi. Thus, this 'essence of Egypt' is far removed from the Egyptian archaeology that was so precious to Mariette. Quite to the contrary, such presentations are based upon dreams and fantasy, combining buildings from many different periods, thus becoming a reflection of 'Egyptomania' (Price and Humbert 2003: 22). After an 'archaeological' birth, *Aida* – as with other artistic fields – could not easily be modernized. In addition to the elaborate outdoor productions, spectacular decoration also occurs within smaller settings, as in the Sonja Frisell productions at the New York Metropolitan Opera (1989), or Hugo de Ana's highly original staging in the Teatro Real of Madrid (1998). Following this principle, certain productions – even in Verona – go much further than simple liberation from convention. In 1987, the designer Pietro Zuffi conceptualized *Aida* as a series of colour mosaics (Figure 3:8 col. pl.):

> … decorations, costumes and accessories cut out in small squares and resembling the artificial drawings created by computers. This tended to evoke either an 'art deco' bathroom (the apartment of Amneris) or New York by night (the Nile Act).

(Sirvin 1987: 29)

The costumes themselves, which are often very fanciful, are more-or-less complementary to the decor. The use of inaccurate or out-of-place hairstyles is currently fashionable, with royal crowns and nemes being worn by most of the cast, while the tunics employed suggest a Greek or Roman – rather than Egyptian – connection.

Lastly, the impositions made by directors upon the cast and singers – often based on fanciful ideas about Ancient Egypt – only add to Egyptologists' amusement. The appearance of naked slaves (who often hover in the background of Amneris' apartments) is not inappropriate, but was it really necessary – as in Orange – for Tutankhamun's mummy to exit its sarcophagus in order to arm and decorate Radames (*Le Monde*, 16 July 1983)? But such recreations – even more traditional versions – can be used to convey social messages, as in Luca Ronconi's production (Scala of Milan, 1986; decorations by Mauro Pagano). The director chose "an archaic, pre-pharaonic atmosphere. Egypt is depicted as an inhospitable land, enclosed between immense rocks criss-crossed with faults: a land that remains to be discovered" (Venturi 1995: 52). In particular, the socio-political aspect is omnipresent and – for the sole profit of the pharaoh – slaves are shown moving gigantic colossi in a manner similar to that seen in Sir Edward John Poynter's (1867) 'Israel in Egypt' (Figure 1:2 col. pl.; Humbert 1994: nos. 238, 386–388). In addition, beggars follow the pharaoh's chariot during the procession to commemorate the Triumph of Radames, collecting the alms which the sovereign is parsimoniously scattering about him.

Egypt reinterpreted, or the art of adaptation

In 1961, Wieland Wagner was one of the first directors to transpose *Aida* into an abstract setting at the Berlin Deutsche Opera: "a primitive and tribal world, a society obsessed with death and the occult powers" (Lafon 1984: 23). "Brechtian Aidas, Freudian Aidas, Aidas as the victim of Nazism, Fascism and Stalinism emerged a few years later" (Lafon 1984: 23).

Subsequently, *Aida* has frequently been assimilated into the period of its creation:

> The 19th Century has become an integral part of the play, insofar as it has strongly influenced the writing, and even the plot, by imbuing the librettist and the musicians with a strong – and peculiarly nineteenth-century – self-certainty which has since been challenged time and again. As in plays written by the German playwright Bertold Brecht – who is considered to be the inventor of the way people distanced themselves from the theatrical process – the lyrical theatre also invites us to reflect on contemporary artistic creations. It thus challenges traditional ways of thinking by holding up a critical mirror lacking any reassuring complaisance.
>
> (Pousaz 1999: 29)

Jamie Hayes' 1997 Belfast production illustrates this approach:

> He shifted the action rather feebly from the original Ethiopian-Egyptian hostilities to the Franco-Prussian war. 1870 is indeed the time of the opera's composition, but there the 'insights' stopped.
>
> … The Triumphal Scene was turned into a champagne party, though at least the ballet music allowed for Egyptian-style entertainment. The trouble with such a specific updating is that the text, especially in *Aida*, undermines the concept at every turn.
>
> (Allison 1997)

In contrast, Götz Friedrich's and Pet Halmen's productions (Berlin's Deutsche Opera, 1982/1988) set the action among the archaeological ruins in which Mariette lived, against a background of unfolding European wars. Fifteen years later, the same Pet Halmen chose a very different approach for the more intimate setting of Staatsoper

Unter Den Linden in Berlin (1995): he located the action at the turn of the last century, amongst the showcases of the Cairo Museum. Egyptologists meet there, some mysteriously disappearing while the opera's characters leave the showcases. Through the developing plot one can thus find elements of *Belphegor*, *The Evil Spells of the Mummy* and the *Adventures of Indiana Jones*. This creates a marvellous sphere of activity which fires the spectator's imagination and offers the possibility of several parallel interpretations.

There are other ways of integrating the 19th century into productions of *Aida*. Nicolas Joel and his designer Carlo Tommasi (Staatsoper of Vienna, 1992), for example, decided to incorporate David Roberts' artwork into their adaptation. The Egyptian temples are thus depicted as ruins, or half-buried in sand.

Egypt according to taste, or the art of transgression

Today, the evolution of theatre staging is not restricted to *Aida*. The director has assumed such a highly dominant role that one may speak of 'Bob Wilson's *Aida*', as much as 'Chéreau's *Ring*'. Due to the universality of its characters and situations, *Aida* lends itself to this rather well. Similarly, its 'Egyptian' setting is also completely adaptable, both in terms of 'Egyptomania' – which lends itself to scenic spectacles – and for more timeless creations:

> In the last few years, a plethora of 'high tech' productions have appeared on theatre stages. These adaptations regard themselves as progressive, depicting scenarios in which the popular masses are manipulated by the media, and where the pharaoh becomes a press magnate exercising his power over the whinging masses by means of a skillfully targeted propaganda. The soldiers are wearing modern battle dress, tanks replace the dromedaries and the processions become a pretext for an extravagant array of dresses that famous dressmakers have designed for the ladies of the elite. Bottles of whisky or champagne replace swords and laurels, while slaves are transformed into political prisoners with the appearance of international terrorists … In many cases, the ballet is delegated to the role of background music, as – for example – in Hamburg, where it was retransmitted through loudspeakers while war casualties are receiving their medals and traitors are killed.
>
> (Pousaz 1999: 29)

Admittedly, some of the results can be frightening. Aprile Millo refused to sing *Aida* in Frankfurt when she learnt that "the heroine was to be depicted vacuuming on the edge of the Nile, and conversing with Radames on the telephone" (Verdino-Süllwold 1991: 29). Nonetheless, it is amusing to see Amneris being massaged in a Turkish bath by a gigantic slave in Jean-Claude Berutti's production (Nantes-Angers-Rennes, 1998–1999).

Antony McDonald's production – presented in Edinburgh in May 1999 – is equally representative of the modernist genre and, as amusingly observed by Rodney Milnes (1999):

> There's a pyramid on the Festival Theatre's front gauze, and that's more or less it for Egypt … Is it right to send up the Triumph Scene and the dance sequence? The people of Thebes assemble with their picnic cool-boxes and build little Tupperware pyramids before rushing around the stage to the ballet music with petrol cans, bits of car, a Hoover, a TV set and a drip-feed. Earlier, the ladies' chorus entertained Amneris by

> brandishing fashion magazines at her. It was all agonizingly chic, but was it relevant
> to, let alone worthy of, Verdi? … I'm not saying this was the silliest, most ill-conceived
> opera production I've seen recently, but it's on the shortlist.

In 1997, at the Cologne Opera, Gian-Carlo del Monaco used the idea of the Franco-Prussian war of 1870 as a starting point, and then decided to stage the action largely within a virtual reality intergalactic war, in a cyberspace of computers and circuits which owe much to Michael Scott. The scene in which a ballet of mobile phone-brandishing yuppies stand in an ocean of smoke-effects and salute the Egyptian victory – in front of a giant screen of stock exchange prices – was received with whistles from the public (*Die Welt* 1997).

The most daringly political production of the piece can be found in the Moscow Helikon and Bolshoi Theatres (May 1997). Under the direction of Dmitri Bertman, the latter offers a curious adaptation that did not meet with unanimous approval. In it, the choruses and orchestra are dressed in lugubrious black costumes and a naked slave is greeted with a fascist salute (in a manner reminiscent of Pasolini). The director's justification for this – and other minutiae of the production – was that "this is not a modern interpretation of *Aida*, but a traditional interpretation that implies a conflict between life and the omnipresent totalitarianism in the Verdi work" (*Corriere della Sera* 1997).

This vision differs somewhat from that propounded by David Pountney, at the Bavarian National Opera of Munich (1996):

> … the abstract visual world in which it all happened was something quite
> extraordinary. Robert Israels' decor suggested a scenery store: half a dozen huge flats,
> a pair of trucks with faint depictions of human, detectably female anatomy (a navel, a
> neck: Pountney sees the opera as a study of two kinds of woman, the fleshly and the
> spiritual), all shifted slowly, continuously, noiselessly by an army of supernumeraries.
>
> (Milnes 1996)

However, a vision similar to that of Dmitri Bertman was produced in Geneva (1999) by Francesca Zambello, with stage decor by Alison Chitty. They intended

> … to show the unbearable crushing power of a totalitarian political regime on
> individuality, becoming inhuman even within the great propaganda demonstrations
> where it likes to put itself on stage.
>
> (Pousaz 1999: 30)

As for the framework of the action, there is no longer the need, in this context, to be Egyptian. According to the producers, one no longer seeks exoticism in Egypt, and it has become necessary to find a plausible alternative. In consequence, why not

> … place it in a future which will perhaps be ours one day? On the other hand, the only
> thing we can be sure to find there is man's irresistible need for self-destruction in
> fratricidal wars; it is the perpetual suffering of individuals crushed by a system which
> exceeds them.
>
> (Pousaz 1999: 30)

Hence the presence of cars – with non-futuristic appearances – in an otherwise fantastical environment.

The importance of staging: how to find a happy medium between the spectacular and the intimate

This question found different answers depending on place or epoch; furthermore, perceptions of Ancient Egypt have not ceased to evolve, as can be seen by the recent influences of the cinema and comic strips. However, spectacle can also accommodate intimate scenes, just as an intimate production can survive outside of extravagance. It is all a question of balance, aiming to carefully identify and define the limits of a genre. Extravagance represents a major danger, a comic departure, and it is possible that the deployment of the ridiculous risks destroying the image of Egypt, and even that of *Aida*. Time has shown that this has not happened. The risks are more to do with poor concepts – whatever the creative principles – rather than with contemporary meanderings.

Auguste Mariette himself quickly realized how difficult the project was:

> To recreate Egyptians like the ones we usually see in theatres is not difficult and, if only this was required, I would not interfere with it. But to combine the ancient costumes provided by the temples, and the demands of the modern stage, constitutes a delicate task. A king may look very beautiful with an enormous crown on his head when he is made out of granite; but as soon as one needs to apply this to flesh and bone, as well as to make him walk and sing, this becomes a nuisance and one should be wary … not to generate laughs.

(Abdoun 1971: 4)

Avoiding ridicule at all costs was Mariette's constant concern, and may perhaps have led to his wish that his name should not be linked with the production, in the event that it should be a failure. He was particularly afraid that certain singers might refuse to cut off their beards and moustaches:

> Could you imagine seeing the king of Egypt with a turned up moustache and a goatee? Go to the Boulaq Museum and visualize such an appendage on one of our statues. You will see the effect that will have.

(Abdoun 1971: 75)

His fears proved justified, and the facial hair that the actors had refused to remove were indeed the laughing stock of the critics on the night of the premiere.

The ballets were also likely to provoke a strong reaction: "let us pass on Jacques Fabre's colourful dance routines [in the 1983 Orange performance], clearly inspired by aerobics or other gym activities …" (Meunier 1983). It seems that even though the ballets were not overly extravagant, they often bordered on the kitsch.

The revival at the Paris Opéra in 1968 – to celebrate the arrival of the great Léontyne Price – was worthy of 'Hellzapoppin' and the Marx Brothers. However, such failure remains extremely rare. Indeed, *Aida* has the potential of rapidly becoming the archetype of a genre which finds it difficult to avoid the ridiculous:

> For little more than a century, skirt-wearing tenors and painted sopranos (in order to appear Ethiopian) have loved each other under cardboard palm trees. If the voices are beautiful, the public accepts convention, unless the pyramids start collapsing, the felucca on the Nile begins squeaking like an old tram and the trumpets miss their cue.

This is what happened at the Palais Garnier in 1968, and the presence of Léontyne Price in the title role did not prevent the catastrophe. One 'Hey, here comes Asterix' as the chorus-singers (who were disguised as soldiers) entered was enough to start a memorable roar of laughter. The stage decorations dated back to … 1939.

(Lafon 1984: 23)

In such contexts, it would surely be worth using an intimate approach. It becomes necessary to find a new interpretation. One solution consists of completely erasing the large-spectacle approach, while keeping the exotic and Egyptian 'atmosphere'. This was Franco Zeffirelli's approach in Busseto. It is difficult to truly understand the complexity of relationships between the four principal protagonists if one has not seen *L'Aida Racontata da Franco Zeffirelli*. In this film, the famous director explains[5] Verdi's work to a group of young singers, including those who will be performing at the performance celebrating the centenary of Verdi's death. In it, one can discover the prime importance of the intimate scenes, which are utterly lost in rooms that are too large. Zeffirelli's film also reveals the importance of light and modulated singing, which tends to be adversely affected by large performance halls that demand a permanent *fortissimo* from all voices. A small room such as the Busseto makes it possible to rediscover Verdi's work in a very different light.

Another way of approaching the aspect of intimacy is to make people distance themselves from the stage by shifting effects between the music, the decoration and the acting, so as to create a delicate chemistry. Elijah Moshinsky's production (set decoration by Michael Yeargan) at London's Royal Opera House (1994) mixed varied cultural elements on a virtually undecorated stage: armour, headdresses and Japanese weapons, primitive masks, signboards, Egyptian furniture and sumptuous costumes that cannot be linked to any one period. This curious amalgam created a sense of cultural non-specificity (and 'distance') which is beneficial to an appreciation of Verdi's work, as well as to the acting of the performers.

This is also the method followed by Robert Wilson, who tends towards the more abstract approach previously favoured by Wieland Wagner. He acknowledges this connection:

He saw abstraction in everything. To this day, it is difficult to convince the singers that what they are doing is abstract. This is not part of their background. Nowadays, however, people are able to appreciate a painting by Rothko for its form or its colours, without necessarily understanding what it means. I think that in the theatre it is possible to listen to and appreciate music without seeking any further meaning.

(Hermans 2002: 8)

Robert Wilson's staging of *Aida* in Brussels (Théâtre de la Monnaie, 2002) shares this perspective: in front of a bare set, reduced to its simplest expression but nonetheless presenting some elements that firmly contextualize the action in Egypt (i.e. archaeological artefacts and a panorama of the temples at the edge of the Nile), the director instructs his performers to carry out measured movements and gestures, which could be described as 'wooden' and 'stereotyped':

As he likes to admit, he practices an 'autistic' theatre, a theatre that does not deliver an explicit message, nor imposes an interpretation, but one which generates images that allow spectators the freedom to create their own associations, to let one's own imagination interact with what is occurring on the stage.

(Hermans 2002: 9)

What was his approach with regards to *Aida*, and does it solve the problems that are discussed in this chapter? This is less than certain:

Wilson starts from an architectural plan which he fills with abstract scenes entirely centered on the poetic aspect. Each one of his spectacles carries the mark of a refined aesthete. He always chooses an empty stage and places man within a gigantic framework that is almost cosmic. The spectator is transported to an imaginary world where metamorphoses, dual meanings and unusual associations dominate. A world of fairytales where geometry appears to be variable, often resembling the world portrayed in "Alice in Wonderland". In Wilson's approach to theatre, the characters appear to be driven by magical forces without any apparent motive, similar to puppets and their invisible strings. The background is always a horizon against which objects and actors are clearly defined.

(Hermans 2002: 9)

Although Wilson's approach seems to have a profound emotive impact on most audiences, it can also provoke a feeling of unease. The characters appear to be lost, and the performances often become stale.

Conclusion: *Aida* today, or the evolution of a concept

Like Mozart's *Magic Flute*, *Aida* draws the crowds and ensures that producers fill their halls, whatever their scale. Nonetheless, if such traditional representations continue to be highly successful with the public, only continuous research is likely to encourage the evolution of the staging and lead to a deeper understanding of both the characters and the work itself. Would Mariette have been shocked to see Amneris half-naked on a table, in the hands of a muscular masseur? Such a question is no longer relevant. *Aida* will only be able to survive if it adapts to changing times, in terms of both aesthetics and psychology. The current evolution in productions of *Aida* shows that directors and designers still possess – in this respect – reserves of imagination that are likely to provide enchantment to future generations of spectators. The only limits to their extravagance appear to be financial, as money may be the only resource which is coming under strict control. In 1988, the Metropolitan Opera of New York envisaged a lavish production of *Aida* by Franco Zeffirelli. In the event, this was replaced by a much less expensive version by Sonja Frisell. Perhaps it is this contingency which will – finally – save *Aida* from uncontrolled excesses.

Notes

1   Against the wishes of Verdi, the Busseto Theatre – built between 1856 and 1868 and inaugurated on 15 August 1868 – replaced an older theatre on the same site.
2   This performance was filmed on 27 January 2001 (RAI-TDK) to commemorate the anniversary of Verdi's death.
3   These include Giza from 1902 and, more recently, in front of the pyramids; in the temples of Luxor and of Hatshepsut in Deir el-Bahri (from 1987 to 2000); in Macerata (Sferisterio, since 1921); in Rome (in the Thermal Baths of Caracalla from 1937 to the end of the 1980s, 9,000 seats); in Orange (Roman theatre from 1936 to the present, 8,000 seats); in the

Avenches amphitheatre (Switzerland, 1995); Sofia (Battenberg Square, 1997); Athens (Odéon of Herodotus Atticus); Pula amphitheatre (Croatia). Other notable settings such as Paris (Stade de Colombes in 1930; Palais Omnisport de Bercy – with 13,500 seats – in 1984 and 1993; Stade de France/Saint-Denis, with 78,000 spectators at the 2001 performance), Shanghai Stadium (40,000 spectators in 2000), Madrid (the Las Ventas bull-ring, 1996) and London (Earls Court Exhibition Centre, 1998; and 'in the round' at the Royal Albert Hall, 2001), have served to perpetuate the notion that *Aida* is first and foremost a huge-scale opera.

4   The painters Despléchin and Lavastre painted the backdrops for Acts 2 and 3, Rubé and Chaperon those for Acts 1 and 4 (cf. Humbert 1994: nos. 275–277, 426–428; see also Humbert 1985: 101–104).

5   Text accompanying the DVD of the performance (see n. 2).

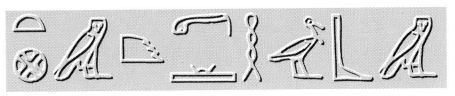

CHAPTER 4

VICENT LLEÓ'S OPERETTA: *LA CORTE DE FARAÓN*

Covadonga Sevilla Cueva

The score for *La Corte de Faraón* was written by Valencia-born Vicent Lleó (1870–1922), a composer of *zarzuelas*[1] and a theatrical impresario. Lleó had been interested in composition from an early age, and showed a predilection for the *zarzuela*. Indeed, many of his pieces were inspired by local popular music, as well as by Spanish music in general. In 1896 he moved to Madrid and began working as an orchestral director, later becoming an impresario for Madrid's most important lyric theatres. He eventually became the proprietor of the Eslava theatre, which he then used to present all his compositions.

The premiere of *La Corte de Faraón* took place on 21 February 1910, and was hailed as a great success by both critics and the public. It was performed in Madrid for two years and then toured throughout Spain. Its success derived from a combination of frivolity, raciness and innuendo that had great public appeal. Condemned as irreverent and banned during the Franco era, it was not performed again until after the dictator's death. Unfortunately, recordings and new productions are rare – even though with time it has lost none of its freshness.

La Corte de Faraón was originally presented as a 'biblical' operetta. However, due to its relative shortness, musicologists classified it as belonging to *Género Chico*. Some even classified it as *Género Ínfimo* (i.e. minute), a euphemism used to describe works of racy character, generally lacking in quality (Alier 1985: 11). Nonetheless, though the text has no literary pretensions, being very simple and seeking to provoke a smile by its use of innuendo, the same cannot be said of the music and orchestration. In several places, these reach high levels of beauty and refinement. At the time, theatre crowds mostly sought to be amused and distracted. In order to address this demand composers usually combined popular melodies, light pieces and revues. The score for *La Corte de Faraón* includes an introduction and eight musical numbers, leaving very little room for dialogue. According to Alier, it reflects a multiplicity of styles, including influences from Viennese operetta *The Tale of the Three Widows*, elements of Spanish folklore (the dance of the *garrotin* – a popular dance typical of southern Spain – which is the subject of the pharaoh's dream) or the 'popular' revue (the *Ay Ba!* verse; Alier 1985: 17).

Guillermo Perrin and Miguel de Palacios wrote the libretto for *La Corte de Faraón*. They were inspired by the French operetta *Madame Putiphar* (Paris, 1897), which was composed by Edmond-Marie Diet and scripted by Ernest Depré and Léon Xanrof. The plot was taken from the story of Joseph and Lotha, Potiphar's wife, and involves the themes of infidelity and unsatisfied passion commonly found in literature. The story resembles the myth of Phaedra and Hippolytus, and the 'Tale of the Two Brothers' of pharaonic Egypt. The satirical manner in which the characters and situations are depicted produces an excellent text, full of twists. The text is never vulgar, in spite of the numerous innuendoes, insinuations and theatrical gestures.

Interestingly, the beginning of *La Corte de Faraón* appears to be a parody of the opera *Aida* (Spanish premiere in Madrid, 12 September 1874) (see Humbert Chapter 3, this volume), which it particularly resembles in the trumpet portion of the Triumphal March. In the operetta, the scene is likewise called "Ritorna Vincitor". In both Verdi's opera and *La Corte de Faraón*, a military parade precedes the arrival of a victorious general, but the differences between the two are nonetheless great. The price paid by Potiphar – the arrow wound that prevents him from consummating his marriage – is the basis for the whole scenario of *La Corte de Faraón*.

One of the operetta's comic elements is the depiction of the characters and the allocation of the music and voices. Specifically, all the male leads are 'ill-treated'. The general Potiphar – a tenor – is made ridiculous by his 'condition', despite being presented with a certain nobility. The pharaoh – a comic tenor or baritone – is portrayed as a faint-hearted alcoholic who is dependent upon the queen. Both the queen and Lotha are depicted as strong-willed yet unsatisfied, while "chaste Joseph" [*sic*] – another comic tenor – irritates the audience by constantly boasting about his 'innocence' and ingenuity. The female characters – particularly the queen, Lotha and Sul the 'Babylonian' – are given more importance than the male protagonists. The Spanish humour in *La Corte de Faraón* is visible in all aspects of the operetta, from the depiction of the characters to the satirical treatment of a biblical story.

As Benavente (1942) noted after the operetta's premiere, this work only develops the original story and does not go beyond what is expressed within it. The authors' main intention was to amuse the audience, in a country where – although the weight of the Catholic Church was enormous – the people enjoyed laughing at themselves and all that surrounded them. Some of Benavente's comments are highly relevant:

> *La Corte de Faraón* is no more daring than the biblical texts. The authors have cleverly removed any crudeness. No one would thank the artists if they wanted to hide theirs. Let us admire the Lord in his works! It will not be difficult to find a mystical meaning in the Babylonian song, which we will soon hear coming from the lips of many senators … Unfortunately, the Catholic Church has lost much of the humour and artistic sense it had during the Renaissance … In the front row I saw many of the serious men who usually adorn brotherhoods and processions.

> (Benavente 1942: 648)

Depictions of Egypt in *La Corte de Faraón*

Egypt's contribution to the operetta is limited to providing a setting in which the story takes place. Despite the light-hearted nature of the subject matter, the authors spent a great deal of time developing the stage sets in order to recreate what they considered to be 'typical' Egyptian scenery. However, the end result is a mixture of Egyptian and

Oriental designs that were fashionable at the time. The events take place in the town of Memphis and included settings in the temple of Isis, Potiphar's residence, the royal palace and the temple of the Apis. The day after the premiere, critics described the costumes and scenery as "pharaonic":

> What a beautiful score and what splendid sets are those of the Corte de Faraón! …

> The most enthusiastic, sincere and ardent applause ever to deafen the Eslava theatre heralded the musician and the set-designer, both of whom hail from Valencia. Dear Lord, this world does hold many beautiful things!

> Similar praise must go to the painter. The five sets he created are beautiful – truly pharaonic, both splendid and fantastical. One cannot aim to achieve a higher standard in art, in terms of relevance, quality of the perspective and detailing.

> > (*La Correspondencia de España*, 22 January 1910)

Elements of Egyptian architecture are clearly represented in the sets, including many characteristic features of the pharaonic period: obelisks, carved cornices crowning the walls of buildings; columns and capitals in the style of the pharaonic period. Some of the reliefs depict the pharaoh making offerings to the gods, and hieroglyphics are visible everywhere. In the second scene, Lotha's nuptial chamber includes features that, judging from 19th century orientalist paintings, one might associate with a harem: Lotha is lying on a chaise-longue surrounded by her female guards, slaves and servants. Palm trees and the façade of a Ptolemaic period Egyptian temple can be seen in the background. Similar Egyptian-themed decorations are incorporated in all five sets. The painter's imagination runs riot, the sets being lavishly decorated using a multitude of colours. Authentic features were obscured by fantastical elements. No wall space was left undecorated, and male faces adorned with horns were represented on 'Hathor-like' capitals. This was not authentically Egyptian, but complemented the operetta's story (in colloquial Spanish, a man is said to have horns on his head when his wife has cheated on him). Despite only having access to black and white photographs of the first production, it is possible to appreciate the incredible impact the staging would have had on the public, as was noted by the arts critic of *La Correspondencia de España*.

The costumes and ornaments reflected similar influences, and tended to represent a mixture of authenticity and fantasy. However the designs were also constrained by what was considered to be morally acceptable at the time. In consequence, the Egyptian elements – such as a crown with an uraeus, pectoral ornaments, the queen's and Lotha's vulture skins or the nemes of Potiphar's assistants – were sometimes difficult to recognize. The costumes of the female characters hinted at sensuality – without offending the moral conventions of the time – and were closer to the clothes of oriental dancers than to those of Egyptian women. Furthermore, the oriental exoticism suited the biblically-inspired theme of sacred prostitution in ancient Babylon and the free love practised by its women (see Appendix, p. 68, and especially the verse *Ay Ba!*).

The text reflected the same influences as those inspiring the music and scenery, with some of the characters having Egyptian or biblical names. The Greek names of Egyptian divinities – such as Osiris, Isis and Anubis – were often introduced into the dialogue, thus taking advantage of their sonority to produce amusing metre. The text referred to biblical Babylon and to the 'Neo-Assyrian world' in the 'Babylonian' melodies, particularly in the *Ay Ba!* verse sung by Sul. The popularity of this verse was such that politically satirical stanzas were added in later performances.

The dialogue and staging of *La Corte de Faraón* presents a vision of Egypt that combines elements from the pharaonic period with 19th century orientalism. This interpretation is derived directly from the writers' pens and the painters' brushes. Lleó created an amusing spectacle; a satire of human passions based on a biblical story that takes place in Ancient Egypt. In *La Corte de Faraón,* Egypt is depicted as a distant and mysterious land, full of sensuality and exoticism. This was precisely what the public expected.

La Corte de Faraón: reflection and satire of Spain in the early 20th century

The late 19th and early 20th centuries were difficult years for Spain. This can be partly attributed to the fact that the method of government – characterized by regular and peaceful transitions between conservative and liberal parties – was generating a great deal of internal tension between social groups. Such governmental process, created by Cánovas del Castillo, was initially regarded as the best way of promoting the country's internal development, becoming fully established in 1881. Nonetheless, the situation in Spain was also influenced by international events. Inappropriate colonial policies caused the emancipation wars of the Philippines (1896–1897) and Cuba (1898). Such difficulties had a catastrophic impact both on public morale and the economy, and is traditionally known as the 'Disaster of 98'. The poorest segments of society were the worst affected. There was an acute shortage of manual labourers, a direct consequence of whole families being decimated in the war. Today, it would be difficult to accept such a catastrophic failure in the political system (Tuñón de Lara 1993: 386). From 1917, the old social and political structures were in decline and the 'Disaster of 98' prompted profound intellectual and ideological divisions among the population.

Morocco was also the cause of some concern to the Spanish government. From the war of Africa (1859–1860) onwards, public support for intervention in North Africa began to wane (Morales Lezcano 1988: 120–121). France also had interests in the region, and tried to move in from Algeria. Between the conference of Madrid (1880) and that of Algeciras (1906),[2] successive Spanish governments had no coherent policy on Africa. Apart from the military and a smattering of politicians and intellectuals, general opinion favoured a policy of non-involvement. This position increased from 1893 (the war of Melilla) onwards; after the events of 1898, Spanish society showed very little interest in Africa.

In the first decade of the 20th century, the Spanish government adopted a series of policies aimed at addressing its internal political problems. Trends included an increase in the social influence of the working class and in the greater popularity of associations of all kinds. This eventually led to a new cultural movement, dubbed "Regeneracionismo", that was openly critical of the values which had dominated the preceding period. The Catholic Church and the army saw a substantial increase in their powers and influence. The Church received the returning members of the clergy who had been abandoned in overseas colonies after the wars of emancipation, and received the backing of the conservative government in placing them in positions traditionally occupied by the middle class. Little by little, a dislike for the clergy grew and a progressive secularization of society can be identified.

The government's interest in Morocco also favoured the army. Political actions became more defensive. Judging from the conference of Algeciras (1906), Spain appeared to have lost much of her independent initiative, and seemed only to respond to the activities of France and other European countries that had interests in Africa (e.g. Morocco, Gibraltar). The Spanish army suffered a number of setbacks in the Rif region and at Melilla, and was defeated at Barranco del Lobo in July 1909. Between 1907 and 1910, public opinion openly opposed Spanish intervention in Africa. Such lack of support was mainly due to the army's conscription of numerous men to fight wars that failed to produce tangible results. Furthermore, the 'Disaster of 98' was still fresh in the public memory, and several incidents had demonstrated the inadequacies of Spanish army officers.[3]

The most significant and violent event – the *Semana Trágica* (tragic week) – took place in July 1909, during which an uncontrolled mob burnt and destroyed several of Barcelona's churches and monasteries.

The *Semana Trágica* signaled the end of an era in Spanish history. Social unrest was rife, and workers agreed to a general strike similar to those of preceding years. Antonio Maura's government failed to introduce the economic, social (salary revisions) and political (electoral) reforms that had been demanded by the people, and which were urgently needed to remedy the country's ills. The campaign against intervention in Morocco, launched by the left wing parties, found support amongst the general public. Nobody wanted to serve in Morocco, particularly when it became generally known that a certain sum of money could guarantee immunity from conscription. Supporters of soldiers who had been conscripted for Morocco started a mass public demonstration in Barcelona, with crowds spontaneously filling the streets and burning churches and convents. The army took control and declared a state of emergency, thus provoking a general insurrection. The government launched a brutal repression that ended with 17 people being condemned to death, with four executions, including that of the renowned intellectual Ferrer Guardia. Maura's conservative government ended with the *Semana Trágica* and brought about a period of liberalism.

La Corte de Faraón was staged for the first time in February 1910, six months after the *Semana Trágica*. From all points of view, it was great success. An analysis of the libretto reveals that behind the biblical story lies a critique of Catholic morals and the Spanish Church of the previous few years. The public's anti-clerical feelings added to their enjoyment of the operetta's numerous jokes on the subjects of infidelity, adultery, feminism and the undervalued male. General Potiphar's character, returning wounded from the war, is mocked in a way that could be taken as a reference to Spanish soldiers serving in Morocco. This may have represented a direct satirical attack on the army, the 'honour' of which had recently been similarly 'wounded'. There is also a double meaning in the pharaoh's character. He is depicted as lacking any real power and as being interested only in music, wine and beautiful women. A large proportion of the public drew a parallel between his character and that of King Alfonso XIII. Performances such as *La Corte de Faraón* were quite cheap to attend and dealt with topics of popular interest, as well as aspects of daily life. The audience for such operettas included members of the nobility and the upper and middle classes, but was dominated by the masses. This was not accidental. From all points of view, *La Corte de Faraón* was a product of its time.

Appendix

Scene 1: Ritorna Vincitor

General Potiphar returns to Egypt after his victorious campaign in Syria and is received by the court in Memphis (Figure 4:1). As a gift from the pharaoh and his queen, Potiphar is awarded a wife, Lotha (Figure 4:2) – the "virgin of Thebes" – who arrives accompanied by the High Priest. After the general reluctantly accepts his gift, the entire court proceeds to the temple of Isis to celebrate the wedding. Potiphar complains about his misfortune to his two assistants, Seti and Selhá, admitting to the fact that he has a war wound that precludes him from carrying out his matrimonial duties. His two assistants then purchase a slave – named Joseph – from the Ismailites, who Potiphar then gives to his wife.

Scene 2: Joseph's coat

Lotha awaits her husband in the nuptial chamber. In accordance with Egyptian tradition, three widows then arrive to instruct the newly-wed as to how she must act towards her husband. Potiphar arrives, but is very preoccupied as he does not know what he is going to do during his wedding night. He ignores Lotha's innuendoes and begins an account of his military feats, whilst waiting for dawn to break. At sunrise, the general departs rapidly to rejoin his army. After the enormous disappointment of her wedding night, the "Potiphara" tries to seduce Joseph. He defends his chastity and ends up running away, leaving Lotha clutching his coat in her hands (Figure 4:3). Hurt by his rejection, she begins to scream, accusing him of having raped her.

Scene 3: "De capa caída" (Of a fallen coat) [4]

The queen and her royal cup-bearer try to make the drunken pharaoh fall asleep by bringing in dancers and singers to play Babylonian melodies (Figure 4:4). Sul (Figure 4:5) – a famous star of the time – sings the famous *Ay Ba!*. After the pharaoh has fallen asleep, Lotha enters demanding justice, Joseph pleading his innocence. The king leaves his wife to resolve the problem and goes down to the garden to sleep. The queen immediately falls in love with Joseph, frees him, and tries to seduce him in front of Lotha. Furious, Lotha denounces the queen's actions. Joseph, whose arms are being held by both women, manages to free himself and jumps through the window.

Scene 4: The pharaoh's dreams

Joseph lands next to the king, who is sleeping in the garden. The king wakes up and tells his cup-bearer that he has just had a very bizarre dream. Joseph interprets it: in the future, women, dressed in light garments, will dance the *garrotín*. The slave shows a vision of this dance to the king, who, admiring Joseph's wisdom, promises to make him the Viceroy of Egypt. The queen, Lotha and Potiphar suddenly enter the garden

Figure 4:1 General Potiphar enters Memphis (© Martin. Comedias y comediantes, February 1910 special issue, Biblioteca Nacional de Madrid).

Figure 4:2
Lotha, Potiphar's
wife (© Nieto.
Comedias y
comediantes,
February 1910
special issue,
Biblioteca
Nacional de
Madrid).

in search of the escaped slave. The king proclaims Joseph's innocence and accuses Potiphar of being the cause of his wife's indiscretion, as he had not fulfilled his duties as a husband.

Scene 5: The Apis ox [sic]!

The entire court is gathered in the temple of the Apis for Joseph's investiture ceremony as Viceroy of Egypt. The pharaoh and Potiphar, each holding one side of a bull's horns, express wishes for Joseph's prosperity. The operetta finishes with a grandiose scene in which the Apis is glorified, and the new Viceroy is acclaimed (Figure 4:6).

Figure 4:3   Joseph loses his coat (© Martín. Comedias y comediantes, February 1910 special issue, Biblioteca Nacional de Madrid).

Figure 4:4 "De Capa caída" (© Martín. Comedias y comediantes, February 1910 special issue, Biblioteca Nacional de Madrid).

Figure 4:5   Sul the 'Babylonian' (© Nieto. Comedias y comediantes, February 1910 special issue, Biblioteca Nacional de Madrid).

Figure 4:6 The Bull ("ox") of Apis (© Martín. Comedias y comediantes, February 1910 special issue, Biblioteca Nacional de Madrid).

Notes

1   *Zarzuela* is a composition combining music and drama, in which the text is alternately spoken and sung without any interruption in the flow of argument. It constitutes the Spanish equivalent of the French *opéra comique*, the Italian *operetta*, the German *singspiel* or the English musical. While the *zarzuela* originated in the mid-17th century, its modern reincarnation dates to the 19th century and was a great success with the Spanish public. A new genre – the *Género Chico* – appeared during the 1860s. These compositions were shorter and of a lower quality, and aimed to amuse the public. The subject matter usually featured popular themes; in the early works the text was mostly spoken, with music being secondary.

2   The aim of the conference of Algeciras was to determine the extent of French and Spanish holdings in Morocco. It also aimed to determine the extent to which Paris, Berlin, London and Madrid could influence socio-economic policy in the territory administered by Sultan Muley Hassan (Morales Lezcano 1993: 23).

3   In 1905, the electoral success of the socialists in Madrid and the Catalanists in Barcelona provoked a violent response from some army officers. A joke published in Barcelona's *Cu-cut* journal was interpreted as a slur on the army, which responded by attacking *Cu-cut's* offices, as well as those of the journal *La Veu de Catalunya*. This act of vandalism was supported by the military hierarchy; Montero Ríos' government, fearing military reprisals, sided with the army, and accused the Catalans of separatism.

4   In Spanish, the expression "Of a fallen coat" is used to describe a worsening of affairs, or the thickening of a plot.

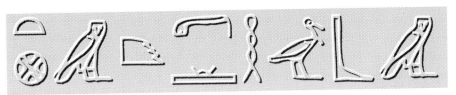

CHAPTER 5

EGYPT IN HOLLYWOOD: PHARAOHS OF THE FIFTIES

Sam Serafy

Hollywood's like Egypt, full of crumbling pyramids. It'll never come back. It'll just keep on crumbling until finally the wind blows the last studio prop across the sand.

(Downey 1992: 96)

So said producer David Selznick in 1951 when the American motion picture industry was confronted with the biggest threat of its history. Despite a booming economy, movie theatre attendance was rapidly dwindling and many were predicting the demise of Hollywood. The enemy was television, which had come into its own in the post-war years: Americans were increasingly opting to be entertained at home. The studios fought back with lavish spectacles with million dollar budgets and casts of thousands. New wide-screen systems like CinemaScope and VistaVision were developed and producers, seeking subjects of suitably epic proportions, were soon drawn to the majesty and splendour of Ancient Egypt. The three major ancient Egyptian epics of the 1950s are *The Egyptian* (1954) directed by Michael Curtiz, *Land of the Pharaohs* (1955) directed by Howard Hawks and *The Ten Commandments* (1956) directed by Cecil B. DeMille. A film set in a historical period perhaps inevitably ends up telling us more about the year of its production than the age it purports to be about. While presenting a reconstruction of ancient times and manners, these films promote American ideals and reflect social and political concerns about the role of women, communism, the Bible and the bomb.

The Egyptian

The Egyptian, produced by 20th Century Fox, is the story of a physician called Sinuhe (Edmund Perdom) who works in and around Egypt during the reign of Akhenaten in the eighteenth Dynasty in the New Kingdom. It is based on the best seller of the same title by Finnish author Mika Waltari (1949) from which the film takes its plot line and characters. The novel itself bears a slight resemblance to the 'Tale of Sinuhe', an ancient Egyptian Middle Kingdom poem (Loprieno 2003: 31–32, 37–38). In the prologue to the film, an introductory narration over scenes of ruined temples and statues proclaims, "the Egyptians were not only builders of monuments. They were human beings no different from ourselves", a statement that actively invites contemporary comparison.

Many of the costumes and interior designs of *The Egyptian* are copied directly from *National Geographic Magazine* illustrations by H. M. Herget which accompanied an article on everyday life in Ancient Egypt, published in Hayes (1941). Racially the Egyptians of both high and low status are white. English actors take the prominent roles, a common Hollywood attempt to lend an air of culture to the historical drama. Black characters never speak and are relegated strictly to the background, occupying menial positions such as servants and guards. As in society, racial separation was the norm in American films. Topographically, Thebes and the Nile region are depicted as barren desert with only a few scattered palms, the sandy locales more in keeping with the character of the present sites of the ancient ruins. The fertile soil of the Nile flood-plain which made possible Egypt's mainly agrarian economy is not shown. The natural world is depicted as hostile, represented by predatory vultures and lions, with many verbal allusions to jackals, snakes and hyenas, and there is little attempt to depict the rich variety of animal life so evident in ancient Egyptian religion and art.

In its portrayal of women, *The Egyptian* adopts the two standard *film noir* character types, the *femme fatale* and the *mother/nurturer*. In the 1950s, the nurturing woman capable of total devotion to a man was the ideal. Conversely, the *femme fatale* is best characterized by her self interest and her drive to acquire money and power (Tuska 1984: 202). During the war years and after, strong women flourished in American films, and were often presented as monsters. This reflected the anxieties of a wartime society in which women had taken control of many positions customarily held by men. The message in the 1950s was that competing with men made a woman hard and aggressive and almost surely doomed to loneliness (Halberstam 1993: 590).

Sinuhe becomes obsessed with a beautiful but wicked Babylonian whore named Nefer. Like the apocalyptic Whore of Babylon she thrives on destruction. Nefer worships the cat-headed goddess Bastet. "There is a reason the god of love takes the form of a cat," Nefer purrs while stroking a Persian feline with a diamond choker. "A cat's paws are soft but they hide claws. A cat takes pleasure in tormenting its victim. Not until the creature is nearly dead will he show pity and put an end to it." Sinuhe's addiction to Nefer leads him to mortgage his parent's property, robbing them of their death rites and their place in the afterlife, and they subsequently commit suicide. Nefer ends up contracting a venereal disease. When Sinuhe informs her that he can save her life but not her beauty, the lesson is clear.

The royal women are also shown to be hard as nails (Figure 5:1). Princess Baketamon (Gene Tierney) and the Queen Mother, Taia, are cynical and twisted by power and ambition. "The gods were perverse," says Taia, "They gave me a son as soft as a girl and a daughter as strong as a man." The image of Diana the Huntress, Princess Baketamon is an expert archer and charioteer, but such skills only serve as further proof of her unnatural masculinity.

By contrast, the humble tavern maid, Merit, who falls in love with Sinuhe and bears his child, is like the model 1950s housewife who selflessly devotes herself to her husband. She never directly criticizes Sinuhe and she responds to his numerous indiscretions with an unflinching expression of doting admonition and always stops short of nagging or taking charge. "Can't you believe in a love that asks for nothing?" she asks Sinuhe. Undaunted by his lack of reciprocity, Merit silently fulfils the role of housewife and mother and, as if to consolidate this position, she purchases and

Figure 5:1   In *The Egyptian* Princess Baketamon and the Queen Mother, Taia, are twisted by power and ambition (20th Century Fox).

occupies Sinuhe's childhood home. Here we see her in her element, performing domestic duties and preparing a fish dinner for Sinuhe and their son. The consummate mother and homemaker, she becomes a key to Sinuhe's spiritual redemption. However, she does display a feisty determination when riled, but Merit's little outbursts are portrayed as funny and charming because she does not aspire to power. When she playfully scolds a servant for lacking manners, he retorts, "Only in Egypt does a woman's tongue take so sharp an edge", a sentiment sure to raise a wry chuckle from 1950s men.

The Egyptian gods are shown as false and, consequently, very little time is spent exploring Egyptian beliefs and customs. "I learned to bend my body to them," says Sinuhe of the gods, "but that was all." A gloomy scene in the 'House of Death' is dominated by great vats of steaming embalming fluid accompanied by the foreboding strains of Bernard Herrmann's soundtrack. "Only condemned criminals and the accursed of the gods seek work in the House of Death," says the foreman to Sinuhe. There is no attempt to portray the elaborate ritual and preparation of bodies. It seems strange that there should be such avoidance and scant treatment of the subject, especially taking into account the public's fascination with it. As the series of 'mummy' films demonstrates (Lupton Chapter 2, this volume), a non-dismissive treatment of the Egyptians' religious beliefs is only acceptable within the boundaries of the horror genre.

Akhenaten's sun worship is shown to be nearly identical to Christianity. Before his death he gives a speech declaring his beliefs:

I see it clearly now. I thought God was the face of the sun. The sun is just a symbol of his warmth, of his creative power. He is no idol, no tangible thing, but the creator of all things, the loving spirit that lives in all our hearts. Nor does my death matter. God is in us all, and one day in his own good time he will speak out in words that cannot be misunderstood.

The Egyptian implies that bountiful evidence of biblical design is all about us. The film begins with Sinuhe as a baby in a reed boat on the Nile, the first of many of the film's biblical allusions.

As a child, Sinuhe assists his physician foster father in his surgery. When the father removes a splinter that is pressing on a patient's brain, he explains to Sinuhe that the patient will now be able to "speak again and walk and live". When young Sinuhe asks "Why?", his foster father mysteriously replies, "No one knows", suggesting the involvement of an unknown force. The ankh is a recurrent image, indicating the cross of life and the symbol of the Akhenaten cult. Large stone ankhs are displayed prominently in pharaoh's chambers and at the Sun temple. The Sun worshippers all wear ankh pendants. In a corner of her home, Merit keeps a little ankh shrine with a burning flame before it. The physical resemblance of the ankh to the Christian crucifix is made obvious. Sinuhe discovers that he is Akhenaten's half-brother and the film concludes with his conversion to the pharaoh's monotheistic beliefs. And just in case anyone still failed to make the connection, a title at the film's conclusion appearing to the strains of a swelling choir reads "These things happened thirteen centuries before the birth of Jesus Christ".

The early 1950s in America were marked by a rapid growth in church membership, especially in the booming new suburbs. There was also a resurgence of evangelical fervour, as spearheaded by the Reverend Billy Graham (Oakley 1990: 326). In 1954 the United States Congress unanimously ordered the inclusion of the words "under God" into the nation's "pledge of allegiance" and in 1955 President Eisenhower signed Public Law 851, making it mandatory that all coinage and paper currency display the motto "In God We Trust". The turn to religious subject matter in the films of this period was also due to the phenomenal success of such Bible-based entertainments as *Samson and Delilah* (DeMille 1949) and *The Robe* (Costa 1953). In these films sin could be depicted without, it was hoped, drawing criticism from religious communities. Despite its Christian fervour *The Egyptian* only managed to earn a 'B' from the National Legion of Decency, the Catholic censorship board established in 1934.

The film presents atheism and nihilism as one and the same. "It is bad to believe in too much like Pharaoh, but it is worse to believe in too little, my friend" warns the belligerent general Haremhab (Victor Mature). Sinuhe meets a grave-robber in the Valley of the Kings who, like the grave-digger in *Hamlet*, explains his atheist philosophy:

Twenty years to build a pyramid or twenty minutes to scrape a hole in the sand, it's all the same. The dead are dead no matter where you put 'em. Immortality? I hold it in my hand. Only the grains of sand will never die.

While bowed in worship in the 'School of Life' Sinuhe asks "Why?". His classmate hushes him: "Sinuhe, be careful, the priests!" Egypt is a country in the clutches of totalitarianism, infested by high priests of an oppressive and corrupt government who stamp out free thought to preserve the ancient order. This grim view of society accorded to the American perception of life in the Soviet Union. Of course, McCarthyism was also limiting free speech in America, especially in Hollywood. During the early years of the Cold War there was a perception that there were Communist spies in cities throughout the United States and that left wing intellectuals were working to undermine the country from within. Hollywood itself became a focus of the 'Red Scare'. In 1947 Dalton Trumbo, Ring Lardner Jr and other members of the Hollywood 10 were imprisoned for refusing to answer questions from the House Un-American Activities Committee about their affiliation to the Communist Party. The Committee again turned its attention to Hollywood in 1951 when a second round of Congressional Hearings to expose Communism in Hollywood took place (Mitchell 1998: AR13). By exploiting Cold War hysteria, Senator Joseph McCarthy had the effect of inhibiting discussion, restricting freedom of speech and promoting conservatism.

Forsaking his principles, Sinuhe leaves Egypt and travels in other lands, plying his medical trade and becoming rich. He cures the Hittite king, who gives him a sword composed of a strange new metal called iron. "This new metal will change the history of the world," Sinuhe proclaims. Sinuhe brings the Hittite sword home to Egypt. He warns the commander of the Egyptian forces, Haremhab, of the war the Hittites are planning against Egypt and presents him with the iron sword. Haremhab immediately comprehends the danger it represents, and he implores the pacifist pharaoh Akhenaten to permit a surprise attack on the Hittites. "Let me strike first. Destroy their cities, their mines and their forges!"

The threat of a foreign power developing superior military technology would have clearly resonated with the contemporary audience. The American monopoly on nuclear weapons ended in August 1949 when the Soviet Union detonated their own atomic bomb. America exploded the hydrogen bomb in 1952 and Russia followed suit in 1953. The United States was finding it difficult to maintain the military edge.

Akhenaten's olive branch diplomacy jeopardizes Egypt's internal and external security and his preoccupation with religious matters leads him to neglect his people and misjudge his enemies. Having conquered the Hittites, the power-hungry Haremhab becomes pharaoh and quickly restores the multi-god system, declaring himself one of them. He reinstates order and returns Egypt to its former military might. While Haremhab is depicted as a despot, like Stalin, who institutes brutal raids on the Akhenaten cult, his character seems more than slightly modelled upon General Douglas MacArthur, the tough imperious field commander whom president Truman was obliged to fire for insubordination in 1951. MacArthur's public challenge to the President highlighted the dangers of giving too much power to the military. Whereas MacArthur's challenge failed because of Truman's strength, Haremhab's succeeds due to the weakness of Akhenaten. By emphasizing the folly of extremes, the film calls for a fit balance of military strength and Christian pacifism. In the end *The Egyptian* becomes a battle for our hearts and minds, for Christian values and American ideals. In a defining speech, Sinuhe renews his commitment to the poor and confirms his conversion to the new religion. Anticipating both Christianity and Democracy, Sinuhe proclaims, "We have but one master, the God who made us all, and in his truth all men are equal".

The Egyptian garnered mixed reviews and fell short of studio expectations at the box office, barely recovering its large budget. The hero in *The Egyptian* is an Egyptian, and although he is often ambivalent toward his homeland, through him we are meant to share some concern for the fate of Egypt. In *Land of the Pharaohs* and *The Ten Commandments*, the heroes are not Egyptian, but slaves of the Egyptians.

Land of the Pharaohs

Howard Hawks's *Land of the Pharaohs*, released by Warner Brothers in 1955, is the epic story of the building of the Great Pyramid at Giza. The exteriors were shot on location in Egypt and literally thousands of Egyptian extras were employed in the crowd scenes. These scenes cut clumsily with the studio bound interior sets of the drama, with the all-American and European cast. Predictably, English actors, here wearing light brown makeup, take most of the leading parts and even the Kushites are white (Figure 5:2). The film adopts many of the same assumptions as *The Egyptian*. Again two opposing female character types are present; the *femme fatale* and the *mother/ nurturer*. Pharaoh's wife, Nailla, understands the fighting and treasure-seeking that keeps her husband away from home for so long, her only demand being that she may mother the son he needs to succeed him. Pharaoh's second wife, the scheming Nellifer, lusts for wealth and power and is intent on destroying the sanctity of the royal family. When a cobra sent by Nellifer threatens her child, Nailla selflessly throws herself upon the snake, dying instantly. Another 'good woman' is Kyra, the slave girl whom Vashtar's son Senta rescues from pharaoh's palace. Senta brings her home, where she enthusiastically takes over the kitchen duties. "Is this what you've been eating?" she remarks after tasting the bland food on the stove. She orders a variety of spices, and demonstrates that a woman's touch was just what the place needed.

Egypt is again shown as lagging behind in technological know-how. To secure his royal tomb from plunderers, pharaoh must look outside Egypt for technical assistance. The master builder, Vashtar (James Robertson Justice), is one of a group of Kushites who were captured by the Egyptians. He agrees to solve the problem of safeguarding the royal tomb in exchange for freedom for his people when the work is completed. Vashtar engineers an ingenious system to seal the pharaoh's tomb and the valuables therein using sand to lower giant stones into place. The film implies that the Egyptians were ignorant of the success of even their own achievements. At the conclusion of the film, Vashtar says of pharaoh, "The Pyramid will keep his memory alive, and that [*sic*] he built better than he knew".

In *Land of the Pharaohs*, ancient Egyptian religion is also constantly invalidated. Vashtar is horrified by its brutality. When soldiers deemed cowardly in battle are thrown alive into a crocodile pit, Vashtar remarks, "Strange religion to deny an afterlife to those who fail in this one". When pharaoh shows Nellifer a special chamber containing treasure plundered from other lands he explains that he has chosen to be buried with these items because they are symbols of his life to come. Since the treasure

Figure 5:2   In *Land of the Pharaohs* even the Kushites are white (Warner Brothers).

pharaoh is referring to is loot won in battle, rather than work crafted by Egyptian artisans, the religious significance is lost. However, unlike the priests in *The Egyptian*, the High Priest Hamar is portrayed as a wise and sympathetic individual and the film even permits him to describe one aspect of Egyptian religion, the purpose of a boat placed in the tomb. But when Hamar officiates at a public mourning of the war dead and the large stone heads of the gods appear to speak, it becomes clear that he is orchestrating the deception. The implication is that not even Egypt's own High Priest believes in the gods.

It is in the concluding scenes that the film's primary purpose becomes apparent. In a merciful spirit, Hamar grants Vashtar his freedom, seeing that his work on the crypt is completed. Thinking she is just officiating at pharaoh's funeral, Nellifer suddenly realizes that she is becoming entombed with the funeral party. As Vashtar's huge stone slabs lower to seal the tomb around her she collapses on the ground, screaming. The pharaoh achieves an afterlife of sorts, in the form of revenge. The Great Pyramid becomes a solemn monument to patriarchal power and moral justice. As slaves of Egypt, the Kushites perform the same narrative function as the Jews do in the biblical Exodus. Vashtar's one demand is to let his people go and, like the Jews, they eventually gain their freedom.

This biblical subtext was about to come resoundingly to the fore in a Hollywood classic which has proved by far the most successful and influential of the films so far discussed.

The Ten Commandments[1]

While audiences were largely indifferent to *Land of the Pharaohs*, they positively flocked to *The Ten Commandments* which, though it cost $13,000,000, became the most popular film of the decade, earning $43,000,000 (Cohn 1993: A102). It was Cecil B. DeMille's second attempt at telling the story, having already made a silent version in 1923. The 1956 version boasts sound, colour and 'state of the art' special effects including the magnificent parting of the Red Sea. Produced by Paramount Pictures, *The Ten Commandments* takes place in the nineteenth Dynasty in the New Kingdom and follows the biblical story of Moses and the Exodus, but adds characters and situations gleaned from later Judaic sources as well as popular fictions to flesh out its nearly four hours' running time. Partly because of its massive budget, *The Ten Commandments* does a good job of presenting a cohesive, though extremely theatrical, Technicolor environment for the larger than life characters to inhabit and for the drama to unfold. Ancient Egypt is once again depicted as a desert civilization. Even along the Nile there is no growth other than a few palm trees. Pharaoh Seti is played by an Englishman (Cedric Hardwicke) and the great majority of the cast are white Americans, with the exception of Russian born Yul Brynner as Seti's son Ramesses II. Brynner makes an appropriately exotic Ramesses and he contributes much to the credibility of the film. Blacks are shown mainly in the background and nearly exclusively in servant roles. However, the film does include one striking break from tradition when the beauty of a black Ethiopian Princess is emphasized and she is allowed a brief speaking part.

Moses, Prince of Egypt (Charlton Heston), is set to marry Princess Nefertari (Anne Baxter) who spends her time enjoying the leisure of palace life. She murders her old servant Memnet when she threatens to reveal the truth of Moses' origins. When Moses discovers his Jewish heritage and chooses to live amongst his enslaved people, she fails to convince him to return to the palace and accept his royal destiny. She reluctantly marries Ramesses and goads him on to pursue Moses and destroy him, deriding him for being outwitted by the god of a slave while casting aspersions on his manhood. By contrast, Moses' wife Liala, the daughter of a Bedouin tribesman, is shown in domestic duties, spinning wool, serving meals or lighting spiritual flames. She remains supportive of her husband's mission, even when he has no more time for her. "Nothing from some is worth more than gold from others," she assures him. Again we are offered the model of the selfless housewife and mother and her selfish counterpart who is wicked because she tries to fulfil her own needs.

The film reflects the attitude of the Bible, which casts the Egyptians as villains and the Hebrews as heroes. The film shows little respect for the artistic and technical achievements of Egyptian society. Even before he learns of his Hebrew heritage, Moses treats the slaves with compassion and he gets results, proving the chief Egyptian architect wrong by ordering the raising of a huge obelisk without it breaking. According to *The Ten Commandments* it is Moses and the Israelites who are responsible for Egypt's architectural wonders.

Cecil B. DeMille was an ardent anti-Communist and the main force behind the Loyalty Oath adopted by the Director Guild in 1950. In an opening introduction Cecil

B. DeMille calls *The Ten Commandments* "the story of the birth of freedom". He continues:

> The theme of this picture is whether man should be ruled by God's law or whether they [*sic*] should be ruled by a dictator like Ramesses. Are men the property of the state or are they free souls under God? This same battle continues throughout the world today.

The film creates deliberate parallels between Ancient Egypt and a 20th century totalitarian state. The Hebrew slaves are dominated by brutal Gestapo-like, bullwhip-cracking slave drivers who address them as "dogs". Egyptian architectural style is equated with that of Nazi Germany and the Soviet Union, monumental in scale but spiritually destitute. It would have been virtually impossible for audiences in 1956 to view *The Ten Commandments* without making the analogy with 20th century Jewish history and the atrocities of Nazi Germany and the founding of the state of Israel. At the time, Gamal Abdul Nasser was president of Egypt. He had allied himself with the Soviet Union and was openly hostile to Israel. *The Ten Commandments* goes some way toward reassigning blame for the Holocaust onto the biblical enemies of Israel. Fundamentalist Christians, convinced of the imminent Apocalypse, saw the Jewish return to the Holy Land as the fulfilment of biblical prophesy. Nations opposed to the formation of the Jewish State, the indigenous Palestinians and their Arab neighbours, including Egypt, could now be viewed, with their pharaonic counterparts, as enemies of God's plan. Ancient Egypt pays heavily for its treatment of the Israelites. God and Moses and the special effects team at Paramount subject Egypt to a series of lethal miracles. The Nile waters turn to blood and hailstones burst into flame as they touch the ground. Ramesses dictates a royal edict to murder the Jewish first-born of each house. The plan backfires as God sends a creeping pestilence to slaughter the Egyptians' first-born, including pharaoh's own son.

Again, the Egyptians' gods are depicted as powerless. Ramesses himself does not believe in the gods of Egypt and he only asks their help as a last resort in a desperate and futile attempt to revive his dead son. "Moses' god *is* God" says Ramesses, finally admitting defeat. Pinned with his people against the Red Sea by pharaoh's army, Moses summons a column of fire through which the Egyptians cannot pass. He then commands the water to part to provide a retreat for his people. Once the Israelites are safely across, the sea comes together again, drowning the charging pharaoh's army in an awesome display of destruction. Moses is in complete command of the elements. He is able to harness powerful natural forces and their awesome, unbridled ability to destroy. By having the one true God on his side, Moses has the military upper hand and a God-given sanction to destroy the enemy. It must have been reassuring to religious Americans in the Cold War to be reminded that God had previously come out against totalitarianism.

The parting of the Red Sea, like the splitting of the atom to unleash destructive forces, ensures freedom to the just as it obliterates the wicked. Inflicting death on the enemy in retaliation for human rights abuses is not only justified, it has Divine sanction. After the first successful test of the A bomb at Los Alamos, President Truman wrote in his journal, "It may be the fire destruction prophesied in the Euphrates Valley era, after Noah and his fabulous ark …" (Patterson 1996: 6). Truman was responsible for the bombing of Hiroshima and Nagasaki and for pressing ahead with the H Bomb program.

While Moses is busy receiving God's law, a Hebrew double agent called Dathan (Edward G. Robinson) arouses discontent among some of the Israelites and instigates the fabrication of an idol in order to appease pharaoh and return to Egypt. They build a golden calf complete with horns and, significantly, an Egyptian style sundisk. (In the 1923 version the disc was inscribed with Egyptian hieroglyphs.) Scenes of sin and debauchery ensue about this false god. Moses returns and hurls one of the stone tablets at the calf, igniting an explosion that forges a fiery chasm in the ground, into which Dathan and the idolaters fall to their deaths, a conclusive demonstration of God's ballistic precision.

While wide-screen innovations helped to keep cinema alive through the 1950s, television was clearly thriving and by 1960 all the major studios were producing content intended exclusively for television (Anderson 1994: 7; Schadla-Hall and Morris Chapter 14, this volume). The studios were also able to sell or lease their extensive back catalogue of movies to television, and a whole new generation grew up watching fifties wide-screen movies cropped to fit the box. Today, while *The Egyptian* and *Land of the Pharaohs* still occasionally turn up on classic film channels and have been made available on video, *The Ten Commandments* has become an American religious touchstone and it is usually broadcast annually on network television during the Easter and Passover season, influencing new generations. A screening in the year 2000 on the ABC television network was the eighth most watched programme in America for the week of 10–16 April: astonishing popularity for a 44 year old movie (Bauder 2000: 7c).

In *The Egyptian*, *Land of the Pharaohs* and *The Ten Commandments*, the rich detail of ancient Egyptian society are seldom explored. Egyptian accomplishments are trivialized while their human rights abuses are emphasized. Their artistic achievements are reduced to a greed for gold objects, and technological innovations are shown to come from outside of Egyptian society. Egypt's fertile Nile Delta is not shown and there is little indication of the keen observation of the natural world so evident in ancient Egyptian artistic and religious creations. Egyptian religious beliefs are employed to stress the superiority of biblical teachings. Pharaonic rulers are shown to be either dangerously ineffectual or brutal and corrupt, and the depictions of the totalitarian Egyptian state serve to underscore the wisdom of American ideals. The films emphasize the similarities between 20th century cultures and the ancient world to prove that the ancients were "just like us". By grafting their own political and social constructs onto depictions of past cultures, these films affirmed what audiences already assumed, or needed to believe.

Note

1   Permission to reproduce a still from *The Ten Commandments* (Paramount Pictures) was unobtainable due to unspecified legal reasons.

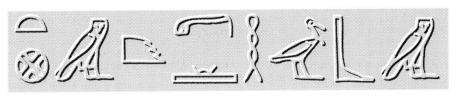

CHAPTER 6

LOST IN TIME AND SPACE: ANCIENT EGYPT IN MUSEUMS

Sally MacDonald

Ancient Egypt in museums

The western public's fascination with Ancient Egypt is considerable; so considerable that it is often taken for granted. Those analyzing recent visitor surveys at London's British Museum comment that, "as might be expected", the Egyptian antiquities attracted most favourable remarks; many more than any other display or feature in the museum (Caygill and Leese 1993: 13). In the report on the most recent survey (April 2000) the researchers concluded that "visiting the Egyptian exhibitions is the main reason why one third of all visitors come to the museum, particularly so for Europeans and parties with children" (information from British Museum Visitor Services Department).

Research carried out in London in 2000 aimed to explore the nature and limits of this fascination. The research (Fisher 2000a) took the form of a series of focus groups, allowing respondents to explore and develop their ideas and perceptions within a stimulating but non-threatening environment. Five groups were selected: one of children aged 9–10 who had studied Ancient Egypt at school; two groups of people who had visited Egypt (one group of backpackers, and an older group who had been on a cruise or organized tour); and two groups of UK-born people aged 25–45 (one white and the other non-white) who had never visited Egypt. Each group contained 6 to 8 respondents and each discussion session lasted between 60 and 90 minutes. The research was commissioned to inform developments at the Petrie Museum of Egyptian Archaeology, University College London. The topics covered were, however, of a very general nature and form a useful basis for an assessment of any museum with substantial ancient Egyptian collections.

Most museums have complex narratives and some displays may bear comparison with books, films or theatrical sets, but they are constructed quite differently and should not be assessed in the same terms. The constraints imposed by the content and scope of the collections, the museum building, the nature of the institution running it, will all contribute to determining its narrative. Still more significant will be its level of funding; displays are expensive and even the wealthiest museums may have to redisplay their galleries in a piecemeal fashion, taking into account the interests of their sponsors. Presenting a consistent, coherent story will not always be possible. At the British Museum, for instance, the sculpture galleries date from 1981, the Sackler galleries of Egypt in Africa and Early Egypt from 1991 and 1992, the John Addis Islamic gallery from 1999, the Roxie Walker funerary galleries from 2000, and a new gallery – 'Understanding Ancient Egyptian Culture' – will open in 2005. Meanwhile the opening, in 2001, of the central Great Court has altered circulation patterns through the museum, so that visitors now enter some of these galleries from a point other than that originally intended.

In some museums, staff programme events, educational activities and temporary exhibitions help to counterbalance gaps or weaknesses in the displays. Comprehensive, published interpretation strategies are rare, however, particularly in those museums perceived to have important collections. While science centres and children's museums – which tend to be concept, rather than collections-led – have pioneered visitor studies and the development of didactic interpretation strategies, art and archaeology museums have tended to adopt a more passive approach. This can be viewed positively as acknowledging multiple viewpoints and ways of learning, or it can be seen more cynically. A prestigious collection is still the most powerful marketing tool for a museum, and hence vital to the careers and security of its staff. Regardless of the museum's educational imperatives, this will normally ensure that attention is drawn to what the museum holds, rather than to what is missing.

While museums cannot claim to offer universal or seamless narratives, what they do convey is an authority, an air of authenticity and scholarship, derived from owning and showing 'the real thing' (Pearce 1995: 387–392). Wildung (1995: 5–6) believes the interaction between the visitor and the ancient artefact is particularly powerful, giving the visitor/observer the illusion that the observer and the observed artefact are contemporaneous. Amal-Naguib (1990: 85) also reflects on proximity and distance in the museum:

> Looking at Predynastic pottery, at Nofret sitting beside her husband, at the geese of Meidoum, at Sheikh el Balad, at the daughters of Akhnaton, and at so many other artefacts, puts us in a perspective of time and space. They are so different, they are so near and yet so far.

Myth and paradox

> We'll see the actual body, Tutankhamun, loads of gold.
>
> (child aged 9–10)

The focus group findings suggest that, for general audiences, "Ancient Egypt is a concept. It is not only a country. It is not purely history. It is not just a tissue of myths and artefacts. It is an amalgam of all of these; a magic terrain where myths may be real. The concept is created by school, media, archaeology, myths and museums, and is completely self-contained and satisfying" (Fisher 2000b: chart 16).

Throughout the discussions with the different groups, certain 'mythic themes' cropped up repeatedly: death; power; wealth; treasure; religion; monumental building; slavery; command of the heavens; creativity; extinction (Fisher 2000a: 20). Researchers felt that the respondents' fascination with Ancient Egypt and Egyptians was founded on a series of apparent paradoxes:

- Clever but death-obsessed.

- Powerful but non-militant.

- Peopled by pharaohs and slaves.

- Great achievements but sterile goals.

- All-encompassing but disappeared without trace.

The living dead

Much of the evidence we have for the ancient Egyptians' way of life derives from their funerary rituals, their tombs, their bodies. Burial artefacts constitute a substantial proportion of most museums' collections and are heavily featured in displays. In some galleries, such as Swansea's Egypt Centre, funerary artefacts are displayed to help illustrate ways of life. In other displays, this predominance of grave goods leads to a heavy narrative emphasis on death and belief. To modern western eyes this desire to channel so much wealth and effort into funerary rituals is both absorbing and incomprehensible:

> I'd like to see how they get mummified, see a dead person in their tomb.

> (child aged 9–10)

> Being and nothingness. A grandiosity.

> (non-white adult)

Our reaction to mummified bodies in museums epitomizes this ambivalence. At once evidently ancient and astonishingly well preserved, they seem both dead and alive. Perhaps the mummy's long history in western fiction (Lupton Chapter 2, this volume) derives from the western fascination with this paradox. Museum displays of mummies tend towards either the scientific or the spiritual. At the British and Manchester Museums the mummies are heavily interpreted, surrounded with information panels on the results of CAT scans – computer generated portraits – emphasizing their importance as objects of scientific study (and see Schadla-Hall and Morris Chapter 14, this volume). In other displays, whether for ethical or dramatic reasons, mummies and coffins are displayed in surroundings more evocative of their original contexts. At the Nubian Museum in Aswan, mummies are shown in a separate gallery, kept darkened until the visitor enters and then slowly illuminated.

At the Allard Pierson Museum in Amsterdam a basalt coffin in the centre of the display areas is the only ancient object visitors are allowed to touch. Coffins or mummified remains are often presented as the focus – the centrepiece of ancient Egyptian displays and final destination of the visitor, who, like the romanticized archaeologist (or despised grave robber), must penetrate several outer preparatory layers before coming upon the body itself. Is this metaphor accidental or deliberate? As Amal-Naguib (1990: 83) comments, "Egyptian collections and their curators together are myth-makers … [A]lthough museum curators remain essentially theorists and are restrained by professional ethical norms and scientific training, they induce dream and fantasy in others". Consciously or unconsciously, curators draw on fictional representations when compiling displays. Why else would so many coffins be displayed upright, as they appear in traditional mummy films?

Popular culture exerts a powerful influence on modern perceptions of ancient religious belief. On the one hand, researchers found, participants in the focus groups respected this evidently deep belief in the afterlife, even if they did not understand or share it.

> The Ancient Egyptians were more spiritual than us. They had so many different gods. The same as the American Indians.
>
> (Nile cruiser)

At the same time several participants made references to the occult – the 'mummy's curse' of romantic fiction – and were curious as to the relationship the ancients may have had with the spirit world. The researchers noted that "the supernatural adds a delicious shiver to the other more rational appeals of Ancient Egypt" (Fisher 2000a: 22–23).

> Apparently the last voyage [sic] of the Titanic was used to transport some stuff out of the tombs. How creepy is that?
>
> (white adult)

Archaeologists and grave robbers

The idea of the curse in western popular fiction rests on thrilling concepts of discovery and trespass. Participants in the focus group discussions were clearly captivated by the idea of dashing archaeologists discovering hidden treasure – Indiana Jones and Howard Carter are both powerful role models. Focus group participants, both children and adults, were almost wholly positive in their view of archaeology, seeing it as a virtuous search for artefacts with a 'Boys Own' appeal. The researchers commented: "Everyone has a tale somewhere of someone who found buried treasure and … a small quiet dream that one day it might be them" (Fisher 2000a: 45).

> I would like to find a flight of stairs in the rock. They found the Anubis seal and there were four rooms blocked off.
>
> (child aged 9–10)

> They don't give up that chance they'll find something. It's a hobby and the achievement of finding something becomes an obsession. Your moment of glory.
>
> (Nile cruiser)

Some of the young men in the focus groups appeared to view ancient Egyptian funerary practice as a kind of game, "as though the Egyptians had buried their artefacts, daring future generations to find them" (Fisher 2000b: chart 38). There appear to be strong parallels between people's descriptions of archaeologists and fictional representations such as the 'Tomb Raider' computer game (see Schadla-Hall and Morris Chapter 14, this volume).

The children consulted as part of the research were likewise full of enthusiasm and a desire to participate, regarding Ancient Egypt as "bursting with life … a magnificent adventure playground" (Fisher 2000b: chart 8):

I want to see a tomb, go into a tomb, get the curse of the mummy.

(child age 9–10)

They had mummies in Egypt. I would have tea with them if they came to life.

(child age 9–10)

Pyramids and pharaohs

For almost all participants, the pyramids were the ultimate icon, apparently demonstrating the power, knowledge and other-worldliness of their builders (Humbert 2003). Their scale is a proof of power and durability, and the unresolved debate surrounding their method of construction is seen as evidence of a higher knowledge, now lost.

> When the Americans moved Abu Simbel … the Egyptians had it built so that as the sun rose, it stayed looking at the real king. It's off-centre now.
>
> (Nile cruiser)

> At age 8 they must have been doing S-level science.
>
> (white adult)

And yet there is a tension between the need to understand, and a feeling that to do so would spoil the secret, that reality might be less thrilling than the unknown.

> I'd like to know how they built, like [sic] their pyramids and got everything perfect. The dimensions are so intelligent, it's scary.
>
> (non-white adult)

Many museums house monumental sculpture and architectural elements that convey a sense of Egypt's ancient temples and tombs. The British Museum sculpture galleries, with their dramatic staging of colossal sculptures, and the Metropolitan Museum's reconstructed Temple of Dendur, both evoke the sheer awe-inspiring scale of monumental ancient architecture.

> Egypt, its beauty and the size of its monuments, like huge cathedrals, you feel so small in comparison.
>
> (non-white adult)

> I've been to the British Museum. How did they move those big things?
>
> (non-white adult)

Numerous books and television documentaries of the last 20 years have addressed such questions. How did the Egyptians build the pyramids? Are the pyramids aligned with the stars? Were aliens involved? But museums almost invariably refuse to acknowledge, let alone engage with, these popular discussions, controversies and fantasies. Occasional displays, such as the Museum of London's prehistory gallery which opened in 1995 and featured Raquel Welch in animal skins on the introductory panel, use iconic images to encourage people to question stereotypes (Beard and Henderson 1999: 51). But such displays are rare, at least in archaeological museums. Perhaps curators feel that to engage with popular culture in this way would be to demean the institution and its message. Visitors to the temporary exhibition 'Ancient Egypt: Digging for Dreams', that did include 'alternative' voices, were pleasantly surprised by its willingness to address such issues and by its questioning narrative (MacDonald 2002: 106).

The researchers found, not surprisingly, that participants' reverence for the pyramids and monumental buildings extended likewise to the pharaohs who ordered their construction, almost as if they had superhuman knowledge or contact with divine powers.

Their royal families were part god.

(non-white adult)

The established Egyptological chronologies inevitably lay emphasis on kingship and kingdoms, and much museum labelling reinforces the idea of the power of the pharaoh as a positive force for stability and continuity: The 'Late Dynastic Period' label in the British Museum sculpture galleries is one example: "The New Kingdom was followed by a period in which the unity of Egypt gradually disintegrated, and this weakened condition left the country open to foreign invaders."

The people taking part in the research, particularly those who had been to Egypt, could cite a few royal names: Tutankhamun, Nefertiti, Cleopatra, Ramesses (Rice and MacDonald Chapter 1, this volume). Named individuals help to personalize this otherwise anonymous culture, although none of the participants had any idea of dynastic chronology. Researchers commented that whereas Roman emperors were imagined as power hungry and aggressive, pharaohs were imagined as "calm, impassive, rising above the fray" (Fisher 2000a: 23).

Some museum displays may contribute to these perceptions. The label for a representation of Sesostris III in the Brooklyn Museum (52.1) reads: "The greatest king of the Middle Kingdom … shown here in the prime of life. His strong, almost brutal features are furrowed, and his eyes are heavy with care … the powerful body … is beautifully sculpted … and the hard, dark stone increases the impression of dignity and royal aloofness." In many art galleries a tendency exists to attribute anonymous works of art to a named artist or studio (Phillips 1997: 98–99). In a similar way, the labelling of anonymous portrait sculptures in some museum displays speculates that they may represent particular pharaohs. The face of a statue (11.150.26) in the Metropolitan Museum is described: "This disdainful face once belonged to a composite statue … the wig and the very close similarity of the face to known images of Queen Tiye, wife of Amenophis III and mother of Akhenaten, make it virtually certain that she is represented here."

Participants in the focus groups were well aware that the media, particularly the film industry, had been crucial in shaping their images of these individuals, and pharaohs generally, although for some, the Bible also had a role:

In the Bible, Egypt is an evil place.

(child age 9–10)

Researchers found a widespread belief that ancient Egyptian society was founded on slavery, and in particular that the pyramids were built by slaves, living in fear of overlords (Fisher 2000a: 25).

I think there were loads and loads of really harsh laws.

(white adult)

What you can see is a beautiful building built by slaves and you're marvelling at who's made it. It's great and sad, that it was all built for one person and so many people had to labour.

(non-white adult)

This reading of Egyptian society, which most Egyptologists would regard as entirely misconceived, is nevertheless powerful. Indeed, taken together, the mythic themes described above had tremendous resonance for all the groups consulted. It would be strange if museums did not attempt to exploit this interest, and most do to some extent. Even in London's Petrie Museum, where cramped accommodation and a predominantly academic audience have resulted in dry and unsensational displays, an upright coffin until recently placed at the top of a dark entrance staircase evoked for many visitors the entrance to a tomb.

The myth made real

For 18 years, between 1961 and 1979, a selection of the finds from Tutankhamun's tomb toured the USA, Canada, Japan, France, England and the former USSR. These exhibitions represented the ultimate museum presentation of these mythic themes: a dark, atmospheric journey, in the footsteps of the cursed Carter, into the sealed, forbidden chamber, stuffed with treasure, of the tomb of a dead boy king. So powerful was this experience in many people's minds and memories, at least in England, that a version of the exhibition was constructed, as a permanent attraction, in Dorchester in 1987.

This exhibition, located in a redundant church on the high street of this small town, occupies a strange middle ground between authenticity and fiction. The opening sections introducing the story of the excavation in 1922 are copiously illustrated with archive photographs, newspaper facsimiles and contemporary quotes, and lead through to further displays introducing Akhenaten, Tutankhamun and ancient Egyptian burial practices. These contain apparently ancient artefacts such as pottery and shabtis – some labelled, others not – alongside replicas, casts and facsimiles (labelled "R", "C" and "fac" accordingly, although in very small text). The visitor is then confronted with a grisly reconstruction of Tutankhamun's unwrapped mummy "based on measurements, photographs, X-rays and computer scans" and "produced by a new British technique … using medical skeletons and actual animal skin", alongside graphic accounts of the first autopsy carried out on the real body (Figure 6:1 col. pl.).

The second section of the exhibition puts the visitor in Howard Carter's shoes. Entering a dark corridor, the visitor is confronted with a tableau of Carter, Lord Carnarvon and Lady Evelyn Herbert while a dramatized sound commentary, including knocking and scraping sounds, recreates the moment of discovery; the "wonderful things" (Wheatcroft Chapter 11, this volume). Through another doorway is a reconstruction of the tomb's antechamber, with replica furnishings stacked as shown in the archive photographs, and even perfumed with "actual samples of the unguents and aromatic oils from the tomb" (Ridley 1998). Next the visitor proceeds to the reconstructed burial chamber, where a second tableau "recreates the moment that Carter separates the outer gold coffin from the inner gold and enamel coffins" (Ridley

1998). An audio presentation describes the scene, praises Carter's achievement and his role as "the instrument of Tutankhamun's immortality", and then invites the visitor to reflect on spiritual matters. As a prelude to several minutes of chanting, drumbeats and dramatized readings of some of the funeral texts in the chamber, the narrator invites the visitor to "listen for a while to the confused hubbub of words that seem to seep from these walls thick with a confusion of inscriptions and prayers … Let's dream in this forest of symbols".

A short display on the 'curse' then leads to the final section of the exhibition, which is set out as a traditional museum presentation, with low but dramatic lighting and individual objects in cases. The labelling here stresses that although all the objects are facsimiles they have been made by craftsmen and artists in Britain and America, using real gold. In fact this is the only section of the exhibition that consciously echoes the 'blockbuster' shows of the 1960s and 1970s. The more dramatic reconstructions and the use of audio have more in common with later heritage site interpretations, particularly Jorvik in York, where a 'dark ride' presentation precedes a more formal museum display.

Whatever its precedents, the Dorchester Tutankhamun exhibition adeptly exploits those themes that contribute to its popular appeal. It is a small exhibition in a small town, but regularly attracts around 175,000 paying visitors each year, about four times the number of visitors to the free Dorset County Museum down the road. Its organizers point to the use of their reconstructions in numerous BBC television documentaries, including those widely used in English schools, as evidence of the authenticity. Certainly, the convenience of these ready-made film sets must contribute to their use for such purposes, which may in turn make them seem more real, thus further blurring the boundaries between reality and myth (and see Schadla-Hall and Morris Chapter 14, this volume).

Icons for sale

The commercial potential of Ancient Egypt naturally extends into museum shops, and most museums with ancient Egyptian collections use images from the mythic themes in their marketing and commercial operations. Human heads – normally royal sculptures or the heads from coffin lids – are most commonly chosen for publicity materials. The Royal Ontario Museum website introduces its Egyptian collections with a gilt coffin head; the Egyptian Museum in Berlin with the famous Nefertiti bust. The three main general guidebooks to the British Museum are all dominated by ancient Egyptian portrait or coffin heads; these images stand for (and help to sell) the museum as splendid, timeless and authoritative.

Museum postcards and souvenirs occupy an interesting grey area, reflecting, in most museums, both curatorial and commercial concerns – what should be sold and what will sell. As with the displays, the selection of objects and images for museum shops will be guided by a number of practical concerns. Certain objects reproduce better in two dimensions, others in three. Licensing arrangements may make it cost effective to reproduce certain objects repeatedly in different formats. And it may be desirable from a marketing point of view to create 'ranges' based on particular objects or types.

It is rare to find a museum whose interpretation strategy appears to cover its entire operation, from the images used on the website through the displays to the souvenirs sold in the shop. Particularly in large museums, these functional areas are managed by separate sections or departments, often with somewhat different goals. The curatorial influence on these products has generally been on the wane over the last two decades, as museums have become more commercially oriented. In most museums, shops have taken on greater prominence. The museum at the Fondaçion Clos in Barcelona is entered through a standard high street shop, selling ancient Egyptian gifts. The British Museum, in addition to four on-site shops, and one round the corner, has an outlet at Heathrow airport, while the Metropolitan Museum has 14 stores in the USA, and a further 12 in Mexico, Europe and Asia. With the advent of internet shopping it is now perfectly possible to buy souvenirs of a visit one has never made.

Beard has commented on the iconic status of the Rosetta Stone, symbolizing at once the British Museum's fame and its indecipherability (Beard 1992: 519–527; Walker Chapter 7, this volume). Despite the unprepossessing appearance of the original object, it currently reproduces and sells well as postcards (four versions), jigsaws, mugs, books, mousemats, candles, paperweights, notebooks, tiles, tea towels, rugs and beanbags. Berlin's 'Nefertiti Head' has a similar iconic status, and appears on a range of souvenirs.

Both of these objects are extremely famous, invariably on show in their respective museum homes, and obvious souvenir material. As souvenirs they help to reinforce the status of the original, and contribute to the marketing of the museums that house them.

The successful ancient Egyptian museum souvenir does not, however, need to reproduce an icon, or even a current exhibit. The British Museum's Gayer Anderson cat – a bronze model from around 600 BC – is enormously popular as a postcard (Beard 1992: 515), and sells well in four sizes as a replica statuette, on jewellery and ties (British Museum 2001), despite the fact that it is currently (2003) off display. At the Metropolitan Museum in New York a large range of children's products are branded with images of William, an Egyptian hippo – 'William is the symbol of Metkids'. One can purchase William artkits, bags, T-shirts, key chains, rubbers, cut-outs and soft toys, but it takes determination to find the original, sitting anonymously, in a case labelled "minor arts of the Middle Kingdom, dynasty XII".

Does cuddly William represent a faintly absurd attempt to project our own fantasies onto an ancient culture, or is he a sign that something – a human element – is missing from the museum's presentation of the ancient world?

Lost peoples

Researchers analyzing the focus group discussions commented on participants' lack of understanding, almost lack of interest, in how ordinary people lived in Ancient Egypt. "There is little sense of human life, of busy people in communities, the way ancient Rome is imagined. Ancient Egypt was an aloof society. It ran with pharaohs and slaves and not much in between. The mummies are as alive as the people" (Fisher 2000a: 13).

It is worth reflecting on the kind of effort that may be required in museums attempting to portray daily life themes. At the British Museum, daily life is covered in the galleries on "Early Egypt" and "Egypt and Africa", but – pending the forthcoming gallery on "Understanding Ancient Egyptian Culture" – do not currently feature in displays about the dynastic period. In other museums, such as the Louvre's ground floor Egyptian galleries, daily life themes are prominent, yet it is rare to find anything more evocative than displays of artefacts grouped by theme. The archaeology of other places and periods has a history of more varied museological presentations: of models, dioramas, and reconstructions (Moser 1999: 95–112). The Museum of London's reconstructed Roman rooms, and the Pepper's Ghost displays of Vikings and Viking artefacts at Jorvik in York are two such examples. Though such interpretations are frequently problematic, they have been shown to be popular with the public in bringing history and prehistory 'to life'. As noted above, tomb contents and funerary material are frequently displayed in a dramatic and evocative way (the displays of the burials of Wah and Sobekmose at the Metropolitan Museum are excellent examples), but the same techniques are rarely applied to daily life displays. Perhaps curators and designers assume that the objects displayed are so attractive and familiar as not to require such contextualization. Or perhaps it is simply too formidable a task.

Interesting experiments are, however, taking place in the field of multimedia, which may have an effect on public perceptions and museum presentations. There are now numerous online 3D reconstructions of ancient Egyptian sites. Although tombs, temples and monumental architecture predominate, reconstructions on a more human scale and with a daily life emphasis are beginning to appear, several of them created by museums. The British Museum's Ancient Egypt website for primary schools (www.ancientegypt.co.uk) includes a virtual temple. The Petrie Museum's "Digital Egypt for Universities" (www.petrie.ucl.ac.uk/digital_egypt) includes reconstructions of settlements at Hammamiya, Naqada and Koptos. The Manchester Museum has produced a reconstruction of the town of Kahun (www.kahun.man.ac.uk). As with other forms of reconstruction, these 3D landscapes are deeply problematic. Though imagined, they can seem powerfully real. Though navigable, they are rarely peopled and may actually reinforce the idea of a dehumanized society. Yet the potential exists to develop them, perhaps incorporating images of the modern landscape, sounds and languages, and to integrate them with museum displays – as the Royal Ontario Museum has done with an animation of a pyramid interior – and thus help to bring the Ancient Egyptians, as we imagine them, to life.

Lost in time

A further difficulty for museums is to convey a sense of the chronology of Ancient Egypt. Researchers commented that among general audiences there was no evidence of an understanding of chronology or sense of historical perspective: "Ancient Egypt is a sealed bubble in which pharaohs, pyramids, slaves, tombs and Cleopatra float around in a rich soup" (Fisher 2000b: chart 7).

Amal-Naguib (1990: 6) comments that "Egyptian collections often impart on the average visitor the feeling that this ancient civilization has stood still". Conveying such a vast chronology is a tremendously difficult task, though most museums with substantial collections attempt it (Fazzini 1995: 38). The Metropolitan Museum manages better than most, with an informative timeline at the entrance to the displays, which are for the most part chronologically arranged. But the label for the opening exhibit, a thirteenth Dynasty statue of Horus (34.2.1), draws attention to continuity rather than change: "The statue was created in the last decades of native rule … it exemplifies the way in which basic Egyptian beliefs and expressions survived through the millennia, providing a seemingly inexhaustible source of strength, beauty and renewal."

Perhaps the most interesting areas to consider are the chronological boundaries of Ancient Egypt. Museum timelines often begin 4000–3000 BC and corresponding displays start – in those museums with relevant collections – with predynastic material. Almost all end or break before 641 AD and the Arab conquest. In both the British Museum and the Metropolitan Museum, Islamic Egyptian material is displayed in physically separate galleries, designated "Islamic" or "Asian" rather than "Egyptian" on visitor orientation plans, and without signage or interpretation that might lead the visitor to make a connection. In both of the above museums the Islamic galleries combine material from across the Islamic world, so that Egyptian artefacts can be difficult to distinguish from Syrian, Iraqi and Iranian. In the Louvre Roman and Coptic Egypt have separate galleries.

The researchers found that among the focus group participants "virtually nothing is known about modern Egypt or times since the pharaohs, and there is no desire to know" (Fisher 2000b: chart 6). Participants made no connection between ancient and modern Egypt, assuming that the ancients had been wiped out or disappeared.

> Corruption at the top and brainless at the bottom. They must have been overrun by other nations. Like the Greeks and Romans.
>
> (Nile cruiser)

As Fisher (2000a: 19–20, 30) summarizes the situation:

> There is little desire to confront the issue of historical integrity. People know the myth, they like it and they want to revel in it. It thrives on never being completely solved. It is entirely in keeping that this world should suddenly and mysteriously have become extinct, just like the dinosaurs ...

> When asked for their opinion of modern Egypt, people tend to look puzzled. They believe it to be just another poor Arab country, indistinguishable from the rest. Modern Egyptians are so unlike the myth of Ancient Egypt that British people tend not to believe that they are the descendants of the ancients.

Those respondents who had visited Egypt seem to have come away with negative and racist views:

> The monuments are too breathtaking for words. It knocks you away and now they can't mend your toaster.
>
> (Nile cruiser)

This sense of disconnection between ancient and modern (Haikal Chapter 9, this volume) bears out the results of research carried out with British Museum visitors in 1999. Visitor exit surveys indicated that while most of those questioned had strong positive associations with Ancient Egypt – 46 per cent of those questioned citing art, 35 per cent monuments – 53 per cent had no associations at all with modern Egypt. The researchers concluded that the layout of the museum's displays "easily confirms visitors' perceptions of a complete separation between past and present in Egypt and allows potentially contradictory images of past glory and present barbarity to coexist" (Motawi and Merriman 2000: 11).

There are of course strong reasons for displaying Islamic Egyptian material as part of the Islamic world rather than as a continuation of the ancient one. But, as Fazzini (1995: 38) notes, this universal cut-off is not generally applied to displays of Nubian material, which often take a broader span, encompassing Christian and Islamic periods. The British Museum's Sackler gallery of Egypt and Africa is one such example, its displays continuing through to 1500 AD.

Lost in space

The 'chronological blinkers' often applied to Ancient Egypt may relate to the way in which it is perceived geographically.

Many museum displays about Ancient Egypt include maps of the Nile Valley, but few include smaller scale maps showing its location in relation to the continent of Africa, to Asia or to Europe (Champion and Ucko 2003: 2–3). Broader perspectives, such as that presented by the Metropolitan Museum's Sackler gallery of Egypt and the Levant, are exceptional. This gallery juxtaposes artefacts from both regions, presenting evidence of artistic exchange, trade, emigration and immigration in texts and artefacts.

Other museums have, within the last decade, displayed their Nubian holdings in new galleries, and attempted to set Egypt within a broader African context. Fazzini (1995: 38) notes displays at the Ashmolean Museum, the Royal Ontario Museum and the Museum of Fine Arts in Boston. The British Museum's Sackler gallery of Egypt and Africa is introduced as follows: "The land of Nubia was the vital link between the ancient Egyptian world and the cultures of equatorial Africa. The objects displayed in this gallery show the diversity of Nubian civilization over 6,000 years, and highlight the great cultural and political flowering of the Kerma and Meroitic periods." Smaller museums have also made efforts to locate Egypt within Africa. At London's Horniman Gallery ancient Egyptian artefacts are included within the new Africa gallery. And at the Brooklyn Museum a small display entitled "Egypt in Africa" draws comparisons between ancient and modern materials and invites visitors to use the library to find out more about such links.

These attempts to locate Egypt are to be applauded but evidence from the research suggests that museums may have to work harder to change perceptions. The focus group researchers found that, particularly for white participants, "Modern Egypt is simply the country you have to get to so that you can physically experience the myth of Ancient Egypt. Many people aren't quite sure where it is, but … this doesn't matter because spiritually they feel ancient Egypt belongs to them too" (Fisher 2000b: chart 26). Furthermore, the idea of Egypt as being an African country was disturbing to some white participants:

> If then, thousands of years ago, they could build them temples, why is it in Africa they are still living in mud huts?
>
> (Nile cruiser)

The discomfort of some respondents with the idea of African Egypt was linked, researchers reported, to a desire to maintain a white Egyptian identity. Most adult white participants in the discussion groups found the suggestion that Ancient Egyptians could be anything other than white profoundly disturbing (and see various chapters in O'Connor and Reid 2003).

> Hollywood makes out they were white Europeans. Why didn't it dawn on me? I assumed they were all white and the dark ones were Nubian slaves.
>
> (Nile cruiser)

> I suppose I want to think that Cleopatra looked a bit like Elizabeth Taylor.
>
> (white adult)

Non-white respondents saw things quite differently. For them Ancient Egypt had a greater role, symbolizing "the theft of cultural capital" by white Europeans (Fisher 2000b: chart 13):

> I went to the library, looking in the African section. It came under European history!
>
> (non-white adult)

Many Egyptologists regard a discussion of the skin colour of the Ancient Egyptians as at best irrelevant and at worst racist (North 2003), and most museums would baulk at discussing the question in displays. The research nevertheless indicated that this is a live issue for general audiences. White western Europeans are, perhaps, looking for their roots among the earliest examples of recorded history, and are anxious to identify with a potent and attractive Ancient Egypt. If that Ancient Egypt is located in Africa, or even in modern Egypt, they become visitors rather than inheritors. These issues are pertinent to the chronologies and geographies museums choose to present.

Conclusion

Western museums with ancient Egyptian collections do not have to work hard to make their collections popular. They can take advantage of, and draw inspiration from, decades of popular culture in literature, films, television and advertising. They can assume that their visitors enter the displays already familiar with certain aspects of Ancient Egypt, and enthusiastic to explore. What this research indicates, however, is that some of those same visitors bring deep-seated misconceptions and unpleasant prejudices, which most museums might wish to change. The challenge is to exploit the subject's popularity while questioning some of the assumptions on which that popularity is based.

CHAPTER 7

'ACQUISITIONS AT THE BRITISH MUSEUM, 1998'

Julian Walker

In 1998 I started observational research in the Egyptian galleries of the British Museum as preparation for an artwork installation. My initial questions were: What do visitors to the British Museum do? What do they want, and what are they offered? As the research progressed I focused on the nature of three acts: touching iconic monuments, being photographed nearby iconic monuments, and purchasing replica souvenirs.

Visitors to any museum participate in the ritual of 'being there'. They come to be in the same space as the objects and as such are tourists to that particular space, participating in the secularized ritual of visiting the museum with its 'iconic objects' which, as Pausanias points out, has been part of tourism since Classical times.

The notion of an aura of the authentic, projected onto the art object, as proposed by Walter Benjamin (1992: 211) is applicable to the museum object, by virtue of the ritual of visiting; this is particularly the case when the object may be thought of as iconic.

The creation of 'iconic status' for items in a collection is a product of the desire for communal possession and stems from roots which may be anecdotal, political, or based on the common experience of size, fear, survival or beauty. If it is accepted that frequent visiting adds to the iconic status of an object, then frequent photography of the object by visitors may be seen to further this process. If it is not just a private experience – a recording of a moment in someone's life – then it may be an act of confirming how the processes of mechanical reproduction through print, film, television and 3D reproduction reify the according of iconic status. If so, we can see that the act of visiting the objects produces further objects, namely the replica-souvenir and the video or photograph.

The Rosetta Stone became a focus for the activities that interested me. At the time of my research it was located in such a way that the visitor was directed to it through a series of spaces which functioned as funnels: from the width of Great Russell Street through a small entrance within the cast iron gates, up towards the grand portico, but through a small door which led onto a large area without objects, along a narrow corridor past a shop to the spacious entrance to the Egyptian Gallery, and finally between massive sculptures to the stone itself. Before this physical experience begins, the visitor is already well aware of the stone's fame and its location within an

Figure 7:1   Detail of 'Acquisitions at the British Museum, 1998' (© Julian Walker).

internationally renowned museum, a link between object and location by which each increases the status of the other. The visitor is in two spaces simultaneously, the space of the Rosetta Stone and the space of the British Museum.

The iconic status in this case is based on awareness of the stone's role in decoding the hieroglyphs; the visual aspect of the object practically seems to imply that it was made with this in mind. Its fame and this visual aspect belie the relatively minor importance that the stone in fact played in the decoding of hieroglyphic text (Budge 1950). The stone has come to be about the decoding of the hieroglyphs just as much as it is about the textual content in three languages, dealing with honours, taxes and revenues. In the same way, the replica-souvenir is about visiting the original and authentic stone; it has this story projected onto it.

Beard's (1992: 521) view of the Rosetta Stone, itself a metonym for Egypt, is that "it appears to centre our understanding of the past in language and texts; if we accept the moral of the 'Rosetta Stone Story', then the culture of Ancient Egypt was revealed to us only through the decipherment of its strange hieroglyphic script. Language and writing is seen to take precedence over artefact". This view passes over the pre-decipherment activities and descriptions of hieroglyphs by those such as Herodotus, Strabo, Pausanias, Pliny the Elder, as well as many others, including medieval Arabic scholars and those working within European culture (Ucko and Champion 2003). The body of knowledge, erroneous or not, to which they contributed, and the interest it engendered must presumably have influenced Napoleon to take the company of *savants* on his expedition in 1789.

Adkins' (2000) book on the decipherment of the hieroglyphs, significantly called *The Keys of Egypt*, also takes Egypt to be about linguistic mediation, mediation of itself through the need to decipher the hieroglyphs and then itself as mediation. Beard's (1992) observations of the activities of visitors, who spend as much or more time reading the information panels behind the Rosetta Stone as they do looking at the stone itself, lend credence to this view; the panels offer a mediation, a decipherment not of the text of the stone, but of the nature of the stone. Yet visitors do not come primarily to read about the stone; their intention in coming is to be with it, to partake of its authenticity and 'realness'.

It is possible that the replica being offered for sale acts as a 'stamp of importance' conferred by the museum shop, an insurance against the visitor not knowing the degree of its value. This in itself may act as an incentive to view the object, much as the recognition of a famous name on a picture-label in a gallery 'informs' us as to how much time to invest in looking at the picture (Walker 1997: 261). The replica and the souvenir tell us what the museum feels we should take special note of, what we should mark our visit by purchasing; it is perhaps significant that the souvenir shop is on the way in as well as on the way out. In the British Museum in 1998 the visitor had to pass by three souvenir shops on the way to the Egyptian galleries. The sight of the souvenir seems to say, 'This is what you want. We've got it, and you can have it too'.

The artwork installation 'Acquisitions at the British Museum, 1998' was presented as a museum display. Based on the observation of how visitors use iconic objects as cultural landmarks to be photographed with, it used photographs of visitors having their photographs taken, enlarged and turned into sculptural objects (Figure 7:1). This was set against a video which showed a pair of hands moving over the surface of two display cases in the ground floor Egyptian gallery and over the rail surrounding the Rosetta Stone. Interspersed with these three activities the camera traced three short narratives: a small, elongated resin sitting cat, replica of the Gayer-Anderson cat, is carried through the gallery and leant against the original object; a small blue ceramic hippo replica is carried in and set in the case where it touches the faience hippo (ca. 1900 BC); and a small resin replica of the Rosetta Stone is brought in and laid on the original. At the time of the project these represented the three most purchased replicas in the British Museum shop.

While the first of these may be purchased for a mix of aesthetics and feline association and the second for aesthetic/humorous reasons, it seems likely that the third is purchased for reasons of respect for, and excitement at finally getting to see, a famous and important object and to be able to show evidence of that visit. Though small, it references a major cultural object in a way that the first two do not. Any of the three, if purchased as a gift, may boast to another the purchaser's power to visit a distant place; the Rosetta Stone replica may in this case carry an educational message, or a confirmation that both giver and receiver belong to a particular level of cultural familiarity.

All three are recognizably Egyptian in terms of their cultural origins. The rich ambivalence that surrounds our relationship with Egyptian culture seems more alluring than the patent intellect and representative figurativeness of Greek culture, and the triumphal aggression of the Romans. For the museum visitor, this relationship is founded as much on the physicality of the material remains that connect us with Ancient Egypt, as on our knowledge of the civilization.

Museum objects are the interface of fascination with Egypt. The Rosetta Stone in itself is perhaps the most well known icon in terms of acting as a conduit for the understanding of ancient Egyptian culture. And yet it is in a sense also the antithesis of what it promises: the fact that the texts were "of limited use" (Adkins 2000: 214) in the process of decipherment indicates that the value of the stone lies in its physical presence, its role as a metaphor for the passage across time, and as a metonym of Egypt itself. Time also plays a large part in the fascination, both the length of time between the present and the perceived time of Ancient Egypt and the duration of the ancient Egyptian civilization itself. Here Egypt becomes a conduit to the past, the state of preservation of its objects and images condensing time so that one can easily imagine oneself in the 'now' of 4,000 years ago. But at the same time there is the vast length of the period of Egyptian civilization, the magnitude of its monuments, the extent of its infrastructure and self-awareness.

The idea of Egypt frequently balances one concept with its opposite: scholarship and mystery, a cultural location in both Africa and Europe, an ambivalent status in the Bible, most notably in the story of Moses leading the Hebrews out of bondage in Egypt contrasted with that of the infant Christ's escape to Egypt and the fear/pleasure reaction to the alleged curse associated with, or projected onto, grave-goods and, by association, their replicas.

Two other areas of activity add to this fascination with Ancient Egypt. First, there is the long history of Egyptian design, influencing fashion, architecture, clothing, jewellery, etc. from the Roman period onwards (Vercoutter 1992: 54), a sort of 'design plundering'. Napoleon Bonaparte's appropriation of the bee as a symbol of his status to supplant the Bourbon fleur-de-lys indicates a desire to reflect some of the power of the pharaohs on himself (Adkins 2000: 41), but implicit in the desire for a 'Napoleonic' hegemony is the desire that the bee should be primarily 'Napoleonic' and secondarily pharaonic. His intention may at first have been homage in the act of borrowing and using the motif, but imperial aspirations imply a desire for immediate association to take the place of referral.

Second, there is the role of Egypt as incidental prize for France and Britain between 1798 and 1803, a site of conflict for control of the fast route to India (Jeffreys 2003: 1–3). Despite Napoleon Bonaparte's contingent of intellectuals his prime motive for the invasion of Egypt was to disrupt Britain's most profitable trading link and to establish a base for military operations to the Indian subcontinent. Following the Battle of Aboukir Bay, the departure of Napoleon Bonaparte and the French evacuation, the British forces left Egypt in 1803, leaving a sublimated conflict between excavators and removers of relics that lasted 50 years; though nationals of other European countries were involved, this appears primarily to have involved French and British agents. The tussle over the Rosetta Stone, though dating from the period of military conflict, 1801–1802, provides the most famous example of this. The hieroglyphs themselves equally became a site of Franco-British rivalry, the prize of their first decipherment still contested between supporters of Champollion and Young.

This fascination may be said to find its expression in the process of removal, the copying of images by Denon and others, but primarily in the taking away of objects. Egypt had in a sense always fed off itself long before Mohammed Ali sanctioned the activities of Salt, Drovetti and Belzoni. The history of the material culture of Ancient Egypt is a history of pillage and removal that runs simultaneously with the history of the burying of objects, for which there is evidence from as far back as 2000 BC when King Merikara told his son that he had been involved in looting tombs. The 'Book of Buried Pearls' (Vercoutter 1992: 59), a guide book for likely treasure sites and a manual of how to overcome the magic protecting them, was written in the Medieval period but was still circulating at the beginning of the 20th century as suppliers sought to satisfy the European demand for objects. Yet, because of the vastness of Egyptian material culture the popular perception seems to be that the sands of Egypt will continue to supply objects almost indefinitely; there will always be something left undiscovered and the processes of removal do not detract from the original. The same pattern of taking away without detracting from the integrity of the whole can be seen in the purchase of replicas from the British Museum shop; as part of the continuing story of the Gayer-Anderson cat or the Rosetta Stone, they are in a sense part of the object, yet their purchase and removal does not detract from the original – rather it is made greater by these processes.

What people do in the galleries may be considered as acts of self-affirmation and awareness. Visitors to the British Museum, especially those obviously on tourist trips, usually spend a very short time in front of most objects in the museum; even major iconic objects elicit a response time that appears to have more to do with recognition and collecting than study or appraisal. Being photographed in front of or near to a famous object is an integral part of this kind of museum visit. The role of the photograph taken in this way is to express the need to 'mark' the act, to create evidence of the person's desire to be associated and in part identified with that object and site. When we examine what exactly is being recorded in these photographs, it is seen that people tend to have their photographs taken standing next to, near or in front of iconic objects which are free-standing: large Egyptian statues, the Rosetta Stone, the façade of the mausoleum from Halicarnassus, the marble statues from the Parthenon, the winged bulls from Assyria. People rarely have their photographs taken standing by objects behind glass, however well known the object: the Portland Vase, Lindow Man, the Sutton Hoo treasures, the Battersea shield, or the Leonardo cartoons. The person visiting the museum-object is prevented from touching the object by a barrier either physical – glass plate, line of rope, high plinth, metal bar – or mental/cultural – shyness, the fear of being observed and told off, respect, a printed notice, some idea of conservation. However, with the exception of the glass barrier, the potential for physical contact exists and a direct line could be drawn in the air between the visitor and the object. At the time of this project the Rosetta Stone was mounted on a stand and surrounded by a metal bar at waist height, set 60 cm from the stone. An invigilator was seated nearby acting as a warning presence, but rather than preventing visitors from touching the Rosetta Stone, he would gently reprimand people after they had touched it, implying a complicity in, or at least an awareness of, the need to touch (and see Walker 1996: 17). If a large iconic object is being touched as a physical link to something further back (i.e. nearer to a source) there may be some notion of a goal for which Egyptian statuary is the conduit.

If touching is prohibited, it then becomes more necessary to have physical evidence of having been in the presence of the iconic object or in the space of the museum. Quite apart from what Sontag (1980: 24) describes as the "compulsion to photograph; to turn experience itself into a way of seeing", there is a specific act repeated over and over in this situation – the photographing of the person with his/her outline overlapping that of the object. The image of the person photographed is mixed with the image of object, the photograph unites them. Game (1993: 145) quotes Barthes: "Significantly, [the form of] mediation in photography is corporeal … Bodies touch without clear boundaries between them." As well as becoming united in space, they become united in time; Sontag (1980: 67) quotes Berenice Abbott: "The photographer is the contemporary being *par excellence*; through his eyes the now becomes the past."

If identification of the subject matter of a photograph dominates perception of it, then the photographs of visitors standing by objects must be about the conjunction of identities, visitor with object. But the photographs mentioned above show a different reality from the perception of visitors themselves to the galleries; they see the British Museum as full of iconic objects, while the photographs show that it is full of visitors associating with iconic objects. In many cases the photographs people take will have other people in them, besides the intended person and the object. The presence of these people acts to sanction the act of being there (and see Game 1993: 145). In this instance it is useful to compare the photograph taken by the visitor with the postcard view of the museum and/or its objects provided for sale by the museum. As Beard (1992) shows, whereas the postcard provides an idealized view of the object or museum which the purchaser may use as ground for projection, the snapshot photograph is made without spatial editing, other than the non-interference by other visitors. The photograph becomes reference material for later; the 'now' is the experience of being photographed, later comes the experience of that experience. It is the job of the photograph as 'object' to remind us of the first experience. It also reminds us of our absence and of our ability to control our perception of that absence. The photograph functions as the mirror in the child's game 'Fort! Da!' described by Freud as an attempt to control absence – by repeating presence and absence, the child sends the object/image away knowing he can recall it; in doing so he gains mastery over the absence of his mother. Having a photograph of oneself standing in front of a famous object and being able to look at it later allows one to control the absence of the experience of being in that place by that object, where the place and the object are of sufficient pre-eminence to act as fixed points.

Photography is used here as proof, as the fact/act of light emanating from subject: the photograph is taken to prove that 'this really was so'. It is impersonal, not unlike the museum itself. Writing, always fiction, cannot authenticate itself, cannot give the 'that has been' of photography (and see Barthes 1984: 85; Game 1993: 139).

"The photograph as souvenir is a logical extension of the pressed flower, the preservation of an instant in time through a reduction of physical dimensions and a corresponding increase in significance supplied by means of narrative" (Stewart 1993: 138). The compressing of three dimensions into two allows a documentation of a point of time that has a narrative stretching into the future: the event 'is', the photograph ensures that the event 'will have been'. The impersonality of both the camera and the museum are used to reflect a judgment of the self. "Because of its connection to biography and its place in constituting the notion of the individual life, the memento becomes emblematic of the worth of that life and of the self's capacity to generate worthiness" (Stewart 1993: 139). And the photograph and the replica-souvenir act like the postcard to validate "the experience of the site, which we can now name as the site of the subject himself or herself" (Stewart 1993: 138–139). The snapshot photograph, because of its connections to the family and highpoints of family life (Bourdieu 1996: 19), extends this creation of 'worth' beyond a group of individuals collected in front of an object, to those individuals acting as a family, indicating the worth and identification of that family's aspirations, ideals, values.

The replica-souvenir is a re-creation or re-invention of the space of the original. Its role appears to be to validate the visitor's visit to the museum in the same way that the visit to the museum confirms the self-worth of the visitor. Yet there is a difference in worth between the souvenir purchased on site and the souvenir purchased after the event. Replica-souvenirs may carry the aura of the experience of being in this place by this object: "souvenirs speak of events that are not repeatable, but are reportable; they serve to authenticate the narrative in which the actor talks about the event" (Pearce 1994: 196). Pearce is talking about personal souvenirs not manufactured as such (the shell case from the battlefield, the lock of hair) that may support a narrative. But the authenticating power can be equally applied to the status of the person: if the souvenir is 'proof' that the person went to a place, then the replica specifically provides 'proof' of the person's depth of experience on seeing that object, the need to 'mark' the act, evidence of the person's desire to be associated and in part identified with that object.

By re-creating the space of the original, replicas carry away the aura of the original without loss to the original. Purchasing a replica involves seeing the original, being moved to want a permanent *aide-mémoire* of the experience and purchasing and taking away the replica. The replica is designed to exist at a spatial remove from the original. Yet the manufactured replica miniaturizes the space of the original and thus the possibility of recreating the essence of the experience. The notion that a replica may be seen as more desirable if bought in the same gallery as the original relates the replica to the Christian relic. In the early days of the Christian church, relics were 'manufactured' by placing objects in contact with the bones of the saints, which were then used to consecrate altars of new churches, often on pagan sites. It was perceived that the secondary relic was as powerful as the original. Beard (1992: 507) uses the term 'tourist/visitor/pilgrim' for visitors to the British Museum and though the connotations of sacrifice and redemption mean that the notion of pilgrimage seems excessive, the relationship to religious activity is clearly appropriate. In 1998 there was a shop in the ancient Egyptian sculpture gallery selling material related to the objects nearby. Purchasing a replica-souvenir here indicates the degree of excitement in being in the same space as the Rosetta Stone and other exhibits, a need to manage time and space by purchasing a souvenir before the aura becomes diminished by distance of time and space. A souvenir purchased here carries greater power to validate the experience than one bought in the shop near the entrance or in the forecourt, still less from a source outside the boundary of the museum itself (Stewart 1993: 135).

Stewart's consideration of the souvenir cedes it less power. In her assessment the replica-souvenir replaces the context of origin with the context of perpetual consumption. But its possession is a kind of dispossession, in that the presence of this 'object that is not the object' declares its status as substitution and thus its failure. It declares the experience of itself to be essentially second-hand. "The magic of the souvenir is a kind of failed magic … Instrumentality replaces essence … The place of origin must remain unavailable in order for desire to be generated" (Stewart 1993: 151). This may explain the melancholy of the souvenir, its fleeting nature, the projection of absence into the future, and sense of its having been taken from its home. However, this notion of failure and homelessness may be equally applied to the original object that has been removed from the site for which it was intended, and particularly in the case of grave-goods has failed in its intended role of accompanying the dead person in perpetuity. In the simplest terms, by being dug up, it has failed to remain hidden from the tomb-opener, treasure hunter or archaeologist.

The relic differs from the manufactured souvenir, in that the former is a metonym, while the latter can only ever be a metaphor, with an aura of 'what it is not' hovering over it. Yet as a metaphor the aura of connection with the original is projected onto it, and it is thus under the control of the viewer/owner, who is consequently in a position of power. So while one cannot own the Rosetta Stone, or even a portion of it in reality, by owning a replica one can symbolically possess entirely both it and one's exclusive experience of it. Essentially, then, the souvenir-replica is different before and after its purchase, the time and space of purchase determining value. Similarly, the photograph becomes an object requiring mediation in the form of placing in its own space. It is an object, a touched thing, which never achieves a 'real home' such as a museum, a place where it 'really' belongs. As part of a narrative it will be pasted into an album always requiring a hand to turn the page and reveal it. If framed it takes its place within the displayed narrative of the owner's life.

As trophies of a moment and a site, both souvenir and replica mediate experience through time and space, allowing access to and replicating the greater mediation provided by the museum object itself. Such mediation must surely connect to the casting of Egypt as a land of mystery, whose ancient inhabitants knew something that we do not. It is an 'unknowing' that has taken many forms over the years, from the 'pyramidiots' (Daniel 1981: 117) to the T-shirt on sale in the street opposite the British Museum showing a tourist Anubis with the caption "Egypt, Land of Mystery". The scale of ancient Egyptian monuments indicates an assurance, a self-conscious declaration, which the authenticity of the museum object refers to and leads us towards.

CHAPTER 8

SELLING EGYPT: ENCOUNTERS AT KHAN EL-KHALILI

Fekri A. Hassan

The publication of Baedeker's Egyptian travel handbook coincided with the publication of the handbook for travellers to Palestine and Syria which came out in 1876. The touristic appeal of the region was enhanced by the growing interest in the Middle East on the part of the colonial powers as well as the ability of these powers to secure safe travel. However, the opening of the Suez Canal in 1869 and the efforts by Khedive Ismail, to refurbish Egypt's image to attract Europeans, played a major role in stimulating tourism to Egypt. Originally a collection of articles for Lower Egypt with the Fayum and the Peninsula of Sinai, followed in 1892 by a handbook covering Upper Egypt and Nubia, the two parts were combined in the fourth English edition published in 1898 with major revisions by Professor Georg Steindorff of Leipzig University. In the fifth edition, used here (published in 1902), another major force in tourism was evident – the tourist companies. Travellers were advised not to travel on their own "in a country whose customs and language are so entirely different from their own". Tourists were advised to travel with Messrs Thomas Cook & Son (Ludgate Circus, London) and Messrs Henry Gaze & Sons (53 Queen Victoria St, London).

Travel agents became an economic force of their own, advertising and promoting travel, and thus spreading tourist-fever. By 1985, tourism had become one of the world's huge business undertakings. In 1982, the number of tourists to all countries numbered 279.9 million persons, yielding as tourist revenues 112,500 million US dollars. Egypt's share was rather modest, with a total of 1.423 million tourists, including 664,000 tourists from Europe and the Americas (0.5 per cent of world tourism), yielding 254 million dollars. However, at the end of the year 2000, the Tourism Ministry in Egypt (*Akhbar Al-Adab*, 3 December 2000) announced that the number of tourists had increased to 2.5 million in 1993, and had almost doubled in 1999 to reach 4.8 million persons. By 1993, the income from tourism rose to 1.9 billion US dollars, and in 1999 it reached 3.9 billion US dollars. This placed tourism in the forefront of revenues producing hard currency, contributing 11 per cent of Egypt's GNP and providing 2.2 million job opportunities.

The promotion of tourism in Egypt has become a key element in the national policy for economic development, buttressed by the creation of a Tourist Development Authority (TDA) and the Egyptian Tourist Agency (ETA). Although there is now a growing emphasis on recreational tourism, the lure of Egypt's monumental legacy is a trump card. The promotional advertisement by the ETA in the popular magazine *Archaeology* (Nov/Dec 2000), adorned with photographic vignettes of Abu Simbel, the Temple of Hatshepsut, and the Sphinx, as well as a felucca, reads:

- There's never been a better time to visit Egypt
- See the land where civilization started
- Seven thousand years of culture, religion and timeless treasures await you
- See where Moses received the Ten Commandments
- Explore the Majesty of the Valley of the Kings
- Diving in the breathtaking waters of the Red Sea
- You can do that in only one place on Earth.

In this chapter, my aim is to discuss the role of this economic process in presenting an image of Egypt through the selling of 'souvenirs', with a focus on the transactions at Khan el-Khalili, a marketplace in a neighbourhood dating back to medieval times (Figure 8:1). The selling of souvenirs is one of the elements of archaeological or

Figure 8:1 A view of one of the old Mameluk gates in the Khan el-Khalili bazaar (© Fekri A. Hassan).

heritage economics, which encompasses a broad spectrum of transactions. Souvenirs, as material objects, are of special interest because they serve as a tangible proxy for the image of a country and its past. In the same issue of *Archaeology* cited above, there is an advertisement by "The Gold Pyramid House: The World's Largest Online Egyptian Bazaar, with over 100,000 quality items". The company claims to be "the World's most exclusive supplier of many hard-to-find products and museum-quality reproductions".[1]

Another company offers gold cartouches "handmade in Cairo by craftsmen in ancient Khan el-Khalili". In the same issue, the Bowers Art Museum of California advertises an exhibit featuring "Egyptian Treasures from the Egyptian Museum". Such exhibits, fashionable as a follow-up to the Tut-Ankh-Amen exhibit, not only generate income for the museum from admission tickets, but also from a shop or shops often named with exotic-sounding words, 'bazaar' or '*souq*', set up to sell Egyptian trinkets.

The range of items offered in Khan el-Khalili and related outlets selling Egypt, and the variety of those outlets, indicate the vigorous trade that sustains such enterprises. My concern here lies with the role of souvenirs in image making, which becomes in this case an integral element of money making. The selling of souvenirs is thus not only an active ingredient of a burgeoning tourist industry, it is also a creative force in shaping what Egypt is through the possession of concrete, material emblems of its identity. The promotion of such an identity is both a product of a historical/political gaze, and at the same time the legitimizing force of what Egypt is in foreign eyes – a matter of significant importance in international cultural exchanges and economic activities (as "culture" is used to define markets: e.g. the case of the European Common Market).

Fakes, replicas and trinkets

The range of items offered to tourists in Khan el-Khalili may be classified as:

- Examples or adaptations of folk Egyptian items or motifs: *galabiyas* (gowns), belly-dancer costumes, tambourines, Arab red shoes (*markub*), Bedouin jewellery, silk, silver, brass and carpets.

- Reproductions of museum items: scale reproductions of original ancient Egyptian artwork.

- Adaptations of pharaonic ancient Egyptian motifs in a variety of items, including clothing and jewellery.

- Innovative items inspired by Egyptian art: e.g. playing cards.

- Perfumes.

- Spices and local food items.

In Egypt, these tourist trinkets are often sold in stalls next to archaeological sites or are peddled by sellers who actively pursue tourists. They are also sold in museum shops, mainly at the Cairo Museum, which are privately run. Shops are also located near tourist hotels and on the premises of five-star hotels. In the past, some of these shops in Cairo and Luxor sold genuine artefacts under license from the Egyptian government.

In Cairo, venues selling trinkets to tourists (Figure 8:2) are concentrated at Khan el-Khalili, which is situated in a district close to the Hussein Mosque. In Baedeker's Egypt, this district (referred to as Khân el-Khalîl – see also other transliterations below) was described as a former centre of the commercial traffic of Cairo, said to have been founded as early as the end of the 13th century, on the site of ruined tombs of the Khalifs by the Mameluk sultan El-Ashraf Khalil (several variations on this historical statement are given below). It forms a distinct quarter of the city, and is intersected by a main street and numerous cross-lanes, formed by long rows of stalls of tradesmen and artisans, all covered over. In 1902, it was the headquarters of the silk and carpet merchants and the vendors of trinkets, as well as a brass bazaar, in which many travellers were tempted to purchase. An earlier reference to Khan el-Khalili was made in 1656/8 by de Thevenot, who reported that there was in Cairo a market every Monday and Thursday, which was held in Bazaar street. Khan el-Khalili was at the end of the street, which had an open courtyard where white slaves were sold. Black slaves were sold in a nearby Khan. In the same district was the Lunatic Asylum and a large mosque (Qalawoon Mosque). de Thevenot noted that beautiful carpets were manufactured in this quarter. The carpets were exported to Europe and Turkey.

Figure 8:2   Poorly made copies of ancient Egyptian statues are among the many trinkets sold as souvenirs to tourists (© Fekri A. Hassan).

Lane (1860: 313–317) described various markets (sing. *souq*, pl. *Aswaq*), including the brass *souq*, jewellers *souq*, and Khan El-kháleelee. In the eighth revised edition of Baedeker's *Egypt*, published in 1929, Khan el-Khalili was still the centre of the market traffic in Cairo. The text re-dates it to 1400, founded by Garkas el-Khalili, master of the horses to Sultan Barquq, on the site of the palace of the Fatimids. In the Hachette *Guide to Cairo, Alexandria and Environs*, published in 1963, the founding of Khan el-Khalili is dated erroneously to 1292, on the site of "the tombs of Fatmite caliphes" (for another version see below). It was occupied and then enlarged in the reign of Qansu el-Ghuri. The commerce was mostly in the hands of Iranians and Turks. It was still the place of silk, carpet and embroidery bazaars. Next to Khan el-Khalili one could find the bazaar for tin and copperware, as well as water-pipes (*nargila* or *shisha*) for smokers, red and black terracotta from Qena, the silver and gold bazaar (*Al-Sagha*), and many shops where cloth was made and sold.

Khan was thus noted not for trinkets relating to Ancient Egypt, but to the oriental bazaar that lingered on from its former medieval glory as a market-place for silk, carpets, brass, gold, silver, perfumes, clothing, and shoes. In Parker and Sabin (1974), the founding of Khan is dated to 1382, by Amir Garkas al-Khalili, 18 years earlier than the Baedeker attribution. It was built as a Caravansary. The guide notes that its composition has changed. There is still a considerable variety of souvenirs, antiques and jewellery offered for sale.

In the 1988 American University in Cairo's *Practical Guide*, the following appears under "Antiques":

> The line between antique and second-hand can be thin. Genuine antiquities dealers must be licensed by the government's Department of Antiquities. Best buys are European items. Genuine Pharaonic items are carefully monitored and cannot be taken out of the country without the approval of the Department of Antiquities … The inventory of one of the shops in Khan el-Khalili is said to include old tables, chairs, marble, scarabs, antique Pharaonic reproductions, beads, coins, inlay. In another shop one finds antique brass beds, *mashrabia*, sofas and mirrors, stones, silver jewelry, and musical instruments.

For the last few decades, Khan el-Khalili has become one of the key attractions for tourists in Cairo. Situated in the heart of Mameluk Cairo in the shadow of the Fatimid Al-Azhar Mosque and the Turkish-style minarets of Sayyidna Al-Hussein Mosque (Figure 8:3), Khan is located in the heart of Islamic Cairo. The Hussein Mosque is the principal congregational mosque in Cairo, and the area is swarming with Cairenes and visitors from *Al-Reef* (the country), who come for blessings.

In one of the alleys of Khan el-Khalili is the famous Fishawi teahouse (*Ahwet el-Fishawi*). It has been relocated from its original position in Khan to its new position, but it has retained the large-sized mirrors and bric-a-brac of the 1920s, and the oriental sofas that were once the diagnostic furniture of teahouses in Cairo. The teahouse has become another mecca for tourists in Cairo, who come here to mingle freely with the Cairenes, try a few puffs of the *shisha* (only tobacco, though foreigners often assume that the pipes are stuffed with *Hashish*), and drink from enamelled teapots mint-flavoured tea and *sahlab*. Peddlers walk by, offering their goods, from the (illegal) skin of desert foxes to folding tables and cushions. Flowers, peanuts, handkerchiefs and postcards may be dropped onto your table to oblige you to buy. Some use this as a

Figure 8:3   Sayyidna Al-Hussein Mosque – a principal religious spot for Muslims in Egypt – marks the eastern boundary of the Khan el-Khalili bazaar (© Fekri A. Hassan).

face-saving 'civil' device for begging. Egyptians often use this kind of transaction as a means of charity.

Tourists who are in Cairo for a couple of days or more invariably come to Khan el-Khalili for an afternoon's shopping and to immerse themselves in the exotic mélange of what is fabricated as an authentic Egyptian tourist-targeted experience (Figure 8:4). Several restaurants serve grilled kebab and *kufta*, a delicious Egyptian specialty of charcoal grilled marinated lamb meat on skewers. Some stalls sell sweets, Egyptian 'pancakes' (*fitir*), and desserts. Shopping at Khan el-Khalili thus becomes an experience rather than the simple act of acquiring souvenirs: it becomes memorable, and the items purchased become souvenirs of that experience.

The items sold at Khan el-Khalili range from kitsch to valuable items of silk, silver, or gold. They may also include European antiques. In one dimension, Khan el-Khalili still serves as the modern survival of an oriental bazaar offering the tourist the riches of the East. In another dimension, it is a source of cheap gifts and bric-a-brac. In still another dimension, it is a way of encountering Egyptians and the living Egypt.

Bargaining: the price of dominance

The quality of items sold varies immensely from one shop to another, and so do prices. Bargaining has always been a key feature of buying and selling at Khan el-Khalili, and this adds to the confusion and thrill of the experience. Buying and selling in Egypt

Figure 8:4   Tourists at one of the cafés in Khan el-Khalili (© Fekri A. Hassan).

form social occasions often associated with drinking tea and small pleasantries. The economic transactions thus create a spark of sociability as seller and buyer interact. These transactions in an exotic milieu of lively activities immerse the tourist in an exhilarating sense of discovery. This also highlights the unequal position of seller and buyer. Even in the act of fixing the price of an object, the negotiation of roles and the implication of status-differential are involved. The act of bargaining is an elaborate social interaction since the price does not depend on a fixed, invariable monetary equivalent to the cost of raw material, manufacture, transport, storage, plus a certain fixed percentage of profit. It has more to do with what the buyer could, and should, on the basis of his rank and status, pay. The verbal exchanges, the clothing of the buyer and his body-language determine his social status and how much he can pay. It is disgraceful for a wealthy person to 'rob' the seller by insisting on bargaining to a very thin margin of profit for the seller. By paying a price above average, the buyer gains respect and status, and in a sense maintains social order based on a 'civic' code of charitable and equitable pricing. It is in the light of these remarks that we may read with understanding the advice given in a recent edition (n.d.) of Baedecker's *Egypt*:

> It is normal to haggle, for the seller will always set his first price high enough to leave room for substantial reduction. But though you enjoy bargaining it should be recommended that with the low wage levels current in Egypt prices are likely in any event to be cheaper than at home, and that it becomes a visitor from a wealthier country not to press the bargaining too far.

Trade and ethnicity: Cairo – the City of Liberty

Khan el-Khalili is a special place, perhaps because of its multi-ethnic background. Historically Khan el-Khalili has always been a haven for foreign merchants – Armenians, Jews, Persians and Arabs from North Africa and the Arabian Peninsula. Merchants and buyers from all faiths, creeds, nationalities and affiliations came together to trade, socialize and live. This probably accounts for the friendly attitudes and tolerance shown to others, as well as to what may ordinarily be regarded as aberrant behaviour. Women and men mix freely at Fishawi, until recently uncommon in Egyptian teahouses. Women also can smoke *shisha*, the water-pipe men smoke in Cairo's all-men cafes.

Ethnic pluralism seems to have been, for a long time, a feature of Cairo in general. For example, in 1534, the visitor Graffin Affagart stated:

> Cairo is full of merchants and artisans, each craft has its own quarter. Khan el-Khalili was the quarter for the finest crafts, textiles, silk, and wool from the land of Flanders, and the merchants of Persian carpets. The Khan consisted of three floors. At that time Cairo was three times the size of Paris. Its population consisted of Turks, Arabs from North Africa (*Magharba*), Europeans (*Agam*), Christians, Latin, Room [Turks], Indians, Armenians, Jacobites, and Nestorians. All were allowed to live together in amity enjoying the laws of the land because Cairo was the City of Liberty.

> (Zaki, Abdel-Rahman 1943)

Antiquities and identity

The variety of trinkets and materials in Khan el-Khalili exhibits an incredible mix of styles, tastes and significance. Although the poorly made scale reproductions of Egyptian statues are remarkable by their ubiquitous presence, the oriental goods, mostly brass, textiles and carpets, give the bazaar its air of vanished oriental glory. This is enhanced by the Islamic architecture of Khan and its setting within the centre of Mameluk Cairo. Although a few shops in Khan el-Khalili sell European 'antiques', a word loosely used to refer to 'ancient' or 'pretty' works of art or 'curiosities', that once graced the homes of foreigners who lived in Egypt from the 1920s to the 1950s, or those of high-ranking Egyptians, the majority of such 'antique' shops are situated in central Cairo, in the Europeanized quarters of the Cairo of Khedive Ismail. Many small antique shops are located in the Bank Misr area of Kasr el-Nil and Sherif streets. A few more are to be found on Kasr el-Nil beyond Midan Moustafa Kamel Square and on Hoda Sherawi Street. These shops cater to resident Europeans, collectors, and those who are looking for quality second-hand furniture or household items at bargain prices. English and French-made furniture usually fetches a high price. Some of these shops obtain their goods from families who want to get rid of old furniture or household items (*karakib*) or from itinerant buyers who collect old things from houses, roaming the streets with a small wooden cart, crying *"roba-bekkia"* (an Arabization of *Roba Vecchia*). Such old 'European' furniture (Figure 8:5 col. pl.) is valued by some well-to-do educated Egyptians who find distasteful the furniture commonly sold – either a garish imitation of modern or old European styles, or the 'Arabesque' chairs and sofas with plastic inlay that are difficult to match with other pieces of furniture. Furniture in most Egyptian homes is now mostly European in style, even if locally made, and of affordable materials and quality. Similarly in dress: educated Egyptians (outside the Al-Azhar religious system) have for the last hundred years assumed European dress. The revival of the *galabyia*, the traditional gown worn by men and women, among well-to-do Egyptian ladies was paradoxically inspired by the appeal such costumes had for European and American tourists in the 1960s.

The business of selling and buying 'antiques', souvenirs or old 'junk' is not just a money making economic transaction. It involves the creation of the current cultural orientation, self-imaging, and public 'values', by assigning a hierarchical monetary value to certain objects. Junk and rubbish may be turned into a treasure. The process of the monetary valuation of the past operates within a system of social valuation based on wealth, once related to lineage and the preserve of land-owning families, and in industrial societies related to industrialists and financiers who pass on their wealth and capacity for making wealth to their families or to those they co-opt. In this context, status becomes a function of the display of items that were once, or are, the exclusive monopoly of the aristocracy. Such objects are often superfluous for life-sustaining purposes and survival, but are critical in asserting one's access to power that goes beyond subsistence. The acquisition of gold and precious stones, as well as the products of skilled labourers and objects obtained from distant lands, are marks of distinction and superiority, because their procurement involves a much greater cost than that of commonly available objects. The display or gift giving of souvenirs or goods (a form of potlatch) from distant lands thus becomes the mark of elevated social status. The procurement of ethnic objects – an act that may be likened to head-hunting – may be an act of appropriation and dominance, although in a few cases it may be motivated by identification, confused identity, aesthetic appeal, or sympathy. In as much as displaying mounted antlers or the stuffed head of a moose is a declaration of virility, dominance and the conquest of nature by the masculine power of the gun, the display of 'antiques' from other countries or 'ethnic' souvenirs – which included in Europe and the US the display of mummies (and even their dissection) for the entertainment of guests – is a declaration of social power and prowess.

Antique objects are costly because they are rare objects of social value, and in turn, their social value is enhanced by the demand that increases their monetary value.

How many tourists buy works by modern Egyptian sculptors and painters? How many buy books by literary figures, other than those legitimized for the west and made into a commodity by the Nobel Prize? How many tourists buy functional items such as shoes or Egyptian-made everyday items of clothing?

Dispossessing encounters

Encounters with Egypt as a business were initially based on the appropriation of gold, carpets, silk and other precious 'oriental' goods, as well as, following the discovery of Ancient Egypt, the acquisition by princes, consuls, barons and rich Europeans generally of statues, paintings and whatever could be carried away from Egypt, culminating in the wholesale acquisition of temples and artefact collections (demanded, for example, as a nominal payment for the contribution of foreign missions to the Nubian campaign). Antique dealers were set up to sell antiquities, which they secured from their own excavations. Among such dealers was Solomon Fernandez (ca. 1830–1860), who exploited the necropolis of Saqqarah, and many important objects passed through his hands, including the famous 'scribe accroupi' in the Louvre (Dawson and Uphill 1972).

The effort that began with individual collectors became a means of national rivalry, with national museums in world capitals displaying their loot from Egypt's glorious heritage, and selling in their museum shops replicas and souvenirs. These outlets thus promote the acquisition of objects as trophies (in addition to satisfying the desire for aesthetic pleasures), and set monetary values for such objects. The replicas, being cheaper, become an affordable substitute for the 'real thing' and can be acquired by the not-so-wealthy person. However, the price for such objects cannot be set too low or they cease to have social value.

Making encounters count

The goods and trinkets sold in Khan el-Khalili as replicas of Egyptian artefacts are in general of much lower quality than replicas ordered specially by national museums in Europe or made in their workshops. They are also much cheaper. In a sense they encourage buying because they are a 'bargain', but they are also devalued because they are cheap, and for the discriminating buyer, not well-made. For example, the re-introduction of papyrus into the tourist market since the 1960s was followed by the widespread production of cheap, inferior 'papyrus' made from the leaves of sugarcane, reed, banana and corn, and by competition that has within two decades trashed it as a cultural and an economic good; produced by inexperienced workers, the product is of a very poor quality.

If Egypt were to establish a policy of cultural economic development that made use of archaeological and cultural resources for alleviating poverty and for promoting a better understanding of Egyptian civilization, this would have to be with an eye to the social and symbolic implications of making and selling souvenirs. Not only would it be necessary to improve the quality of replicas and tourist goods and to re-examine the composition and layout of the bazaar, but the range, items and activities associated with selling souvenirs would have to be addressed. Development policy would have to include measures to introduce tourists to the contemporary cultural context of Egypt, as well as a shop-window for its various products. Khan el-Khalili, for example, situated in one of Cairo's medieval book-markets, does not have a single bookshop for tourists. Neither does it have a single gallery for contemporary Egyptian artists. The products in many cases are displayed as finished products; the market, however, could be a place to observe artisans at work, thus enhancing the human element in the making of objects and linking the work to a human face, and to effort and skill.

Egypt must also consider the implications for the lack of proper training and facilities for artisans working in Khan el-Khalili. They should be supplied with appropriate materials and informed of advances in their crafts. Periodicals, manuals and data-sheets should be provided, of methods, supplies, and good practice. The knowledge of master artisans should be documented and their contributions recognized and rewarded. A development programme should work within the existing social matrix, thus requiring a profound understanding of the social texture and of decision-making in the community. Intervention by the government should not be one of replacement or enforcement. It should integrate relationships between the small-business community and the traditional craft workers and governmental organizations. For example, there is no link between the Khan el-Khalili community and a unit established within the Egyptian authority responsible for archaeological heritage in Egypt, the Supreme Council of Antiquities (SCA), the Centre for the Revival and Conservation of Ancient Egyptian Arts (*Markaz Ihiya' al-Finoun al-Misryia al-Qadima*), established in 1982 (Khadry *et al.* 1985). This unit includes an Institute for Archaeological Crafts (*Ma'ahad al-Hiraf al-Atharia*). Although the Centre, *Markaz*, displays its reproductions in the SCA building in Zamalek and some objects are sold in museum shops and SCA offices in archaeological districts, there has been no effort either to market such productions widely or to engage the private sector in a partnership with the SCA in its endeavours, which would allow both the transfer of knowledge from the SCA to artisans in the private sector and the generation of income to sustain, expand and develop SCA training and research activities.

Concluding remarks

From this overview it may be concluded that:

- Archaeologists who hope to elucidate how the past is manipulated or involved in the politics of identity and dominance may wish to examine the hidden dimensions of selling and buying antiquities, souvenirs, mementos, or replicas.

- The purchase of trinkets of archaeological significance by tourists involves complex dynamics involving both the buyer's and the seller's notions of self, 'other', ethics, nationalism, social hierarchy, and worldviews.

- In Cairo, Khan el-Khalili, once a medieval bazaar, is one of the main attractions for tourists. The trinkets and goods offered to tourists in this market place project a virtual reality of an oriental Egypt with degraded scale reproductions of ancient Egyptian statues and other art objects.

- Khan el-Khalili, with its multi-ethnic heritage and its own sub-culture, is potentially suited for fostering a deeper understanding of the various facets of Egyptian civilization and living culture that are often beyond the grasp of tourists, who are drawn as actors in a pre-staged play with a colonial script.

- The mobilization of the past to release the artistic and creative talents of Egyptians is poorly served by the existing arrangements. Measures by cultural-heritage organizations to train, support and encourage young artisans are much needed.

Note

1   A sample of some of their gift ideas includes a life-size sarcophagus, Cleopatra's dress, Tut's chair, Egyptian gowns, belly-dancers' costumes, scarves, vests, shawls, hats, tote-bags, men's ties, purses, Egyptian aprons, wall-hangings, rugs, tapestries, headdresses, masks, chokers, pencil-holders, costume-accessories, armbands, collars, belts, cuffs, wallets, spectacle-cases, magnets, key-chains, boxes, postcards, mosaics, mother of pearl, mugs, ornaments, scarabs, plates, pyramid lamps, perfume bottles, toy camels, thimbles, spoons, crystals, vases, alabaster, soapstone, Egyptian coffee-makers, earrings, buckles, books, colouring-books, wrappings, gold jewellery, mummy-beads, rings, necklaces, cards, book-marks, puzzles, games, stationery, chess-sets, brass items, tambourines, and papyrus.

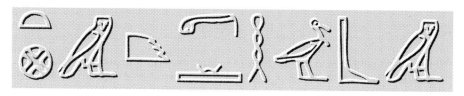

CHAPTER 9

EGYPT'S PAST REGENERATED BY ITS OWN PEOPLE

Fayza Haikal

Bonaparte's invasion of Egypt in 1798 resulted basically from the contending policies of France and Britain over the 'Eastern Question' and clearly marked the country as a focal point for European interests and political intrigue, but it also inaugurated the cultural dialogue between Egypt and the modern western world. In the field of Egyptology as in many others, the expedition's scholars played a fundamental role. With the discovery of the Rosetta Stone in 1799, which was to assist Champollion in the final decipherment of the hieroglyphs in 1822 and the publication of the *Description de l'Égypte* (*Description* 1809–1828), the world's fascination with Ancient Egypt reached one of its highest peaks. Egyptology having been consecrated as a fully-fledged science after Champollion's *Lettre à Monsieur Dacier* in 1822 in which he announced his decipherment of the hieroglyphic system, and the publication of his *Précis du Système Hiéroglyphique* in 1824, scholars worked even more assiduously to understand Ancient Egypt's culture and uncover its treasures.

Strangely enough, the international admiration of, and concern for, antiquities in general and those of Ancient Egypt in particular, had only weak echoes in Egypt itself. Culturally completely Arabized at the time, Egyptians did not care much for pre-Islamic civilizations, which they considered as pagan and therefore unworthy of their attention. Further, not acquainted with their previous language and culture, they could not comprehend their richness or the impact they still had on the Egyptians' current life, and even less their impact on the great religions of the world which they knew and acknowledged. It was at the instigation of Champollion himself, who was distressed at the rapid deterioration of the ancient monuments and at the way they were treated by foreign or local adventurers and excavators, that Mohammed Ali Pasha, the Viceroy of Egypt, had a Service des Antiquités Egyptiennes created in 1835 to try to control the traffic in antiquities in and out of Egypt. This Service des Antiquités was entrusted to a certain Youssef Dia and housed in the Ezbeqieh gardens of Cairo, near the School for Foreign Languages supervised by Sheikh Rifa'a R. el Tahtawy, as were many other newly-created educational institutions at the time. The Ezbeqieh centre was also to be a museum where artefacts found all over Egypt would be collected. Dia Effendi did his best to enlarge the collection, but in fact it soon became a reserve for presents to be offered to distinguished guests of Egypt. Depleted by rulers without real ties to the cultural heritage of the country, and pressed to please European superpowers, the collection's remaining objects were transferred to a room belonging to what was then equivalent to the Ministry of Education at the Citadel. But they did not remain there very long, for in 1855 the Viceroy presented the whole collection to Archduke Maximillian of Austria, as a souvenir of his visit to Egypt.

A few years later, Auguste Mariette, a young French Egyptologist, was sent to Egypt by the Musée du Louvre, to search for and purchase Coptic manuscripts. Instead, carried away by his enthusiasm for and love of Ancient Egypt, Mariette excavated at Saqqarah and in 1851 discovered its famous Serapeum. This fabulous discovery and the treasures he sent to the Louvre allowed him to stay longer in the country and encouraged him to take better care of its monuments. Because France at the time was a leading cultural power and had a great deal of influence in Egypt, in 1858 Mariette was appointed Director of Egyptian Antiquities (Delamaire 2003; Humbert Chapter 3, this volume; Jeffreys 2003: 10). With him, the Service des Antiquités Egyptiennes was resurrected and it began to play an important role in the life of the country. In addition to excavating and establishing laws to regulate foreign excavations in Egypt, Mariette sought a new museum where he could curate and exhibit newly uncovered or collected Egyptian objects. He was allowed to refurbish an old warehouse in Bulaq for this purpose. Unfortunately this museum was flooded in 1878 and had to be closed for repair until 1881. When Mariette died in that same year, he was buried in the gardens of the museum. In 1890 the growing collection had to be moved to a larger space in Giza where it awaited the construction of a new museum, the current Egyptian Museum in Cairo, which was inaugurated in 1902 (Saleh and Sourouzian 1987). Together with the objects he had so lovingly collected, Mariette's own tomb and mausoleum were transferred to the gardens of the new museum as a sign of gratitude towards a man who had served Egypt so well. Today this museum is much too small for the marvellous collection it houses, whether on exhibit or in storerooms. Plans for a new museum to be constructed near the pyramids are now under way.

After Auguste Mariette, the directorship of the Service des Antiquités and the Egyptian Museum remained a French prerogative until 1936. Then the two positions were separated, because the Service in the meantime had developed tremendously, with the creation of inspectorates for antiquities all over Egypt that were put in charge of the excavation and protection of monuments, and with the establishment of many provincial museums in addition to two new important museums in Cairo, for Coptic and Islamic antiquities respectively, and one for Greco-Roman monuments in Alexandria. The Service was also reorganized into different departments to cope with the variety of disciplines and historical periods for which it was responsible. In 1936 Etienne Drioton became Director of the Service, while British Reginald Engelbach was placed in charge of the Egyptian Museum. In 1950, Mahmoud Hamza became the first Egyptian Director of the Cairo Museum, and in 1952 Mostapha Amer was appointed the first Egyptian Director of the Service des Antiquités Egyptiennes. After the 1952 revolution, the laws regulating excavations, whether foreign or Egyptian, publication rights and exhibitions abroad were gradually adjusted to the new conceptions and political realities. Two decades later the Service, this ever growing institution, changed its name to better reflect its status and responsibilities, so that it became 'The Egyptian Antiquities Organization' from the 1970s to the early 1990s, when it was renamed 'The Supreme Council for Antiquities'. It goes without saying that such an enormous institution, with around 20,000 people working for it, carries a certain weight in the country and that it promotes archaeological awareness among the people.

But if Egypt is indebted to Mariette and his successors for having established the Service des Antiquités Egyptiennes on a solid basis to protect Egyptian antiquities at a time when the rulers did not really value this heritage, the young Egyptians who worked with them must not be forgotten. Struggling to establish themselves in a country where priority was still given to foreigners, they strove to awaken pride and interest in Ancient Egypt among their own people. The most important of these pioneers was undoubtedly Ahmad Pasha Kamal, who lived from 1849 to 1923 and who is considered as the father of Egyptian Egyptology.

Ahmad Kamal specialized in foreign languages before joining the short-lived school of Egyptology established by the eminent German scholar Henri Brugsch (1827–1894), who worked in Egypt at the time. He graduated in 1869, and after many different jobs, mainly as a translator of French or a teacher of German in various administrations, he joined the Service des Antiquités, where he first worked as a translator of foreign languages and teacher of ancient Egyptian. He then became the first Egyptian Assistant Curator at the Cairo Museum, where he remained until he retired in 1914 aged 65. His contributions to the museum were many, for not only did he help move the collections to their present location, but he also published its *Stèles hiéroglyphiques d'époques Ptolemaique et Romaine* in two volumes (Cairo 1904–1905) and its *Tables d'offrandes* in two other volumes (Cairo 1906–1909) of the then recently created series *Catalogue Général du Musée du Caire*, published in Cairo by the Service des Antiquités and its successors, and which remains one of the basic resources for Egyptologists today.

Ahmad Kamal was committed to creating new museums in Egypt, and he voiced his views and opinions strongly in *Al-Ahram*, the semi-official daily newspaper of Egypt. Thanks to his enthusiasm and commitment, museums were opened in Assiut, Minya and Tanta, thus setting a pattern to be followed later in other places.

In addition to his famous museum-related activities and publications, Ahmad Kamal joined many archaeological excavations and wrote reports about them and their finds, mostly published in the *Annales* of the Service des Antiquités Egyptiennes. His role in discovering the cache of royal mummies at Deir el-Bahri was also fundamental. Moreover, Egypt is indebted to Ahmad Kamal for encouragement of other young Egyptians to follow in his path, creating a department for teaching ancient Egyptian and civilization at the 'High School for Instructors' known as the Khedeweya school. Among his students were Selim Hassan, Mahmoud Hamza, the future first Egyptian Director of the Cairo Museum, Ahmed Abdel Wahab and others who graduated in 1912. Together with Sami Gabra, Abbas Bayoumi, Pahor Labib, and a few others, they form, after their master Ahmad Kamal, the second generation of Egyptian Egyptologists who, in their turn, contributed to the diffusion of this discipline and of the knowledge and appreciation of Ancient Egypt among their fellow countrymen.

In addition to the many articles he published in French or in Arabic in various fields of Egyptology and to his contributions to the *Catalogue Général du Musée du Caire*, Ahmad Kamal wrote, in Arabic, eight invaluable encyclopaedic books on

Ancient Egypt presenting its history, geography, administration, society with its various classes and professions, religion, archaeology, science, etc. He wrote monographs on Memphis and Heliopolis, and a textbook for students to learn ancient Egyptian with exercises for practice, and a small dictionary, which included Coptic phonetic values for ancient Egyptian words. But foremost of all these is his unpublished manuscript in 22 volumes of a dictionary of ancient Egyptian, translated into Arabic and French, with Coptic and Hebrew comparisons, in which he clearly establishes the relationship between the ancient Egyptian and Semitic languages. He finished his book before the great Berlin dictionary began to be issued (1926–1931) and even before the small one published in 1921 came to be known. Still, when presented for publication the publication committee managed to reject it, although Reisner, one of its three members, wished to publish it. But Lacau refused it and Firth abstained from voting (Moukhtar 1964/1965). In spite of the tremendous progress Egyptology made during the 20th century, the book should still be published one day to testify to Ahmad Kamal's encyclopaedic knowledge and pioneering ideas at a time when Egyptology, not yet fully acknowledged in Egypt, was still the prerogative of foreigners (Moukhtar 1964/1965: 43–57).

When Ahmad Pasha Kamal died in 1923, a whole century had passed since Champollion's publication of the *Précis du système hiéroglyphique* and many things had happened in Egyptology, both in archaeology and in philology. The most spectacular and probably most significant of these was undoubtedly Howard Carter's discovery of Tutankhamun's tomb in November 1922 (Reid 2002). The news provoked a new wave of enthusiasm for Ancient Egypt as well as 'Egyptomania' in the western world. In Egypt it accelerated the process of the rehabilitation of Ancient Egypt that Ahmad Kamal had started. The Egyptian government even thought of re-opening the Khedeweya School of Egyptology which he had established but which had not lasted long. Instead, when the Egyptian University opened its doors in 1925, it was decreed that the Faculty of Arts would have a Department of Archaeology, with two sub-sections, one for Egyptology, and the other for Islamic Civilization, Art and Architecture, where foreign scholars would contribute to the teaching. Graduates of that department form the next generation (third) of Egyptian Egyptologists, and include the pioneer archaeologist of the desert and oases Ahmed Fakhry, Abdel-Moneim Abu Bakr, Guirguis Mattha, Labib Habachi, Ahmed Badawi and others. This department was closed in 1933 and replaced by a three year postgraduate diploma equivalent to an MA, open to all graduates of the Faculty of Arts. In 1954, undergraduate studies were offered again for a BA in Egyptology. Graduate studies were also kept, so that Egyptology finally became a discipline like any other at Cairo University. With the growing number of students wishing to pursue university education, the Department of Archaeology was severed from the Faculty of Arts and became, in 1971–1972, a Cairo University Institute in its own right. In 1974 it developed into the Faculty of Archaeology with three departments dealing respectively with Egyptology, Islamic Civilization, Art and Architecture and the Restoration of Archaeological Artefacts and Monuments. It awards a number of graduate diplomas in related disciplines, in addition to MAs and PhDs in its three main branches (Radwan 1993: 5–7; Reid 1985: 105; see also Sheikholeslami 1986: 30–34, 45–47, 61).

Today, in addition to the Faculty of Archaeology at Cairo University, Egyptology is taught in departments of the Faculties of Arts of most other national universities, in addition to the comparatively recent department at the American University in Cairo, so that between 400 and 500 graduates emerge each year, a number which exceeds that of the annual graduates of all the other universities in the world put together! It is clear that this number exceeds by far all the needs of the country and the potential of universities and libraries, so that it creates many different problems at undergraduate and graduate levels, besides those of unemployment similar to those affecting the whole world. But it also diffuses cultural awareness, and helps to consolidate a trend in Egyptian Egyptology which tries to investigate probable and/or possible survivals from, and analogies with, Ancient Egypt in current life, whether in our language, traditions or beliefs (for evidence of a growing trend, see Haikal 1994: 205–211, 1997: 291–292; Naguib 1993).

While Egyptology was laboriously establishing itself and its proper institutions in Egypt, 'Egyptomania' was slowly developing. Born of the new awareness of a glorious past combined with nationalistic feelings against European influence in general and particularly against British occupation, the search for Ancient Egypt in its own land was a very different phenomenon from international 'Egyptomania'. It was certainly not a search for exotic mystery, esotericism, or even for the simple admiration of the beauty and contribution to the world of a great civilization: the 'Egyptian Revival' (Curl 1994) was rather a search for a long-lost identity, yearning stimulated also by the shock of the encounter with another culture. It represents a longing for a time in which Egypt was great and admired, not subdued by foreign powers; a time of *real* values when, as the legends have it, truth and legitimacy were always vindicated against evil, falsehood and violence. It was a search for a kind of purification and renewal, like the return to the *zp tpi* or 'primeval time' in Ancient Egypt itself, with the perfection of creation and the purity, energy and enthusiasm of childhood. Ahmad Shawky, 'the prince of Arab contemporary poets', was among the first Egyptians to acknowledge Ancient Egypt's glory when he mentioned its great historical moments in his first lyric epic.

This rehabilitation of a long neglected and rejected past is particularly evident in the literature and arts produced in Egypt after the discovery of Tutankhamun's tomb. This sensational event corresponded with a new period of nationalistic dynamism and militant action against the British, who would not evacuate their troops from Egypt in spite of the declaration of independence in February of that year. The wave of international enthusiasm for things Egyptian which this major discovery produced did not remain unnoticed by Egyptian intellectuals who had studied in Europe and were familiar with western culture and ways of thinking. In the historical conjunctions of the time it would have been difficult for them to remain insensitive to their government's indifference to that event which shook the whole world, and from which Egypt should have derived so much nationalistic pride.

Thus, deeply shocked, Mohammed Hussein Haekal wrote a virulent article on 25 December 1922 in his recently founded daily *Al Siyassa* to denounce this negative attitude. This was the first of a series of articles, short stories, or introductions to other people's books in which Haekal presented and defended Ancient Egypt. His writings reveal not only emotional involvement and an admiration which he tries to convey to his readers, but also a deep intellectual commitment and knowledge of the main Egyptological literature of the time. He continued researching as time permitted as he himself says, to understand a culture that he felt linked with the present, because

> no part of the history of a country can be deleted from the total sum which forges its identity. As European culture developed ... without breaking its links with Christianity or ignoring the Classics, so changes in languages or religions which happened in Egypt should in no way sever its present culture from its past; and there is no point in denying this spiritual thread which links the past with the present to continue forever in the future, defining Egypt's historical specificity.

(Haekal 1933: 12)

In addition to descriptions of archaeological sites and the general consideration of ancient Egyptian civilization, Haekal, curiously enough, deals in his short stories essentially with queens and divinities, that is to say, precisely with what needed most defence in his days: women and 'paganism'. He presents them and explains the symbolism behind their stories, the degree of refinement and sophistication they manifest, and the ethics of their great civilization which they reflect. He does this casually, through the conversations of a group of young men enjoying their time of leisure, having tea at the Semiramis or during a party on a *dahabeya* (a houseboat on the Nile). In this way his stories tell not only of Ancient Egypt, but also of the young, intellectual and sophisticated upper class of the country in the 1920s and 1930s.

Haekal was probably the first Egyptian writer to try to understand the culture of Ancient Egypt and make it appreciated by his contemporaries. His enthusiasm was infectious and he was soon followed by others, professional writers or simple amateurs carried away by the nationalistic winds of the time. They wrote historic novels, fantastic interpretations of religious texts, idealized monographs on particular personalities or events. Or they simply chose Ancient Egypt as a setting for their stories and ancient Egyptian names for their heroes to convey messages which they did not always care to voice too clearly. Equally they turned to Ancient Egypt to present eternal values when the symbolism carried by names like Isis, Osiris, Ahmose, Akhenaten or Nefertiti, for example, became apparent.

In this huge output, the literary quality varies tremendously, but they all illustrate the growth of the admiration for Ancient Egypt and its manifestation in Egyptian intellectual life. Naguib Mahfouz, the 1988 Nobel Prize winner for literature, started his career as a writer in 1932 with a translation of James Baikie. He then wrote novels and short stories mainly depicting contemporary life, but a few drew their inspiration from Ancient Egypt. Thus in 1939 Mahfouz published *The Jest of Destiny*, called 'The Revenge of Re' in the recent English translation. This is an 'Egyptianizing' novel in as much as the main hero is none other than the great Kheops himself, all the protagonists' names are Egyptian and the setting, of course, is Memphis.

The story opens with the description of pharaoh resting on a golden throne by a window overlooking the gardens of his Memphite palace in a style which cannot fail to recall in any Egyptologist's mind, Ramesses II resting on his golden throne, in a tent overlooking the city of Kadesh, just before the famous battle which was to lead to the peace treaty between Egypt and the Hittites (Rutherford 2003). Further, the plot is inspired by P. Westcar where a magician foretells the end of his dynasty to the great

Kheops. Mahfouz used this prophecy to present the theme he wanted to develop, namely the power and inevitability of destiny that no one, not even the divine Kheops himself, can prevent, hinder or control. Mahfouz used the theme and the setting, but his plot is pure fantasy.

He used Ancient Egypt again and again, whether in pseudo-historical novels where real historical figures and events appear, as in *The Struggle of Thebes* (Mahfouz 1944), which is supposed to relate the expulsion of the Hyksos, or pure fantasies, as in *Radopis* (Mahfouz 1943), which describes a love story between a pharaoh and a priestess. In *He Who Lives in Truth* Mahfouz (1985) presents the personality of Akhenaten as seen by his contemporaries often in contradictory ways, thereby exposing the relativity of 'Truth'. Finally, as in *In Front of the Throne* (Mahfouz 1983), he reviews important political personalities of Egypt from Menes to Sadat, making them enter Osiris' judgment hall where their deeds are reviewed and their contributions to Egyptian history are weighed and given some kind of assessment, until the god's final judgment.

In fact, none of these books has much to do with real history; they are but a setting for Mahfouz's expression of his socio-political ideas. But what is important here is that they show Ancient Egypt as a source of inspiration in modern Egyptian literature and reveal their author's intellectual curiosity and attraction to this culture (e.g. Mahfouz 2002).

Among the first Egyptian intellectuals to search for symbols in Ancient Egypt is Tewfik el Hakim, one of Egypt's greatest and most prolific writers. In his first novel *Return of the Soul*, written in Paris in 1927 and published in Egypt in 1933, a cry for independence, freedom and identity percolates the drama. Also borne of the confrontation of oriental culture and western policies towards Egypt at the beginning of the 20th century, the title 'Return of the Soul', so explicit by itself, is further emphasized by the introductory reflections of the two volumes, both inspired by, when not taken directly from, the ancient Egyptian 'Book of the Dead'. Volume One reads:

> When time flows towards eternity
> we shall see you again
> Because this is where you are going,
> where everything merges.

In Volume Two, when the story is already halfway to the final goal, it reads:

> Stand up ... stand up, oh Osiris
> I am your son Horus
> I came to bring back life to you.
> You still have your real heart,
> The heart of your past.

Later Tewfik el Hakim wrote further short stories, such as *The Temple Dancer* (1939), and plays such as *Isis* (1955), inspired by Ancient Egypt, where he presents 'eternal' values and their perpetual conflict symbolized by the story of Isis and Osiris and the conflict of Horus and Seth. But here, as he says himself in the epilogue of *Isis*, the idea is not so much to present Ancient Egypt, but rather to induce his audience to reflect on certain realities and discuss the problematic of idealism versus reality, or power and politics against science and worth.

It seems that the trend of using Ancient Egypt as the setting and its heroes, human or divine, as the symbols for eternal concepts in novels and plays, gradually prevailed over the desire to inform or instruct, or even revive, which was clear in Haekal's writing. Younger authors tend more and more to move further away from the original sources, as if their historical or cultural content had become part of the conscious cultural heritage of the educated Egyptian, so that its symbols no longer need to be explained. Moreover, assertion of identity so strongly aroused by cultural and political confrontation retreats slightly in the face of curiosity and intellectual fascination, so that the local response to Ancient Egypt comes closer to its western counterpart. Two books seem particularly relevant.

Gamal el Ghitany's (1992) *Moutoun al Ahram*, whose very title is taken from Egyptological literature since it means 'Pyramid Texts', is divided into 14 spells, some quite long, subdivided by thoughts used as headings of passages and others gradually shorter and shorter until the last one, spell 14, consists simply of a word repeated three times – Nothing, Nothing, Nothing. This rhythm of the book is paralleled by that of the text which, through some 'pyramidology' and folk tales concerning people and the pyramids, describes the fascination that these exert on some of their beholders; a fascination and a dangerous power which can lead to absorption by, and final annihilation in, the body of the pyramid.

Among the stories related by the author, two are particularly expressive. In the first he tells of a family of "pyramid climbers" who lived in a village at the foot of the pyramids. Climbing the Great Pyramid was their business, and the father would teach his son, and only his son, the best routes to reach the top faster and faster. The story ends with the last climber, a young man, kind and pleasant, but always lost in dreams which he would not communicate to anyone: one day he rose early in the morning, climbed to the top of the Great Pyramid and in an ecstatic dance disappeared forever. The other story tells of a group of determined young men who decided to penetrate the secret of the pyramid and who, while advancing within it, gradually diminished in number, lost the sense of time and reality, had visions of paradise and never came out of the pyramid. Thus, the sanctity and symbolism of the pyramids as a passage from this life to the other, from materialism to spiritualism – this symbolism develops as the book progresses so that, when the book is entitled *Moutoun al Ahram* where in Arabic *Moutoun* means both texts (*corpus/corpora*) and 'bodies', the title becomes explicit in the form of the book and its content, as well as in the power of the monuments themselves.

A completely different kind of book is that of Abdel Moneim Abdel Kader's *Mother Apple's Stories*, written in Jedda in 1986 and published 10 years later in Egypt. Set in a place called *pr nwb* which in ancient Egyptian means house of gold, but here referring to Egypt, the story is supposed to take place just after Osiris' assassination by his brother Seth (here called Shet), when Isis roams the land, fleeing from the murderer and in search of the body of her brother. The cast includes other Egyptian divinities, Hathor, Thoth and Maat, but they serve only to give the story some kind of ethereal, fantastic ancient Egyptian flavour. The main protagonists are two brothers, Anubis and Bata, like the two brothers of P. d'Orbiney, and a cow which (in the papyrus) can become a female, symbolizing love, beauty, desire, sexuality and life. The author also includes in his narrative bits and pieces of different ancient Egyptian stories that he translates very literally into the Egyptian Arabic dialect, in order to retain the feeling of Ancient Egypt present in the text. Other elements in his book have nothing to do with Ancient Egypt, but the atmosphere created is totally timeless and unreal, allowing the author any fantasy he wishes.

Ali Ahmad Bakathir, born in the Far East of Arab parents, came to Egypt and wrote a series of plays. His *Akhenaton and Nefertiti*, originally published in 1940, was the first Arabic play in 'free verse', in which he expressed his ideas through historical personalities, gods, heroes and situations inspired by ancient Egyptian literature.

Ancient Egypt has also penetrated the world of opera and ballet, which were themselves new to Egypt in the 19th century. An example of an opera libretto is Mohsen el Khayat's (1996) *Osiris' Throne* which relates the story of Isis and Osiris, but transposes it to modern times, emphasizing the struggle of the 'rightful weak' symbolized by Horus against their overlords, symbolized first by Seth and then by businessmen in general, with hope in the future reappearing with the final vindication of Horus. So far, this libretto has never been set to music.

Salama el Abbassy's libretto for *Anas el Wogood*, on the other hand, was set to music by Aziz el Shawaan and performed in the Cairo Opera House in January 1997. The tale, drawn from the *Thousand and One Nights*, relates the love story of a young soldier and a high official's daughter after the Arab conquest of Egypt. To avoid a marriage of which he does not approve, the father sends his daughter into seclusion in the temple of Isis in Philae, but the young soldier manages to find her. Finally, moved by the courage and sincerity of the young man, the Sultan agrees to give him the girl in marriage, and blesses the young couple.

Tais, another opera inspired by Ancient Egypt, also had its premiere in 1997. Aziz el Shawaan's ballet entitled 'Isis' was also recently presented.

Ancient Egyptians often feature in cartoons and children's stories. But more interesting are satirical cartoons in newspapers and magazines where political personalities are represented as Ancient Egyptians or as talking to them (Figure 9:1). Most famous in this genre are the political sketches of Mostafa Hussein and Ahmad Ragab in the *Akhbar* daily, and those of other artists in the magazine *Caricature*. Such representations not only reveal what Ancient Egypt represents in the caricaturists' eye, but also project the views of their compatriots and how seriously – or not – they take ancient Egyptian culture and its symbols.

If nationalism and the search for identity triggered and dominated the search for Ancient Egypt in the literature of the 1920s and 1930s, they also activated its manifestations in the art and architecture of the period. Thus, a few years after his death, when Egypt wished to honour Saad Zaghloul, its great national hero who died in 1927 after having fought for Egypt's independence, the idea of erecting for him a 'pharaonic' mausoleum presented itself quite naturally (Haekal 1930) as the best expression of grandeur, immortality and particularly of a specific Egyptian identity. The monument was built on Mansour Street in the centre of Cairo with proper 'pharaonic' architectural elements, adapted to a more contemporary structural concept (Figure 9:2). The entrance is dominated by two Egyptianizing columns with lotus bud capitals and an architrave with the famous winged disc of Egyptian temples. A cavetto cornice covers the whole structure while toruses run along all the

Figure 9:1   Ramesses II statue complaining to Farouk Hosni, Minister of Culture, on being hired to stand at the central railway station in Cairo.

tapering walls (Price and Humbert 2003: Figure 1.11 col. pl.). In the garden, stone containers or vases for plants have adopted ancient Egyptian shapes and decorations and the cast-iron enclosure fence of the garden has further Egyptian motifs. The mausoleum was built in 1931, by the architect Mostafa Fahmy Bey.

A few years later, King Farouk had a rest-house built for himself in Giza, near the pyramids, in the 'pharaonic' style of those who ideologically were his ancestors

Figure 9:2   Saad Zaghlouf mausoleum (© Fayza Haikal).

(Figure 9:3 col. pl.). This lovely little building is decorated with all the symbols of kingship and divinity: winged discs, cobra snakes, statues of the king as pharaoh, reliefs representing the king on a chariot, hunting wild animals, symbols of chaos and evil, coloured glass windows depicting boating parties, a theme which is also taken from ancient Egyptian wall scenes, or literary texts. To crown it all, Farouk had his name written in hieroglyphs in cartouches on the doors of his rest-house, and 'boundary stelae' in the garden mark the borders of the royal resting place. Had the king remained in power longer, it would not have been totally surprising if he had ordained for himself the building of a tomb with pharaonic ornaments, or even pyramidal in shape.

Many years later, after the 1973 Egyptian-Israeli war, Egypt used an ancient Egyptian symbol to immortalize the soldiers who fell on the field of honour. Indeed Sami Rafei's splendid memorial to the Unknown Soldier, erected in 1974 on the Autostrad Avenue in Nasr City, is an open, right-angled pyramidal structure made of granite and concrete which reaches firmly and proudly to the sky (Figure 9:4 col. pl.). The wings of the pyramid are inscribed with one composite name formed by juxtaposing many names picked at random to represent the Unknown Soldier. This inscription is written with the simple forms of the kufic script, which beautifully match the straight lines of the pyramid, so that the combination of an ancient but modernized shape with a medieval Arabic script confers upon the monument a certain aura of eternity.

One of the most important state monuments, namely the highest constitutional court of Egypt, has been built on the Maadi Corniche in a strong Egyptianizing style (Haikal 2003).

Other official buildings and institutions such as universities and national companies have taken ancient Egyptian symbols and designs for their logos, either for their intrinsic symbolism – such as Thoth, god of learning and wisdom for Cairo University, or the sun god's falcon and obelisk for Ein Shams University – or for their Egyptian qualities, such as an Egyptian queen to represent Bank Misr or a modernized falcon head for Egypt's national airline Misr Air. This is probably an off-shoot of the 'search for identity' trend of the inter-war period, during which most of these institutions were created. Ancient Egyptian artefacts and monuments to represent the State are also common on stamps, coins and bank notes (Figure 9:5), or medals – for what could be more Egyptian than a pharaoh or an Egyptian queen, even if some of their most beautiful statues have strayed into foreign museums?

In sculpture, the first and most important manifestation of the return to ancient Egyptian themes and forms is Mahmoud Mokhtar's statue known as 'Egypt's Revival', or better, 'Egypt's Renaissance' (Figure 9:6). This took Mokhtar almost 10 years to complete (1919–1928), and now stands opposite University Bridge in Giza. Essentially Egyptian in its size, material and symbolism, this huge red granite statue represents a sphinx, symbol of the grandeur of pharaonic civilization, rising at the side of a woman, Egypt, proudly removing her veil to reveal the awakening of the nation. As Karnouk (1988: 15) writes, "the narrative quality of the statue is clear; it juxtaposes two pictographic determinatives in one sentence … Like a hieroglyph it calls for an objective and collective reading of the image … therefore the communicative potential of the statue was great, and the public response overwhelming and diverse".

Mokhtar is the first major Egyptian sculptor since the Ancient Egyptians, and his works are a clear revival of their great art. His statues, whether in Egypt or in France where he studied, testify to that fact, as much as his public monuments. His marble 'Nile Bride' of the late 1920s, now in the Musée Grevin in Paris, represents a beautiful maiden with an ancient Egyptian royal headdress and delicate jewellery. Almost all his female statues wear ancient Egyptian attributes, in addition to their typical features and the perfect polish and simplicity of their forms, so reminiscent of Egypt's

Figure 9:5   Egyptian currency (Egyptian one pound note).

Figure 9:6   Mahmoud Mokhtar's statue, 'Egypt's Renaissance' (© Fayza Haikal).

most classical styles. As for his early 1930s bronze reliefs on the granite base of the monument to Saad Zaghlul on the island opposite Kasr el Nil Bridge, they are almost modern interpretations of scenes of ancient Egyptian life in the fields, and of mourners at funerals. The statue of the national hero stands on a high pedestal, itself in the shape of four Egyptianizing columns.

If Ancient Egypt is undoubtedly present in Mokhtar's work, it becomes more subtle in Adam Henein's 1965 bronze 'Dynastic Bird' or 1978 bronze 'Silent Watch', the names, shapes and very souls of which are clearly inspired by ancient divine hawks and block statues (Karnouk 1995: 64–65). Samir Shoukry's 'Head of a Statue' (1992), now at the Nile Hilton shopping quadrangle, is also clearly inspired by ancient Egyptian statuary.

The 1996 'International Biennale' of Cairo showed some interesting works of younger Egyptian artists, among them 'Wire mummies' by Mohammed Abdel Hafez. Mummies in Ancient Egypt were made to preserve the body and help the people overcome death. But the deceased were also evoked in banquets and songs to remind the survivors that life upon earth is not eternal and to encourage them to enjoy it while they can (e.g. 'Songs of the Harper', see Lichtheim 1973: 113–117). With his 'Wire mummies' the artist conveys a similar meaning, since the use of this cold modern material for his artistic expression emphasizes the inevitability, sadness and finality of death.

While Egyptian atavism and phantoms emerge clearly in Fathi Ahmed's woodcut prints 'Egypt's Eyes' (1978) and 'Mothers' (1981) for example (Karnouk 1995: 102–103), a completely different attitude with respect to Ancient Egypt is manifested in Ramzi Moustafa's painted wood 'Osiris and Isis' (Karnouk 1995: 83) of the mid-1980s or Esmat Daoustashi's 1990 painted wood screen 'King and Queen' (Karnouk 1995: 70), where elements from many cultures are combined in a colourful Egyptianizing pastiche of royalty. In these two works, austerity, spirituality or even deference are replaced by humour and perhaps some kind of cynicism towards 'values' which were thought of as being eternal.

If Ancient Egypt is present in some of Ragheb Ayyad's paintings, like his 1934 'Works in the Field', where the scene is painted in different registers above each other to express depth but without real perspective (Karnouk 1998), specific Egyptian motifs or symbols appear only later in easel paintings. They manifest themselves clearly in works like Effat Nagui's 1960 'Universal Men' (Karnouk 1995: 69) where a good half of the painting is directly inspired by the ceiling of the burial chamber of Seti I. Alexandrian artists Farouk Wahba and Sarwat el Bahr have also exploited mummies and pyramids. Farouk Wahba's mummies are rather more promises of life, as his titles 'Canvas Relief' painted with hieroglyphic inscriptions on well packed bundles (late 1980s) and 'Resurrection: a mummy half way out of the tomb' (1990), suggest (Karnouk 1995: 74–75). The same hope appears in Sarwat el Bahr's 1984 'Ancient Rituals', where light shines above the pyramid. In his 'Mummy Assemblage' of the mid-1970s, a Coca-Cola drink painted on the chest of the mummy points to the future rather than to the past (Karnouk 1995: 75–76).

Nostalgia, the sense of time and its effect on humans are often expressed by the presence of ancient Egyptian artefacts or monuments in the works of artists, particularly those who have lived abroad. For example, this appears in Ahmad Mahmoud Morsi's painting, presented at the last Cairo 'Biennale', in which enigmatic human figures perform music and dance rituals by a pyramid while a bird (perhaps the soul) comes out of it.

Again, nostalgia and the effects of time are a recurrent theme in Abdel Ghaffar Shedid's work in which Ancient Egypt is omnipresent, whether with its material or spiritual symbols, pyramids and broken statues or birds and other sacred animals. This is the case in, for example, his 1987 'Renaissance' and 1988 'Morgana the Fairy' or his 1990 'Men and Cosmos' or 'Nubian Island I and II', so much so that one has the impression that ancient Egyptian symbols are Shedid's principal tools for expression. In paintings where broken pieces are shown, as in his 1987 'Excavations' or 'Ostraka' or in Ahmad Abdel Karim's painting presented at the 1996 'Biennale' which display a combination of many Egyptianizing drawings, one wonders whether they should be read as symbols of destruction, or rather of reconstruction and revival of the past, as on an excavation site. As so often with figurative art, interpretation is in the eye of the beholder rather than clearly revealed in the intentions of the artist him or herself!

As everywhere else, the Egyptian search for its past is also present in film. It appears in a light and humorous way in Fatin Abdel Wahab's 1963 *Nile's Bride*, for example, where an ancient Egyptian princess reveals herself to a young archaeologist who wakes her up, thus leading him into endless troubles. It is nobly represented by Shadi Abdel Salam's 1975 film *The Mummy*, an account of the discovery of Queen Inha'py's tomb in 1881. In order to prevent violation of their actual mummies after their own tombs had been robbed, kings of the New Kingdom had been reburied there during the twenty-first Dynasty. This tomb had been discovered by the Abdel Rassul family, who for generations had been living off the traffic in its treasures until they were denounced by their youngest heir, who preferred to reveal the cache to the police rather than see this violation continue. The splendid rendering of the boy's awakening apprehension followed by his inner conflict when he decided to betray his family to protect his cultural heritage, is only surpassed by the perfect rendering of Egyptian artefacts, jewels, coffins and other pieces of furniture in the tomb, and by the general atmosphere that prevails in the film. Abdel Salam's detailed study of ancient Egyptian culture also manifests itself in his shorter film *The Eloquent Peasant*, which is a transposition to the screen of parts of an ancient Egyptian tale (Loprieno 2003: 36–37).

The 'minor arts' have also responded to the call of Ancient Egypt. Pottery, furniture, jewellery and advertising have their great artists who draw their inspiration from Ancient Egypt, for the love and appreciation of its beauty, making exact or stylized copies of recognized artefacts, or reusing well known motifs in new combinations. Commercial appeal has also contributed to the diffusion of ancient Egyptian art (Hassan Chapter 8, this volume). In this case the quality of the production varies considerably, from real works of art to very poor imitations, which are little better than caricatures. This commercial appeal has also affected the architecture and decoration of many bazaars, shopping arcades and international hotels (Figure 9:7 col. pl.), in response to, and exploitation of, tourists' predilection, rather than a genuine cultural concern for Egypt's cultural heritage.

'Egyptomania' and the manifold consequences of that heritage play a vital role in the economic life of the country. They have a more important international cultural presence than scientific archaeology. For indeed, if the Supreme Council of Antiquities has more than 20,000 persons working for it today, to administer, study and preserve monuments and sites, it is still international 'Egyptomania' in its broader sense – the attraction of Ancient Egypt in general – which forms the base of the tourism industry, one of the pillars of the Egyptian economy (El Daly Chapter 10, this volume). And this very economic importance is perhaps the major factor that stimulates both the authorities and the masses to respect their cultural heritage. It is true that the love of Ancient Egypt is often stimulated by Egyptology and new discoveries, but it is not always the case, for it also thrives on dreams, imagination and fantasy and it should never be allowed to be disappointed by harsh scientific realities. If Egyptology proves, like science in general, to be an excellent bridge for international relations when diplomatic relations are tense or severed because of political situations, it is clear that without international 'Egyptomania', Egyptology's job would be more difficult.

Ancient Egypt is now fully present in our lives and its legacy weighs heavy on our shoulders. To protect and preserve its material heritage is an inescapable concern, not only for Egypt but for all the civilized world. There is no chance that it can again be forgotten. The pharaohs have made it; their culture is resurrected. Long live Egypt, 'Egyptomania' and Egyptology.

Acknowledgments

It is with much emotion that I dedicate this chapter to the memory of my friend Dr Abdel Aziz Sadek, whom I first met when we were both studying Egyptology at Cairo University. Because Azzuz shared with me the love of art and beauty and a deep interest in everything Egyptian, I feel that he might have enjoyed it.

I wish to thank my assistant Hesham Elleithy for helping me to gather the material and the photographs.

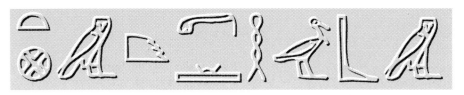

CHAPTER 10

WHAT DO TOURISTS LEARN OF EGYPT?

Okasha El Daly

How is it that, in this age of atomic fission, space shuttle, and other wonders, each year many more thousands of people from all over the world visit Egypt to see its ancient temples, tombs and cities? Why have vast crowds waited patiently for so many hours at the British Museum, the Louvre and elsewhere to see the treasures of Tutankhamun? What is it that makes the demand for university degrees, for extramural courses, for exhibitions, for films and books concerned with the civilization of Ancient Egypt so intense, above all in English-speaking countries? Other ancient cultures cast their spell; but Ancient Egypt exerts a special hold on the public imagination.

(Smith 1983: 5)

No serious research has, to my knowledge, been attempted on the subject of what tourists get out of their visit to Egypt. Reputable travel firms do, of course, ask customers for feedback, and though this will include questions on the quality of the guides and guest lecturer, if there has been one, they cover mainly matters of marketing interest to the tour operator and nothing about the learning or spiritual experience of the journey which may even inspire some visitors to continue their study of Ancient Egypt.

This chapter is informed by my 20 years or so as a registered Egyptian guide, but also by my academic training in Egyptology, by my current research into medieval Arabic visitors to Egypt, and by my attendance at conferences of the Association for the Study of Travellers to Egypt and the Near East (Starkey and Starkey 1998).

It is worth considering some of the differences between present day visitors and visitors from the past, for these may explain the availability of non-academic materials that currently exist in the public domain.

Most visitors to Egypt today are tourists, according to the IATA definition (Leiper 1979), although there are still a few 'travellers' and expatriate workers and, of course, very important, although relatively small in number, the academics and archaeologists whose work is concerned with Ancient Egypt. Most tourists have a very small space of time in their lives for Egypt and their most probable means of communication about their experience is to a limited domestic circle, via film, postcards and small reproduced artefacts including jewellery, reinterpreted to meet modern tastes. These days, tourists are likely to use word of mouth to encourage others to follow them in their experience. I must exempt from this vast group a relatively small but significant group of visitors who, for example, study for Diplomas in Egyptology in their spare or retirement time and who visit Egypt year after year, even twice a year. Prior to the 1950s, many visitors clearly had time to write books, diaries or long descriptive letters, or to use a talent for painting. Some of these have been well described (e.g. Clayton 1982; James 1997; Manley 1991; Pick 1991; Saad el Din and Cromer 1991). Some fell in love with Egypt and became, so to speak, 'Egyptianized'. The best example of this breed is Lucie Duff Gordon who lived in Luxor as *Bent Balad* – 'native woman' – among the local people, who adored her. On her death in 1869, the whole of Luxor mourned her (Frank 1994: 5; Gordon 1865; Pick 1991: 170 ff). There must be many other interesting accounts, verbal and visual, hidden in attics, though many more will have been destroyed. Of course a great number of academic books and papers on Ancient Egypt are still being produced, together with many unscholarly but best-selling histories and novels.

But how do present day visitors compare with visitors of previous ages, and were their aims and perceptions the same? I believe mass tourism to be different in nature to that of earlier times. As Baqader (1997) noted, the basic tourism industry focuses on sensual pleasures that start with the letter *s* – sun, sea, sand, etc. (cf. Cohen 1984; Crick 1989). It is responding to the consumer society with its ferocious appetite for the pleasures of the flesh. But consumerism is not limited to experiencing sensual joys, it also manifests itself in acquiring souvenirs of the host country. Souvenir-hunting is not a new phenomenon. Ancient Egyptian artefacts, deposited long ago in western and Arab homes and palaces, suggest that travellers always took home mementos of their travels, whether bought or gifted (for the effect and use of such Egyptian materials see Harris and Harris 1965; Roullet 1972). Jewish merchants in Egypt were in the business of producing souvenirs (Brown 1739: 323 ff), which must have been for distant European markets but maybe also for sale locally (cf. Dannenfeldt 1959: 16 ff). Certainly by the 1800s family businesses around Luxor, some still functioning today, were busy forging 'genuine antiquities' even 'genuine mummies' for sale to travellers (Wakeling 1912: 113 ff). Mummies and even parts of mummies seemed to be particularly in demand and were offered to visitors, from Al-Baghdadi at the end of the 12th century to Pietro Della Valle in the early 17th century. The urge experienced by some visitors to Egypt of wanting to dig up mummies can be seen from the accounts of many early travellers searching for them (Dannenfeldt 1959: 17 ff). Pietro Della Valle, who visited the country in 1615–1616, shortly after arriving in Cairo rode to Saqqarah where he "divided up his workmen to dig in different places and set up his tent in the middle, determined not to leave before something was found". In the end he had to be content with buying two mummies from a local peasant who took him to the nearby mummy-pit to see them for himself. He was so proud of his two mummies that he put them on display in Cairo before shipping them to Messina (Holt 1998: 20).

Travelling of course predates written records, and so we can only surmize about what travellers, particularly from other parts of Africa, from Arabia and from the northern shores of the Mediterranean, came to Egypt for, and what they did when they were there.

The first visitors that we know about in any detail, mainly through their writings, are the Greeks. Alexander conquered Egypt in 330 BC and the Ptolemies subsequently ruled the country, adopting many aspects of Egyptian religion and culture. There are many graffiti of Greek names as far south as Philae, some with dedications not only to the reigning pharaoh but also to relatives and friends. There are also letters arranging for accommodation with friends whilst attending religious ceremonies and festivals. However, we cannot usually tell whether these are travellers or expatriate workers (Maehler 1992, 2003; Thompson 2003).

At this time Egypt was regarded as a great centre of civilization, of religion and of science. A number of well known Greek scholars are purported to have spent time in Egypt (Tait 2003: 29, 31, 33) in order to learn, but also, it has been suggested, to add to their credibility as sages. These include Thales, reputed to have been the first to measure the height of the Pyramid of Kheops, Plato, said to have visited with a group of scholars during travels after the death of their teacher Socrates, and Pythagoras, who is believed to have spent 22 years of his life in Egypt. There have been suggestions that the evidence for some of these visits is not above question (Tait 2003), although it is generally accepted that Plato did indeed visit and there are certainly numerous complimentary references to Egypt in *The Republic* (Daumas 1984; Kákosy 1993). Plato, in various works, also made mention of Egyptian art and music that show his knowledge and appreciation of them (Davis 1979).

The writings of Herodotus about his travels are well known (Harrison 2003). An interesting study by Ball (1942), himself an advisor on desert surveys who spent 34 years studying maps of Egypt, describes and compares the detailed geographical, geological and cosmological studies of Herodotus, Strabo, Pliny the Elder and Ptolemy.

After the victory of Octavian over Cleopatra in 30 BC Egypt became, not a province of Rome, but a personal fiefdom of the Emperor, and Romans both visited and settled in the country. Roman festivals replaced many of the older ones, though the popularity of Isis and Osiris remained strong, and the cult of Isis spread even to western Europe (Harris and Harris 1965; Rice 1997; Roullet 1972; Witt 1971). Military and administrative functionaries from Rome visited important sites in Egypt, continued each autumn the festival for the flooding of the Nile, and left a great deal of graffiti to record their visits (Thompson 2003; Van 't Dack 1983).

The next large corpus of work deriving from visitors to Egypt is by medieval Arab/Muslim writers, in the main written in Arabic. They cover subjects such as religion, participation in extant practices and scholarly debates, excavation, surveying and recording ancient sites, descriptions of the flora and fauna, and, most significantly perhaps, discussion and efforts to decipher the ancient scripts. These travellers and scholars were doubtless encouraged to visit Egypt to study its wonders, by the many positive references to Egypt in the Quran, as well as by the Quran's general exhortation to travel in order to learn from and about others (El Daly 2003). Add to this the fact that Muslims travelling through lands under Islamic control were never perceived as strangers, since "every Moslem was always at home among other Moslems" (Rosenthal 1997: 35 ff). The medieval scholar Al-Zarkashi wrote a treatise on the subject of the requirements of the traveller, where he counted among them the need to learn about and from the countries visited (cf. Gellens 1990; Netton 1996; for Arab travel accounts of Egypt see Abbas 1992; El Daly 1998, 2000; Haarmann 1991 cf. Vantini 1975).

Travellers came from the west as well as from the east, many of those from Spain and North Africa passing through Egypt on their way to the Red Sea to find a passage to Mecca, and recording the sites they had visited, particularly the pyramids. There were also Jews and Christians making the journey to Egypt (e.g. Rabbi Benjamin of Tudela d. 1173 and William of Tyre d. ca. 1185) (Babcock and Krey 1943). But few other visitors from Europe made the journey to see the pyramids (Cannuyer 1984a, b).

For whatever reason, though visits to Egypt must surely have continued, particularly from Arabia and the rest of the Muslim world, there are fewer extant documents or records from the beginning of the 16th century until the arrival of the French in 1798. This period coincides with Turkish rule of Egypt but there appear to have been few Turkish travellers referring to the antiquities of Egypt (Haarmann 1976, 1991, 1996). It also coincides with the height of the western European Renaissance and Enlightenment, with their humanist approach to the arts and sciences (Dannenfeldt 1959; DuQuesne 1999; cf. Iversen 1961; Wortham 1971a). Only relatively few Europeans are known to have visited Egypt at this time, for example John Manderville, Pietro Della Valle and William Lithgow, although scholars such as Kircher were studying and making advances in the interpretation of hieroglyphics, from Egyptian monuments and Arabic manuscripts brought to Europe by Romans, crusaders, travellers and merchants (Roman 1990; Ucko and Champion 2003; Volkoff 1970).

The next flood of visitors came as a result of European colonialism and expansion, particularly by the French and the British (Jeffreys 2003: 7–8). It was under the reign of Mohammed Ali Pasha that a sea and overland route from London through Egypt to India was established in 1830, when Waghorn obtained a concession from the Egyptian government and carried the mail between London and India (Conner 1983: ch. 10). Soon tourists followed, leading the Egyptian ruler in 1845 to establish an agency to look after them. This agency was known as *maslahit al-murur*, the Traffic Agency. The first decree to organize and regulate tourists in Egypt, including the work of *turgmans* or *dragomans* (interpreters), was introduced on 8 May 1849 under the ruler Abbas Pasha I. Native and foreigners alike were allowed to work as guides and had to obtain a signed statement from the tourists at the end of their work to show that the guests had been satisfied with their services (Diab 1994).

It is with the opening of the Suez Canal (1869) and shortly afterwards, in September 1882, with the British occupation and protectorate, that we see the beginnings of present day tourism. Thomas Cook played an active part in this, including the commissioning of Wallis Budge, then Keeper of Egyptian and Assyrian Antiquities at the British Museum, to compile a guide book especially for the use of their passengers on Nile cruises (Budge 1897). Those who wished to travel independently were still able to contact local *dragomans* to make all the required arrangements, at a cost, and those who could not afford this could arrange everything for themselves. One such visitor decided to fill a gap in the market by writing a book for such travellers with the eye-catching title *The Nile Without a Dragoman* (Eden 1871). About the same time, local societies were established to provide scholarly help to the more inquisitive traveller (Sadgrove 1998).

From the 19th and early 20th centuries there is a vast corpus of travel writings, supplemented by paintings. These include diaries, letters and publications, many of which are in English (Starkey and Starkey 1998). There are details of visits to sites and the adventures of getting to them, but comparatively few attempts to discuss the significance of the sites. The representations of living Egyptians were mostly as servants and, if depicted at all, they tended to be as shadowy men in *gallabeyas*. Yet some European travellers did enjoy "attempting to live as the Egyptians did, in adopting local dress and customs, yet anxious to assert their native identity" on special occasions such as Christmas (Conner 1983: 149). While some British in Egypt – for whatever reasons, perhaps even as disguise (Usick 2002: 66–67) – were donning *qaftan* (Figure 10:1 col. pl.) and *tarboush* (as was Lord Leighton even at home), Egyptian officials and the better-off were wearing "frock-coat, waistcoat and trousers" (Conner 1983: 149).

The romance of the discovery of the tomb of Tutankhamun resulted in the spread of some knowledge about Ancient Egypt, leading not only to greater numbers of wealthy visitors, including travellers from the United States, but also to the development of a fashionable decorative style, and the appearance of Egyptianized architecture (Humbert and Price 2003).

Partly as a result of World War II, partly as a result of film and television, and also as a result of British soldiers, no longer at war, making contact with ordinary Egyptians during the protectorate (which ended only two years after the Egyptian Army revolution in 1952), the 1950s brought Europeans a greater awareness of other cultures (cf. Hopwood 1989).

However, the single most important factor for visitors to Egypt has been the development of cheap and easy air travel, as well as the Egyptian response to the demands of the growing tourist industry. Everywhere in the world, 'Egyptian' brings the response, even from small children, of 'The Pyramids!' while adult western responses also include 'Tutankhamun' and 'Mummies' (Lupton Chapter 2, this volume; MacDonald Chapter 6, this volume). However, perhaps for the first time in nearly 4,000 years, people today visit Egypt without even setting eyes on a pyramid, partly due to the development of cheap sun-and-sea holidays on the Red Sea, and more recently due to direct flights to Luxor for a week of cruising on the Nile.

The vast increase in tourism has of course had a beneficial effect on the Egyptian economy generally (Hassan Chapter 8, this volume). Partly in response to increased tourist numbers the Department of Antiquities has made many more sites accessible, some excavated by the growing number of young Egyptians studying their ancient heritage (Haikal Chapter 9, this volume), although many more are excavated and published by foreign academic institutions. Some of these are within major sites long visited, such as Memphis or Giza.

For a number of reasons Egypt is finding it difficult to keep abreast of the expansion and expectations of the tourist industry. For example, many of the older guides are graduates in Egyptology, and others are mature people of other professions who have studied their history with great passion. At some time all have had to pass an exam and have had to join the Guides Syndicate, first in order to gain a permit, and then to renew it every five years. The Syndicate acts as a professional body, and runs lectures, debates and visits for members to keep them up to date.

One response to the increase in tourism has been the creation of a number of Schools of Tourism, mainly in the private sector. They cover all aspects of tourism, but have had great problems in finding sufficient numbers of teachers with adequate knowledge to teach Egyptology. Entry standards to such schools are not always rigorous and so over the last 10 years large numbers of licensed guides have emerged, many of whom are charming and entertaining and do an excellent job with the many tourists who want only the briefest overview of Egyptian culture and monuments. It remains important to match the right guide to the right kind of tour, and travel agents both in Egypt and in the home countries of the tourists could do a better job of matching special interests to the right guide.

The explosion in tourism has also led to another development that currently has unforeseen side effects, namely the vast increase in the number of travel agencies. Competition should be good for the consumer, and in many ways it is. But travel agencies quickly learned that they would make more money if they invested in shops and factories manufacturing anything from gold jewellery to T-shirts. Then of course, tour groups are directed to specific shops (Figure 10:2 col. pl.), which in many cases provide the only opportunity for tourists to meet local people, but is seen as a waste of time by some. This is a great pity since the level of ignorance on the part of most tourists regarding modern Egyptians is widespread. One is reminded of an observation made by Clarke (1983: 109): "Any Englishman hearing a party of Egyptian Arabs in conversation, and being ignorant of their language, would suppose they were quarrelling." On the positive side of course is the increased employment that tourism has created. An interesting side effect has been research into and revival of traditional crafts that might otherwise have died out.

Many tourists will know only of the Giza pyramids, the Cairo Museum, and the tomb of Tutankhamun, and will feel deprived if these are missed. A week's cruising from Luxor to Aswan will include the temples on the way – Luxor, Karnak, Edfu, perhaps Esna, Kom Ombo and Philae when they reach Aswan. Also essential is a visit to the Valley of the Kings, where people will queue for long periods to see the small tomb of Tutankhamun, which often means that there is little time to visit the more spectacular tombs of more important pharaohs. Few tours visit the Valley of the Queens unless they have arranged to see Nefertari's tomb, though many will stop at one or other of the Tombs of the Nobles. Few tours have time to visit the workmen's village of Deir el-Medina or the many splendid temples on the west bank. Longer tours based around Luxor may include a northern detour to Dendera and Abydos, accessible again, although security measures in place can still cause frustration, to guides even more than to visitors. The sites of Beni Hassan, Amarna and Hierakonpolis are still almost impossible for groups to visit, but there has recently been a significant improvement to the way security officers deal with the demands of tourists and guides, and small groups with special interests can often visit them by prior arrangement.

Aswan has always been seen as a sleeping place for Philae and Abu Simbel, but in recent years the tombs of the Nobles on the west bank have been opened, and, more recently, the Nubian Museum. The Nubian sites rescued before the flooding of Lake Nasser were, until 10 years ago, virtually impossible to visit, but there are now at least five cruise boats, each visiting these sites twice a week. Those on boats between Aswan and Luxor cannot visit the interesting, and recently cleaned, tombs at El Kab, but even those in coaches usually view this splendid site only in passing from the road.

Figure 1:2 'Israel in Egypt', oil painting by Sir Edward John Poynter, 1867 (© Guildhall Art Gallery, Corporation of London).

Figure 1:3 'Egyptian' block printed linen furnishing fabric, designed by Kolland for G. P. and J. Baker, 1923 (© G. P. & J. Baker).

Figure 1:8 Princess of the Stars, 1999 (© Meiklejohn Graphics, UK). The picture illustrates a pre-millennial tendency to link the achievements of Ancient Egyptians with extra-terrestrial interventions.

Figure 3:2 Scene of Radames' Triumph in the Verona production of *Aida*, 2002 (direction and stage settings by Franco Zeffirelli) (© Jean-Marcel Humbert).

Figure 3:5 *Aida* in Verona, 2001 (direction and stage settings by Pier Luigi Pizzi) (© Jean-Marcel Humbert).

Figure 3:8 *Aida* in Verona, 1987–1988 (direction and stage settings – "a series of colour mosaics" – by Pietro Zuffi).

Figure 6:1 Children viewing a copy of Tutankhamun's unwrapped mummy, on display in the Tutankhamun exhibition, Dorchester. In the background is a copy of Tutankhamun's gold mask. Artefacts from two different parts of the museum have been combined for this publicity shot.

Figure 8:5   Shop in Khan el-Khalili selling old European style furniture (© Fekri A. Hassan).

Figure 9:3   King Farouk rest-house at Giza Plateau (© Fekri A. Hassan).

Figure 9:4   Unknown Soldier war memorial at Medinet Nasr (© Fayza Haikal).

Figure 9:7
Entrance to Three
Pyramids Hotel in
al Haram St, Giza
(© Fayza Haikal).

Figure 10:1 Oil painting by Jean-Baptiste Borely (1819) of the Honourable Charles Irby in 'Turkish' *qaftan*. Note the Temple of Philae in the background, and the statue of a priest of Amun (now in the British Museum) in the foreground (© Fine Art Society, London).

Figure 10:2 A local home/workshop in Luxor, decorated for the tourist trade
(© Okasha El Daly).

Figure 12:1 Hoarding for Crüwell tobaccos (© Archaeological Museum, Strasbourg).

Over the past 15 years many more sites in the Memphite area have been opened to tourists. Saqqarah of course has been visited for many years, much to the surprise of many tourists who discover that there are more than three pyramids in Egypt! Now the pyramid sites of Dahshur and Abu Sir can be visited, though this would usually be done during a second or later visit to Egypt. Meidum and nearby sites, although seldom visited, provide a pleasant day out from Cairo, and the more intrepid can set off into the desert to rediscover the almost hidden pyramids and the barely excavated small temples of Lisht. Fayum has a wealth of interesting antiquities and is an easy day out from Cairo, but its main visitors are Cairenes visiting its lakeside resorts.

Desert travel has always held romance for some, and there are occasional tours to the Kharga Oasis which is being slowly developed to receive more visitors. More tourists are following in the supposed footsteps of Alexander to Siwa; they are usually connoisseurs rather than first-time visitors. Thanks to the recent spectacular discoveries by Zahi Hawass and his colleagues of the Valley of the Golden Mummies in the Oasis of Bahariyah in the Western Desert, there are now a growing number of groups heading that way.

Alexandria is now regularly on tour agendas and will doubtless become even more popular as a result of the French/Egyptian underwater excavations and the opening of the new Library there (Butler 2003). Much work has already taken place to make sites more interesting and accessible to visitors. There are a number of important sites in the Delta and surrounding area, but with the exception of Rashid, Tanis, Tel Basta and the Coptic monasteries in the Wadi Natrun, they have not yet been well prepared for visitors.

Virtually every tourist to Cairo will visit the Egyptian Museum. Some will be taken to old Coptic Cairo where a leisurely stroll brings invitations to visit many unofficial, but sometimes very interesting, sites (Horbury 2003), but few, even Cairenes, know of the dramatic Coptic site next to the *qariyat al-zabalin*, hidden in the Maqattam Hills facing the Citadel. Its rock churches are no less interesting than the modern carvings and arena for present day services (Hassan Chapter 8, this volume). It is also the site of the burial of many well known figures in Islamic Sufism, such as Dhu Al-Nun Al-Misri and Ibn Al-Farid, and therefore attracts numbers of Muslim visitors. Cairo abounds with medieval mosques, some ruined, but each with its own special interest, and other medieval buildings including the old eye hospital, restored 15th/16th century houses and the 12th century walls and gates, but few tourists are taken off the (fairly narrow) beaten track of Khan el-Khalili, in spite of recent investment to make many of these sites safer and more accessible (Hassan Chapter 8, this volume; Netton 1996: 145 ff).

Some of the most popular sites are under threat from the sheer impact of so many visitors, although in some instances more money could help to protect them. It may be significant that there has been no great outcry either at the special charge of LE100 (around £10), or the restricted access to the restored tomb of Queen Nefertari (150 visitors are allowed only 10 minutes' access each day). Perhaps, therefore, the Egyptian Antiquities Department needs to be bolder. But at the same time it cannot take too many risks with the lifeblood of the Egyptian tourism industry. It is not just a question of the economy. There is a complex web of relationships that develops between visitors who first come to Egypt as tourists and local Egyptians (Hopwood

1999); some take an interest in supporting charities, most notably those looking after animals like Brooke's Hospital for animals, as well as orphanages and schools for children. Some visitors get involved in trying to solve some of the problems that they feel their home countries were responsible for creating. A current example is the issue of the estimated 23 million mines buried by the warring factions during World War II in the Western Desert, which still kill or maim a number of people and animals every year (*Al-Ahram*, 24 December 1998: 3).

Educating travellers about the countries they visit has been a concern for many years. Recent conferences have had the topic of education high on the agenda (Elbert 2000: 9). According to the British campaign group 'Tourism Concern' this subject continues to generate interest today (Wells 2001). It is worth asking what the role of the Egyptian guide can be in educating tourists who do not necessarily learn in a structured academic way during their visit – though some may be inspired to read and study on their return home.

The aims of a guide leading a group of present day travellers should differ from one group to another. Until recently, tourists visiting Egypt went there primarily to see the pharaonic antiquities of the country, with an almost total lack of awareness of anything else. So the guide's normal practice is to go through a set of specific historical talks as a background to each site. As it is presumed that tourists have only a passing interest in historical explanation the guides normally keep such information to a minimum. Guides often have a perception that some nationalities are more interested in serious knowledge, these being the British, the French and the Germans. Perhaps the reason for this perception derives from the fact that these are the countries most associated with the creation of modern Egyptology. These countries also happen to be among the four sending the largest number of visitors to Egypt. The figures published recently by the Egyptian Ministry of Tourism for the period from January to July 2001 shows the top 10 countries according to the number of their nationals visiting Egypt as: Germany 467,384, Italy 408,693, United Kingdom 206,674, France 203,908, Saudi Arabia 149,381, Benelux countries 133,413, Russia and Commonwealth countries 129,868, USA 128,929, Scandinavian countries 121,899, Libya 87,893. This same report shows that, in the year 2000, tourism generated a total income to Egypt of £2.5 billion.

Many of my groups were associated with academic institutions such as universities or major museums (Figure 10:3). I therefore always assumed that such visitors would be interested in the country's history in its entirety, although the itineraries with which I had to cope did not support my assumption. Nevertheless, I aimed, within the constraints of time and given itinerary, to present a background survey of the whole history of Egypt, showing its continuity. Notwithstanding the glamour of the pharaonic sites and artefacts, I tried, with varying degrees of success, to show that later phases of Egyptian culture are also very important. The main problem here is that most of these itineraries focusing on pharaonic monuments are designed by guest lecturers accompanying the groups, and as most of these tend to have backgrounds in Egyptology, they seem to wish to avoid anything beyond the 'Egypt of Egyptology' or 'Egypt of the Pharaohs'. It is not that other monuments do not interest the visitors, it is simply that knowledge of them falls outside the expertise of most Egyptologists, who are expected to give background lectures about the sites and therefore choose to ignore non-pharaonic sites altogether. The traditional

Figure 10:3   The author exchanging views with Ancient History Professor Margaret Drower in front of students from the USA (© Okasha El Daly).

itinerary of tours is rooted in pre-arranged mass tourism itineraries, as can be seen from Budge (1897: vii–viii), who states in the preface to the fourth edition of his guide book:

> Experience has shown that the greater number of travellers in that country are more interested in history and matters connected with Egyptian civilization from BC 4400 to BC 450, than with Egypt under the rule of the Assyrians and Persians, Greeks and Romans, Arabs and Turks. It is for this reason that no attempt has been made to describe, otherwise than in the briefest possible manner, its history under these foreign rulers, and only such facts connected with them as are absolutely necessary for a right understanding of its monuments have been inserted.

Another reason may be found in what Fahim (1998: 10) calls the "Oriental representation of Egyptian culture" on the part of Europeans where the Islamic/ Oriental side of Egypt was for many Europeans a subject of ridicule and amusement, while the pharaonic aspect was highly regarded and its themes widely adopted in European architecture and decorative art. However, many early European visitors to Egypt also fell under the spell of its Islamic heritage, to the extent that back at home they sought to emulate masterpieces of Islamic art and architecture. At Leighton House in Holland Park, London are reproductions of the interiors of some of the Mameluk buildings of Cairo where Lord Leighton spent time; the house itself was described as "Quite the eighth wonder of the world" (quoted in Findlater 1996: 4 n. 1; see also Conner 1979; Danby 1995: 176 ff; Sweetman 1988).

A second aim of my tours was to present some flavour of contemporary Egyptian issues. Most guides tend to avoid discussing politics or religion for fear of offending the sensibilities of their guests. Egyptian rules of hospitality dictate that one should not disagree with a guest. I take the view that it is the tourist's right to know as much about these issues as their time and inclination allow. It can sometimes be a daunting task, particularly with regard to politics, as most members of tours belong to the so-called educated middle classes. British groups sometimes have a tendency to glorify British colonial history and its supposed benefits to Egypt. I sometimes felt that I was walking on a bed of thorns, trying to explain what should be obvious: that Egypt is not just a landscape dotted with glamorous monuments, but contains a people and a culture with the same human concerns and needs as everyone else (Figure 10:4). An interest in the local people seems to have been more normal among 19th century visitors to Egypt, "who were often as concerned with the life of contemporary Egyptians as they were with the remains of Ancient Egypt" (Starkey and Starkey 1998: 3–4). But back then visitors were not constrained by itineraries designed by travel agents with profit as their overriding concern. I tried within these constraints to create some understanding of modern Egypt and Egyptians so that once back at home the traveller could better follow and understand local news coverage of some of the issues.

Religion can be another thorny issue, but I tried to give an overview of the Egyptian Jews, the Coptic Christians, and Islam, as few tourists are aware of their significant contribution, particularly of the Egyptian Coptic Church, to the development of religious thought and practice in the west (Horbury 2003). Equally, most tourists have a very limited knowledge, if any, of Islam or of the science and scholarship of the Arabs who played a well documented part in advancing the civilization of the Mediterranean and beyond. I also tried to show that the relationship between Islam and the West was not always, as commonly perceived, that of war and

Figure 10:4   The author involving local Egyptians in a foreign tourist visit to the Meidum pyramid site (© Okasha El Daly).

aggression; it was more often than not a cordial relationship built on mutual respect and co-operation (Hunke 1960; Watt 1972).

My third aim was to encourage visitors to pursue further study of Egyptian culture, either on their own or in academic institutions. To further this aim I provided handouts with reading lists on various subjects, or even books when I could afford to do so. I also provided names of suitable academic institutions, although many of them offer only fairly limited courses on Egypt, always focusing on the more glamorous aspects of its pharaonic past. Some students complain, and rightly so, of the lack of availability of a more comprehensive treatment of the subject.

Some of my personal reminiscences illustrate my points. For example, a few years ago, I took a group of teachers from Lambeth to spend a week in Egypt not so much to learn about its antiquities, they having done this at home, but to observe closely the modes of life in a city such as Cairo, as well as in a small village on the edge of Luxor. This experience was remarkable for all of us. We called unexpectedly at a house of a *fellah* and were greeted by the family as if we were long lost friends, and the *fellah's* mother, the head of the household, welcomed us in and sent for her son who was in his field. As it was lunchtime we were naturally invited to share the meal with the large family of about 12 people. The teachers were inquisitive, so questions about every aspect of the family's life and work were translated by me, and answers conveyed back. They took down notes and drew pictures. They even asked the host about the cultivation of various crops and he at one point stood in the middle of the courtyard with his hoe, digging up the earth to show us how sugarcane was cultivated – to the delight and amazement of the teachers. I also invited the group, by prior arrangement with the Ministry of Education in Cairo, to visit Badrashain Secondary School on the road to Memphis. This is the school that I myself attended, before university, and one of my teachers, who was by then the headmaster, warmly welcomed us. After the usual hospitality, we were allowed to visit any classroom and talk to students and hand them a prepared questionnaire. The Lambeth teachers were impressed with what they saw and of course I was very proud of my school. We then moved on to a private school so that they could see a different system of management. The Egyptian teachers enjoyed meeting this energetic group of British teachers. Needless to say, the girls and boys at both schools were so well behaved that the British teachers almost wanted to stay there! They asked one of the students about their attitude to their teachers and the student pointed out some beautiful Arabic calligraphy on the wall that reads: "Stand up in glorification of your teacher as the teacher is almost a Prophet."

Many African Americans and African-Caribbean British see Ancient Egypt very clearly as part of their heritage, and are moved by and proud of the ancient splendour with which they feel they have a right to associate themselves. Many active African Americans currently arrange regular pilgrimage tours to Egypt and even hold international conferences there (Carruthers and Harris 1997; MacDonald 2003).

Other groups include those who are immersed in ancient Egyptian religion, and believe that they practise it, such as large groups of Rosicrucians, mainly from the west coast of the United States, who until a few years ago were allowed to remain for the night in the Temple of Abydos and inside the Great Pyramid.

An Irish Catholic priest, visiting with a lively group of compatriots, became quieter and quieter until, towards the end of his visit, he told me how shaken he was about the teachings of his Church and its interpretation of the Old Testament. He had seen in Egypt just how much of his Christianity derived from "pagan" Ancient Egypt. A similar impact of Egypt caused famous travellers like Harriet Martineau and Florence Nightingale to delve deeply into their religious doubts and convictions (Rees 1995: 90).

A sophisticated, educated English woman told me after her return home that, during our visit to the Church of Saints Sergius and Bacchus in Old Cairo (Gabra 1993: 118 ff), when looking at the steps to the small dark crypt where Jesus and the Virgin Mary are reputed to have sheltered, she suddenly realized the truth of Christianity and became, and has remained, a born again Christian.

I also remember the many Jews from Europe and the United States who are disturbed not to find any reference in any of the temples or tombs of their existence, or of Moses and his life story, or of their assumed slavery as a group under pharaoh.

And above all, I remember the reaction of many ordinary Europeans as some of them, for the first time, realize that the present cultural balance in the world was not always so. And every visitor, whether on the first or the twenty-first visit, is overwhelmed by the sheer size of the temples and magnificence of the decoration of the tombs. The overall impression of those who go to Egypt is that they somehow belong to its history and culture. This may be due to certain characteristics of the Egyptians noted a long time ago by the medieval Egyptian scholar Ibn Zahirah (*Mahasin*: 204); Egyptians, he said, were famed for:

> Their sweet tongue, much flattery and kindness to people and love of strangers, they treat them very gently and give them charity and provide them with help to carry out their tasks and support them … Egyptians do not object to people's behaviour and do not denounce them or envy them and do not compete with them but they let everyone get on with what they want to do; the scholar is busy with his scholarship, the worshipper is busy with his worship, the sinner is busy with his sin and every craftsman is busy with his craft. Nobody turns to anybody else to blame them for sin or shortcomings.

It is tempting to try to link this attitude among Egyptians back to their significant spiritual heritage: "… of harmony, of reconciliation and transformation" (Hornung 2001: 201). Many visitors to Egypt return home with sufficient spiritual and material reminders to make them feel really at home, in Egypt!

Acknowledgments

My grateful thanks to my wife Diana for reviewing this chapter with the eyes of a traveller, tourist and critic and for her insightful remarks.

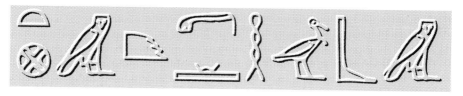

CHAPTER 11

'WONDERFUL THINGS': PUBLISHING EGYPT IN WORD AND IMAGE

Andrew Wheatcroft

There are perhaps two epiphanic moments in the history of Egyptology. Denon recorded the moment in 1798 when the French army first encountered Ancient Egypt. As the soldiers came upon the temples of Karnak and Luxor:

> the whole army, suddenly and with one accord, stood in amazement … and clapped their hands with delight, as if the end and object of their glorious toils, and the complete conquest of Egypt, were accomplished and secured by taking possession of the splendid remains of this ancient metropolis.

> (Gillespie and Dewachter 1987: 13)

From France's encounter with Egypt emerged a monumental publication, *Description de l'Égypte* (*Description* 1809–1828; Jeffreys 2003: 2–3), and the origins of the modern study of Egyptian archaeology.

The other moment is better known. It took place on the day that Howard Carter first peered into the tomb of Tutankhamun. To Lord Carnarvon's anxious enquiry, "Can you see anything?", Carter's immortal (but bathetic) response was "Yes, wonderful things" (Carter and Mace 1954, 1: 96; Ziegler 1994: fig. 2).[1] These two incidents, widely separated in time, suggest that perhaps Egypt's impact was as much visual as intellectual.

Long before the development of scientific archaeology, Egypt was familiar to Europe. This in itself was unusual, distinguishing Egypt from most other ancient cultures in the region. We might compare Egypt with Sumer. Until the decipherment of Sumerian cuneiform in the 19th century, Sumer was unknown; Egypt, by contrast, had been an object of intense curiosity since the Renaissance (Curran 2003). The meaning of hieroglyphics became the subject of constant theorizing and speculation. This was, admittedly, an Egypt adjusted to fit European preconceptions and constructed to fit the intellectual needs of western scholars. Like alchemy, this proto-Egyptology had its own rigorous principles of investigation and analysis. Subsequently, in the same manner that scientific chemistry discredited alchemy, scientific Egyptology also denied its antecedents. But this chapter is not concerned with the *study* of Egypt but with the *publishing* of Egypt. Moreover, considering Egypt as a field and subject for publication reveals certain elements of long-run continuity that extend into the present.

Between Denon and Carter, another significant figure in the developing study of Egypt, Amelia B. Edwards, defined a public face of archaeology: publication. (Another was museum display, and although the two often intersected, it is a topic outside the scope of this investigation.) Edwards, as the Secretary of the Egypt Exploration Fund, had made the Fund's incoherent (and slightly chaotic) book programme her special concern and interest.[2] While others considered the reports published by the Fund as simply a benefit of membership, she saw them as a primary means of promoting research and study. In the Fund's Annual Report for 1889–1890 she reported, "The sale of past memoirs [reports and monographs] is steadily increasing, and as I predicted since two or three years ago, the society has become not only a society of excavators, but important publishers and booksellers". She was herself a successful author, and her book *A Thousand Miles up the Nile* (1877) began a lifelong engagement with promoting Egyptological studies (Rice and MacDonald Chapter 1, this volume). She wrote books, lectured, campaigned, and in 1882 organized the Egypt Exploration Fund, the first independent association for the study of Ancient Egypt. It is perhaps not surprising that she saw publication as the most effective method of fulfilling the Fund's objectives for the dissemination of knowledge and for generating income.

By the time she died in 1892, she had put the Fund's publishing programme on a more business-like footing. A year before her death she had also published *Pharaohs, Fellahs and Explorers*, a collection of the many lectures she had given in the United States to raise interest in Egypt. But with this last book she also did much to establish a strand of popular-but-serious archaeological publishing that has lasted to the present day. The opening lines of *Pharaohs, Fellahs and Explorers* embodied the credo that she had advanced ever since her discovery of Egypt in 1877:

> It may be said of some very old places, as of some very old books, that they are destined to be forever new. The nearer we approach them, the more remote they seem; the more we study them, the more we have yet to learn. Time augments rather than diminishes their everlasting novelty; and to our descendants of a thousand years hence it may safely be predicted that they will be even more fascinating than to ourselves. This is true of many ancient lands, but of no place is it so true as of Egypt. Our knowledge of how men lived and thought in the Valley of the Nile five or six thousand years before the Christian era is ever on the increase. It keeps pace with the march of discovery, and that march extends every year over a wider area. Each season beholds the exploration of new sites, and each explorer has some new thing to tell … Thus the work of discovery goes on apace. Old truths receive unexpected corroboration; old histories are judged by the light of new readings; fresh wonders are disclosed wherever the spade of the digger strikes new ground. The interest never flags, the subject never palls upon us: the mine is never exhausted.

(Edwards 1891: 3–4)

The broad generic categories for publishing Ancient Egypt had been defined by the early 20th century. They still exist today.

- Fieldwork and survey reports.

- Academic monographs.

- Popular scholarly books.

- Illustrated or photographic books.

- Mystical or sensational: fiction and non fiction.

However, what distinguishes publications in the first three categories is an unusually heavy reliance on visual material. It might conceivably be argued that the study of Egypt is a branch of 'art' and therefore the predominance of visual material is to be expected; alternatively, that as a subset of archaeology, it relies on excavation drawings and images. However, I contend that after the production of the Ur-text of Egyptology, *Description de l'Égypte* (*Description* 1809–1828), the underlying cultural expectation was that books on the topic would take a specific visual and textual form.

The University of Edinburgh Library lists 285 items as "Egypt – Antiquities". The collection is not particularly comprehensive, but it is quite strong in the first three categories, and, to a degree, representative of the various types of books published. In terms of content, the different categories varied widely but the high ratio of image to text was a consistent factor. Thus W. M. Flinders Petrie's study of *Diospolis Parva*, published by the Fund in 1901, had a coloured frontispiece, plus 48 illustrations with a text of 62 pages (Petrie 1901).[3] The volume published by the Archaeological Survey of Egypt on the *Mastaba of Ptahhetep and Akhethetep (Saqqarah)* had 34 plates and the volume published by Bernard Quaritch in 1905 on the *Saqqarah Mastabas and Gurob* in 1905 had 45 plates and 50 pages of text. These rough and ready calculations may seem trivial, but they are precisely the factors considered by publishers when planning and pricing volumes.

When the Archaeological Survey of Egypt was launched under the direction of Francis Ll. Griffith, its first published report was on the work at Beni Hassan in 1893. In his Preface, Griffith outlined the Survey's objectives:

> … Our united aim has been perfection. We are proud even of our partial success; but we are conscious that we have not yet raised the work to what should be its ultimate level.
>
> (Griffith 1893: vii)

However, the cost of pursuing perfection, in terms of both time and money, was considerable. The demands of preparing the reports for the press were underestimated and the large ratio of image to text represented a high investment in terms of draughtsman's work (see James 1997: 164–180). It was perhaps unfortunate that Amelia Edwards died when she did, since it is clear that she had a sounder business sense than most of the other worthies who made up the committees of management. Once she had taken over the publications of the Fund, they appeared on time, reprints were put in hand for titles like *Pithom* that sold well, and crucially she developed sales beyond the distribution to the membership. Close relations were developed first with Trench Trübner, a firm then bought out by the Reverend Charles Kegan Paul to form Kegan Paul, Trench, Trübner. Kegan Paul's firm also failed, to be bought up by the more entrepreneurial George Routledge to form Routledge and Kegan Paul. However, the publisher's commitment to Egyptology continued, as it does in its current incarnation as Routledge, a division of Taylor & Francis. An even more significant supporter was the firm of Bernard Quaritch, founded in 1847, and the publisher of many important Egyptological works.

Both Quaritch and the Routledge business (through its Kegan Paul, Trench, Trübner imprint) developed a wide range of books that were scholarly in content, but wider in their appeal than the reports and surveys produced by the Egypt Exploration Fund.[4] Both companies continued to produce highly profitable 'popular scholarly' books, many of which proved to be extraordinarily long lived. Perhaps the prize should go to E. A. Wallis Budge, whose *Book of the Dead* was first published in 1898 and was still in print 100 years later. His study on *The Mummy* (first published in 1893) was also still in print in 1993. The works produced by Quaritch and Kegan Paul, Trench, Trübner provided a model that other publishers seem to have followed, in both Great Britain and the United States. The Society for the Promotion of Christian Knowledge published a translation of the huge text by Gaston Maspero, the doyen of French archaeological activity in Egypt, *The Dawn of Civilization: Egypt and Chaldea* in 1894. It too conformed to the standard of profuse illustration.

Ancient Egypt attracted writers who had no Egyptological experience themselves, but interpreted the published reports and fieldwork. Pre-eminent among them was an enterprising clergyman called James Baikie, born in 1866. At the age of 40, he wrote his first book on Egypt, *The Land of the Pharaohs* (1924), and never looked back. Thereafter, either for his principal publisher A. & C. Black, or his secondary publishers, Baikie published a book almost every year. He could turn his hand to anything – *Peeps at the Heavens* (1911) or *Peeps at the Royal Navy,* a patriotic effort in 1913 – but Egypt was his first love. He never visited the country, but published posthumously his most substantial book in 1932: 870 pages on *Egyptian Antiquities in the Nile Valley.* Baikie fully acknowledged the scholarly researchers who made his books possible, and did much to develop a popular audience for which Egyptologists themselves later published. Most successful was Howard Carter and A. C. Mace with the three volumes of *The Tomb of Tut-ankh-Amen, discovered by the late Earl of Carnarvon and Howard Carter* (1923). These also offered a high percentage of high quality photographs (Vol. 1: 188 pages text and 104 images; Vol. 2: 153 pages text and 140 images; Vol. 3: 182 pages text and 80 images). In the late 1930s and into World War II, Flinders Petrie published a number of popular scholarly books with Bernard Quaritch under the imprint of the British School of Archaeology in Jerusalem.

The problems with publishing fieldwork and survey reports continued. The costs of financing this work grew inexorably, and one indication of the future was that the huge two-volume report on 37 years of work on the Giza Necropolis was published between 1942 and 1955, *at the charge* of Harvard University Press and the Boston Museum of Fine Arts (Reisner 1942–1955). Scholarly work in its purest academic form was less and less likely to achieve a return for a commercial publisher. However, the demand by publishers for good quality Egyptological work that would appeal to a popular audience grew steadily, as these proved steady sellers. I. E. S. Edwards' *The Pyramids of Egypt* (1947) remains in the Penguin list, after many reprints, 56 years after its first publication. Thus, at the beginning of the third millennium, the fieldwork and survey report is in decline in terms of printed volume publication, and is (I believe) now better suited to other methods of more modern dissemination. Paradoxically, this pressure also affects publications at the other end of the spectrum. The size of the dedicated market for introductory texts in the teaching of Egyptology is not large.[5] Increasingly, it forms a module or group of modules within the structure of other courses, and students resist buying introductory texts with a limited use. Here, too, electronic resources are being developed to serve this market. Two good examples are the Egyptology Resources web page by the University of Cambridge (www.newton.cam.ac.uk/egypt), and the *Internet Ancient History Sourcebook – Egypt*, part of a major internet history resource run by Paul Halsall at Fordham University (www.fordham.edu/halsall/ancient/asbook04.html).[6] The academic monograph, last to arrive on the scene, is also a stagnant and static market, with much of its *raison d'être* absorbed by scholarly journal publication. However, popular scholarly books, illustrated books, and mystical and sensational works continue to flourish.

The publishing paratext

The link between image and text was significant in publishing Ancient Egypt from an early date. This was because of the need to explain (to scholar and non specialist alike) a wide range of material culture: epigraphy and papyri (in mysterious and pictographic scripts), architecture, painting, funerary and domestic objects. The compelling interest of hieroglyphs to western culture perhaps stemmed from their tantalizing legibility. Unlike, for example, Chinese pictographs, Egyptian hieroglyphs appeared capable of intuitive understanding, connection and analogy. From the 17th century, epigraphy assumed a priority; in the 19th century it became a *sine qua non*. Griffith, in the first publication of the Archaeological Survey, reserved special praise for a near-contemporary of Champollion, the Scot Robert Hay. He noted that Hay

> was content to amass in his portfolios one collection after another of detailed and minutely accurate drawings, copies of inscriptions, and plans that put to shame most of the contemporaries and later work. And he did this without being able to read one line of the strange characters which he facsimilied with so much care. He was without doubt convinced that such work would be valued by a future generation that would read the inscriptions with ease after the monuments themselves had been defaced.

(Griffith 1893: vii–viii)

This gloomy appraisal, that Ancient Egypt might survive only through the published record, underpinned Griffith's commitment to perfection. But the model for perfection, at least as far as publication was concerned, had already been established. Griffith looked back to the *Description*, but in the history of publication, one needs to go back one stage further, to the work of the erudite 17th century Jesuit, Athanasius Kircher (1602–1680) (Curran 2003: 124–129; Grafton 1991; Hassan 2003: 51, 58). His interpretation of hieroglyphics was erroneous, but it was not unsystematic. Almost single handed, Kircher generated a serious interest in Egypt through his publications. He was a polymath; one of his biographers described him with justice as the "master of 100 arts" (Reilly 1974). In 1650 he supervized the excavation of an Egyptian obelisk discovered beside the Appian Way. It was re-erected in 1652 at his instigation in the Piazza Navona, with Kircher (1650) having already published a study of its inscriptions (Hassan 2003: Figures 2:23, 2:26). Between 1652 and 1654, he published *Oedipus Aegyptiacus*, Kircher's major work on Egypt, in three large folio volumes, profusely illustrated.

What is of concern here is less Kircher's content than the manner of his publication. This is the area that Gérard Genette (1997: 1–2) has described as the 'paratexte' of any publication. He defined this as "what enables a text to become a book and to be offered as such to its readers and, more generally, to the public". This included format, editing, punctuation, chapter structure, typography, notes, appendices, images, translation, marketing and promotion: all the elements that mediate between the authorial text and the consumer. It is the paradigm which defines the genre for the reader: as a novel, a textbook, an academic monograph, an encyclopaedia and so on. It is not difficult for any literate person to differentiate one genre from another by simply recognizing its paratext.[7] In the case of the study of Egypt, any serious investigation from Kircher onwards was paratextually determined to include a strong visual element. The publication of *Description de l'Égypte* (*Description* 1809–1828) defined that paratext conclusively.

The publication of *Description* was an act of state, and on a scale worthy of the Napoleonic Empire (Gillespie and Dewachter 1987). It was one of the largest books ever published, with a paper size called 'Jésus', measuring more than 26 Old French inches vertically and 20 Old French inches horizontally (105 x 75 cm). The volumes contained in total more than 3,000 images engraved on 837 copper plates, more than a hundred of them double or triple fold spreads.

The largest were 40 inches by 20 inches in size. The format of the book, a huge folio called The Great Eagle (*Grand-aigle*) had been selected in 1792 as the format for the national cadastral survey, and there were therefore a number of paper mills and printers used to dealing with work on this scale. It was perhaps for this reason that an even larger paper size, *Le Grand Monde*, was rejected (http://perso.wanadoo.fr/cadastre/aigle.htm). While the name had no Napoleonic connotations, it may well have seemed apposite for this vast national scheme. Nothing on this scale had been attempted before, and no bookcase existed that could contain it. It was possible to order a special piece of mahogany furniture to accommodate the volumes:

> Its pilasters were carved in motifs of temples, lotus flowers, and busts from Thebes and Dendara. Two basilisks framed a winged globe set in a corniche of lotus leaves. There were fourteen narrow shelves to hold the albums horizontally and a vertical slot for each volume of text. The top could be raised to form a reading rack.

> (Gillespie and Dewachter 1987: 1)

The production of the work required more than one and a half million sheets of paper, difficult to manufacture with sufficient accuracy to take the fine line engravings. There were regular disputes between the Commission running the project and the paper makers (Desgranges) over the quality of the vellum 'velin' paper (the highest quality of wove paper) and many batches were rejected. The most difficult task was the production and the printing of the plates, which were considered to be the touchstone of quality for the entire enterprise. The production of the copper plates fell far behind the planned schedule. Only the automation of the process with a machine designed by the head of the Commission, Conté, allowed the work to be completed to an acceptable quality and within a reasonable timeframe. In all, the four Parisian printers chosen to print the plates produced 820,000 sheets, 60,000 of them in colour. A print run of 1,000 copies was planned for of the first, Napoleon, edition, but it was evident that this would nowhere near satisfy the demand. By about 1820, it had become obvious that there was a huge international demand for the work. A. M. Panckoucke

(1821–1830) was granted the right to publish a second edition with the proviso that any profits accruing to the government were to be split between the *savants* and artists involved in the enterprise and a fund to support the sciences and arts, in particular the art of engraving.

The second edition lacked something of the imperial grandeur of the original edition. The text was expanded but then printed in a smaller 8vo format. The plates were reprinted but folded to fit the smaller format volumes. The first versions of the text volumes had been published before the fall of Napoleon in 1815, and he also saw pulls of many of the plates. But he died in exile on St Helena without ever seeing the full extent of the work. One solace were flower pictures from the *Description* that Napoleon cut out to decorate the walls of his house on the island (Wilson-Smith 1996: 276). The restored king, Louis XVIII, continued to support the production as in the national interest and Panckoucke tactfully commissioned the fine frontispiece portrait of the king, the 'Médaille Égyptienne', and had a beautiful new emblematic frontispiece engraved and hand-coloured (to his own design).

Description de l'Égypte (and, further back, *Oedipus Aegyptiacus*) provided the paratext of visual profusion that most Egyptological books have followed ever since. It is fair to ask, however, whether this is an entirely beneficial heritage. By the end of the 19th century, the 'Archaeological Survey' was experiencing great difficulties with the cost of producing images, and finding suitable draughtsmen. The latter problem, together with problems in maintaining quality, had also frustrated production of the *Description*. The problem with images has continued into the present. In my own experience over many years of commissioning works on Egypt for Routledge, issues concerning visual images were the greatest cause of arguments with authors and the invariable source of cost-overruns. The tradition assumed that 'more is better', that the value of a book on Egypt might be judged in part by the number of illustrations it contained. Early popular scholarly books, where the text was the primary concern, often stated the number of images as part of the title, or used a phrase like 'With many illustrations' or 'Profusely illustrated'. The cost issue was a problem from the 17th century, but it has been exacerbated with the late 20th century professionalization of the sale of picture rights. There has been a dramatically escalating increase in the cost of permissions for reproduction.

Changing the paratext

A new model or paratext is therefore necessary for the communication of 'Egypt'. It is notable that the category of mystical and sensational books often sell without any images at all! There are now many ways in which Egypt's past is presented – on television, film and the internet – where a visually dominant element is essential, and 'profuse illustration' may no longer be so necessary for many categories of books on Egypt. In the past, the images used were often meaningful to the author and (I judge) probably meaningless to the reader. Often they bore little or no relationship to the text and they were badly captioned, if captioned at all. It is also possible to create a visual overload, with too many images of a similar type of object becoming tedious to the reader. The tradition which determined that 'more is better' had its origins in a cultural formation where visual images had a rather different role, demonstrating power and value rather than content. Now this element of the image has diminished and the audience for books on Egypt's past are (in this sense) more discriminating.

The reader wants powerful and effective images that enhance or 'explicate' the text. Many books from the past have achieved just such an effect. The numerous images in Howard Carter's description of the tomb of Tutankhamun were grouped in sections at the back of the book. The text was powerful and the images had a great impact, even when poorly reproduced. The cumulative impact of text and image was remarkable. Of course, the 'wonderful things' that he was describing, the excitement of the excavation and its aftermath, made this an ideal topic for a book. But the care with which the various elements within the book have been balanced and co-ordinated make it more effective than many more colourful and visual productions dealing with the same material.

Moving from the abstract to the particular, or from theory to practice, is a process fraught with difficulty. Instructional texts in publishing usually assume a static and settled practice that bears little relationship to reality. The archetype was Sir Stanley Unwin's *The Truth about Publishing* (1926), which reached its seventh edition in 1960.[8] Another example, by the Director of Princeton University Press, Herbert S. Bailey, appeared two years after Sir Stanley's demise. This had reached its third edition by 1990, is still in print, and continues to be read in Africa and Asia as a model for university press practice.

This desire to construct a positivistic 'theory from praxis' is common among publishers, and is itself illusory. Sir Stanley's account can be seen as an imaginative fiction about his own firm, a highly distorted vision of his own idiosyncratic working practice, and of the industry in general. Bailey's account also represents a mismatch between vision and reality, but he nevertheless ran a business of the highest quality and dramatized a central problem in publishing: whether a publisher's work was to be based on whim and fancy ('art') or whether there were inexorable underlying principles to be observed ('science'). Bailey thought both had their place, and who could quarrel with that? However, both of these panjandrums took a rather lordly view of authors, and therein lies the problem of applying their theories to the publishing of archaeology. But there are lessons that can be drawn from the early history of the publishing of Egyptology and from current practice. Furthermore, it is possible to see both opportunities and threats for the publishing of 'Egypt' in the future. I have suggested that since the early days of the Egypt Exploration Fund an idea of publishing practice was embedded within archaeology. It was archaeologists themselves rather than commercial publishing companies, university presses or museums who possessed this model of good practice. It was never formally elaborated into a theory, but it grew by accretion as a form of oral tradition. Perhaps for this reason, during my period of active commissioning, about 25 years, the archaeologists were collectively quite different from the other kinds of author with whom I worked.

Their interest in the physical form of the publication was more informed and articulate. In general terms, other authors were normally concerned about the size of the print run, whether the book was in paperback or hardback format, the overall number of illustrations, and the extent of advertising. Every archaeologist with whom I dealt was preoccupied with specific details of the visual material, captions and the interaction of image and text. It was not always a welcome intervention. The historic tradition of 'profuse illustration', which has always been part of the dominant paratext of books on Egyptology (and archaeology more generally), could create tension in author-publisher relationships. While the cost of producing images, as well as the increasing permission charges, turned publishers against the profuse use of visual material, archaeologists continued to expect large numbers of half tones and line illustrations.

The archaeologists were essentially right. But their insistence, which grew from the fundamental nature of archaeology as a discipline, had to be considered in the light of the changing economics of publishing. It was not always easy to persuade authors to reduce their demand for a large volume of visual material, especially when they often bore the considerable costs of producing the artwork themselves. They did not understand why it was more complex and difficult to produce images with text than to produce text alone. One author whom I prized was immensely difficult over the range of images in his books. Until, that is, he became in effect an archaeological *publisher* as well as an *author*.

Past publications in the field of Egyptology hold many lessons both for professional Egyptologists and for publishers. It is remarkable how static the publishing of Ancient Egypt has remained (and conversely how long-lasting many of the books have proved). However, their longevity often stems not from any exceptional quality but from the lack of a superior replacement. In many ways, the publications have become fossilized, and have not moved forward in the same manner as books in other fields. New standards should mean better and not worse books. A new paratext is needed which can accommodate the current economics of publishing, the changing nature of the audience, and new possibilities of distribution and marketing. In the past, Egyptology publishing was largely inwardly-directed, driven by professional needs, with the odd successful foray into the unknown territory of popular publishing. Now, while Egyptologists can publish and exchange professional information more easily and economically than ever before, they can no longer reach a large popular audience without the skill and guidance of publishers, or TV and film producers, as they could in the days of Howard Carter.

The overall market for 'Egypt', following the changing nature of the audience, has bifurcated, rather than atomized. The demand for 'Egyptological product' has never been greater, yet, paradoxically, professional Egyptologists are now less able to satisfy that demand than ever before. The demands on Egyptologists' time and services have increased exponentially. In the past, professional Egyptologists filled both academic and professional demands, and in some cases, the popular interest as well. This is no longer so easy. The professional demands of employers – whether universities, foundations or museums, to say nothing of audit-obsessed governmental and quasi-governmental bodies that provide funding for research – have reduced the time available for such fringe activity. Professional Egyptologists can actually damage their professional acceptability by achieving popular success. Even writing a textbook for students may be regarded with disapproval.

Publishers too are driven by changed needs. An individual title, however successful, is now less desirable than a flow of publications into the market. While 'list' or 'portfolio' management is not a science of publishing, it certainly makes sense within the current structures of the publishing industry. An odd, random, Egyptology book will increasingly only make sense within a publisher's list if it sits alongside other books which can be marketed to the same audience. The publisher's knowledge of, and commitment to, that audience ought logically to increase with increased investment and market share. The reality is that Egyptology will generally be enfolded within a broader range of editorial and marketing responsibilities. That, of course, is what has always happened. Only a few publishers, past or present, have seen Egyptology publishing as a major component in their list, on a par with, say, new fiction or history. However, the intensity of the popular passion for the subject is just as great (or greater) than these much larger publishing entities. The career of John Louis Romer (1981, 1982, 1993) epitomizes such a popular interest. His passion for Egypt began, like Howard Carter, as an archaeological artist, but through his books and television programmes he has become the best known 'face' in the modern study of Egypt. He has an idiosyncratic style, lambasting the Egyptological establishment in the west and bureaucratic inertia in Egypt with equal intolerance. He communicates a passionate concern for Egypt to those who read his books and watch his television programmes. There are perhaps two ways for professional Egyptologists to regard the Romer phenomenon. The first is to disapprove, on the grounds that even *haute vulgarisation* is unwelcome and harmful. The second is to view it as a 'competitive advantage' in gaining attention and financial support for what is a fringe discipline. Those whom the popular work like Romer's catches as children are often the Egyptology students of the future. The same complaints about vulgarisation that were raised about Howard Carter's 'showmanship' are now being re-directed at John Romer.

Enterprising publishers should see in the popular passion for 'Egypt' an opportunity that can be developed and exploited much more effectively than it is at present. However, the market is not quite what it seems at first sight. The publishing of Egyptology can be seen as a spectrum, ranging from readers who believe that the pyramids were created by aliens from the far recesses of the universe to professional epigraphists. In this spectrum, John Romer and similar authors now occupy a kind of mid point. Romer, through his film, TV and publishing has created what is effectively a new publishing category. Publishers have to choose which segment of the spectrum they wish to occupy.

Within Egyptology, there are now effectively two niche markets. The first, popular, extends from the pyramidologists at one end to Romer-style books at the other. The second extends onwards to highly specialized monographs. Notionally, both segments are part of the same market. In practice, they are not. Understanding the nature of a real, as opposed to an apparent, market is not always easy. Mailing lists cannot usually discriminate one kind of interest in 'Egypt' from another. These differences only become clear within any market when it is expressed in terms of a spectrum. Every niche market has its periphery: setting Egyptology across a spectrum makes these peripheral relationships clear.

The popular extremity of 'Egypt' is closer in marketing terms to areas entirely outside the subject than to the scholarly end of the same spectrum. Using a spectrum structure makes it possible (and sensible) to envisage a larger potential market than the tight boundaries of the niche would suggest. The chosen spectrum depends upon the nature of the publisher. From a publisher's perspective an identity of content should be less significant than the parameters of an identifiable market. Within the spectrum these are cognate publications although they may look very different. Those who buy 'Romer' and become enthusiasts for Egyptology may eventually buy further up the spectrum. For this reason, a list that currently embraces only highly specialized monographic work could consider extending it to a broader audience, while a list that focuses upon the Romer-type material might consider publishing selectively for the higher level. Such publishers would be well placed to produce educational or textbook material.

The popular books depend (as they did in the first half of the 20th century) upon the specialized work of professional archaeologists. Some are still written by working Egyptologists, but to a decreasing extent for the reasons outlined above. The skill of the writer is to interpret complexity for the benefit of a non-professional audience. Conversely, professional works can be made more accessible to a wider audience by adopting the skills of the writer or presenter. Michael Rice (1984: vi) has sensibly observed that archaeology began with the 'diggers', then developed the associate disciplines of the 'classifiers', and now has come to depend upon the 'presenters'. The role of the presenter is to judge the appropriate style or register to explain the same body of Egyptological material to a different audience. The concept of register does not yet feature within the technical vocabulary of either marketing or publishing, but it should. Every publication operates within what linguists would call a different register (Butler 1999), the necessary tonality and approach to achieve the most effective communication. The professional language or structure of abbreviations, jargons, and professional debate necessary for an academic dialogue is rarely suitable for a non-professional audience. The reverse holds true. However, it is possible, using the same body of data, to shift the register in order to make the book more appropriate to the needs of different categories of reader. However, more than a change of tone in the text is needed. The shift extends across the whole range of publishing attributes: text length, design, typography, and use of images.

Matters of detail are important when publishing within the scholarly paratext, but they can become even more significant when re-presenting the same body of content further down the spectrum. Thus, Jan Picton (pers. comm.) has suggested that no book should be published without a simple indication of scale for any object depicted. It could be included within a caption or might be presented graphically. Most professionals in the field would regard this as essential information for an archaeologist but also useful for the non-professional. Yet this is not done as a matter of course. Too few authors provide the information and many publishers are silently grateful to be relieved of an additional editorial and production burden. Yet this is a flaw of the same order of irritation as the lack of an index. Most reputable publishers would not consider publishing a serious book without an index, and they still mutter to each other *sotto voce* that a slew of literals or typographical mistakes is unprofessional. Yet presenting a book with inadequate visual material – photographs of poor image quality, graphics that do not illuminate the text, maps printed at too small a scale, inadequate captions – is an equally grave fault. It is also a source of confusion and irritation to the reader. A professional reader may be well aware that a statue of Ramesses II is huge, while another statuette is the size of child's toy. Television presenters have adopted the old trick of using a human body to give a precise sense of scale. But very few popular books bother to inform about size and scale.

Rice's 'presenter' (the term derives from television) is a much amplified version of the old-style cicerone. If a book is intended for a non-professional audience (including students and their textbooks), both categories – 'presenters' and 'scholars' – have to possess the same attributes: they both have to be fully aware of the scholarly material, arguments or debates, and they need to be able to breach the tightly circumscribed limits of what is considered appropriate in purely professional debates. As a result they are often considered controversial within the academy.

No doubt some sensitive scholars do not want their work to rub shoulders with more popular books within the same list. But for the most part this is not an issue, since most concerned recognize the need to publish more popular work within a scholarly or academic publisher in order to build a bridge. A market relationship is constructed across that bridge, a continuing relationship with the reader. The business aim is that readers become repeat customers, so long as the publisher continues to supply material fulfilling their increasingly complex demands.

Today we should be looking forward, seeing how to continue to enlarge the market for Egyptology. A new paratext should look forward to embracing the hypertextual possibilities that will appear once the 'e-book' has developed to the point of being a usable technology. In any printed text there are limits to the uses that can be made of images. They are static, printed to fixed scale and from a single perspective. With access to electronic digitized images, all these limitations vanish. So too, with instantaneous online access and a form of pay-to-view for images, a vast repertoire of additional material is now available. Imagine an electronic text in Egyptology that looks like a book, feels like a book, but is in fact a point of access to a larger body of material. From the author's perspective, it breaks down the limitations imposed by tight economics of book publishing. From the publisher's perspective, it allows a new degree of imaginative publications. And, from the reader's viewpoint, it allows the purchase of a magical text, one with near-infinite possibilities.

Ancient Egypt is unique in one special sense. The "wonderful things" that Carter saw are equally interesting to scholars and to the interested general reader. There are no inherent barriers between one level of knowledge and another. The two million 'hits' that the Egyptology Resources website received between May 1998 and June 1999 must have covered a very wide range of interests, and from schoolchildren to university Egyptologists. Moreover, the close interrelationship between text and image in the publishing of Ancient Egypt must now address the means of making this relationship flourish. It is not simply a matter of carrying across all the paratextual elements from the old format into the new. The new opportunities of electronic or e-book publishing generate their own opportunities and problems. Within a decade we shall have moved beyond the present electronic incunabula to real electronic books. To secure the future of publishing Ancient Egypt, now is the time to plan ahead.

Notes

1   In fact, to be fair to Carter, he could see very little, since at that point electric light had not been shone into the chamber.

2 I have not been able to undertake archival work in the records of the Egyptian Exploration Society (as the Fund later became known). My conclusions are drawn from the published accounts and annual meetings of the Fund. These, however, are revealing. Each meeting received a full financial statement and reports, and the session usually concluded with a lecture.

3 In each of these examples, I have excluded preliminary and end matter, as well as appendices. Although this is not an ideal arrangement – since appendices may sometimes form an integral part of the text – it does at least provide comparability between books.

4 The publishing company Routledge now has no connection with the imprint Kegan Paul which was relinquished during a company reorganization in the 1980s.

5 The Oriental Institute, Chicago ran a highly successful museum education programme in 1998–1999 that was designed to use improved 'curriculum materials' to replace textbooks at school level. This is a useful low-cost adjunct to internet access.

6 The site also contains an interesting brief account of itself: "History: Egyptology Resources, set up in 1994, was the first web page set up specifically for the benefit of those interested in Egyptology, whether laymen or professionals. From May 1998 to June 1999, the site received in the region of 2 million hits! Media and awards: This page was featured in the July 1995 issue of *Personal Computer World*, the 27 September 1995 issue of *The Times*, and the 26 March 1998 issue of *The New York Times*. Versions: The site began purely as text, although the Egyptology Resources picture appeared fairly soon after. It then went through an intermediate version with a rather over-coloured image map for linking to the pages (about 1995). A change was then made to the black background, first with frames and arrangements, using fewer graphics, was adopted." This is information of great value and more sites should adopt a similar practice. The *Internet Sourcebooks* at Fordham are an invaluable resource covering many aspects of history (www.fordham.edu/halsall/ancient/asbooks04.html).

7 One type of post-modern trickery has been to displace the paratext of one genre with another: so a novel is presented with prefaces, introduction, appendices, and even an index.

8 An eighth edition was published in 1976, "revised and partly re-written by Philip Unwin". This had shrunk back from 350 pages of Sir Stanley's final recension to the more modest scale of his first thoughts. It remains in print in the United States (Unwin 1976).

Acknowledgments

I would like to acknowledge the very valuable help and advice of Michael Rice and Jan Picton in the preparation of this chapter.

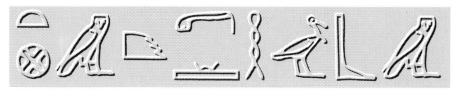

CHAPTER 12

HIJACKED IMAGES: ANCIENT EGYPT IN FRENCH COMMERCIAL ADVERTISING

Bernadette Schnitzler

While commercial advertising is primarily driven by the economic priorities of development and customer loyalty it also offers, within its commercial constraints, "a place that reflects a period's deep tendencies, qualms, myths and modern sensibilities" (Fresnault-Deruelle 1989: 11). It thus becomes a reflection of an age, its mentality, and represents certain aspects of a society. In a direct or subconscious manner the terminology employed in advertisements relates to collective memory, a cultural heritage shared by humanity as a whole. "Advertising imagery functions as an allegory: using iconic elements, it establishes a system of values that constitutes a brand's symbolic or descriptive lexicon" (Fresnault-Deruelle 1989: 11). Thus, through complex psychological processes, this imagery becomes associated with obscure feelings, desires or dormant fantasies: a desire for prestige, originality, to please, to escape … Through the use of clever conditioning techniques, the images become so powerfully suggestive that they push the consumer into purchasing the product. Through buying a product, one also acquires a lifestyle or self-image – a reflection of the images contained within the advert – which fits in with the specific social and cultural context that the advert conveys. The range of idealistic images used to attract consumers can thus be identified. The acquired product becomes a symbol, which identifies the buyer with a particular group, or which suggests itself as a means of social promotion.

The first contacts between advertising and Ancient Egypt can be found from the early 19th century, but mass commercial exploitation of antiquity began in the second half of the century with the growth of international exhibitions, illustrated magazines, newspapers and trade catalogues. The early 20th century saw the diversification of promotional media, with events and publications increasingly targeted at particular consumer groups; the number of ladies' magazines aimed at housewives, for example, grew rapidly from the 1930s (Sullerot 1966). This trend continued throughout the 20th century, and across western capitalist countries a sophisticated advertising industry emerged, developing new media for mass and niche promotions through street advertising, commercial radio and television and, most recently, digital media. Campaigns have often employed a range of interconnected media designed to have a cumulative effect: posters and images, notices and advertisements in the press, product packaging and labels, promotional offers – not forgetting the numerous advertisements that disseminate cultural stereotypes on TV screens worldwide.

This globalization of advertising required the use of imagery and terminology that could be widely understood and frequently also required the need to refer to a common heritage. The Egyptian civilization was considered to be a favourable vector as, along with ancient Greece, it was often portrayed as a 'cradle' of western society. The European fascination with Egypt dates back to the days of ancient Rome, when it was perceived as a flamboyant and mysterious country. Europe's progressive rediscovery of Egypt followed several chronological stages (Vercoutter 1986). It began in the late Middle Ages and Renaissance with the accounts of numerous travellers attracted by its history, monuments and landscapes, followed in the 18th century by the development of the Masonic movement, which was strongly influenced by Ancient Egypt (Hamill and Mollier 2003; Ucko and Champion 2003).

The scholars who accompanied Bonaparte during his Egyptian campaign were another powerful agency in this rediscovery. The publication of the ten-volume work *Description de l'Égypte* – under the direction of Dominique Vivant-Denon, first Director of the Louvre Museum, made Egypt 'fashionable' throughout Europe (*Description* 1809–1828). Egyptian styling heavily influenced early First Empire designers, disseminating Egyptian themes into all aspects of architecture and art (Humbert and Price 2003). The establishment of important collections, such as those of Consuls Drovetti and Salt, helped European museums to accumulate numerous works of Egyptian art. At the same time, images of ancient Egyptian and Nubian monuments were popularized by drawings, engravings, watercolours and – later – photographs. The field of ancient Egyptian history was opened up by Champollion's decipherment of hieroglyphics.

By the mid-19th century, scientific research in this area centred on several important Egyptologists: Young and Wilkinson in Great Britain, and Lepsius in Germany (Jeffreys 2003). In 1836 the raising of the Luxor obelisk in Paris was an event that had an impact far beyond French borders (Hassan 2003: Figure 2:39). The 'Expositions Universelles' of 1867 and 1900 portrayed French colonies and faraway lands, particularly Egypt, as exotic and mysterious and events such as the opening of the Suez Canal in 1869 brought Egypt to the forefront of world news. European trading and sporadic colonization of the eastern Mediterranean (including Egypt) attracted the attention of the general public in the west. This increased exposure eventually led to the development of numerous 'clichés', boasting of the exoticism or quality of oriental products such as tobaccos and textiles. These included 'Filtra Orient' and 'Xanthia' cigarettes and tobacco from the Orient, 'Efka' cigarette papers, and the cotton fabrics, silk goods and perfumes offered under the 'Jumel' brand. 'Crüwell' tobaccos employed vast historical frescos illustrating the glories of the pharaoh (Figure 12:1 col. pl.).

Prominent archaeological discoveries became the subject of extensive press coverage – the discovery of the Deir el-Bahri royal mummy cache in 1881 could have come straight out of a detective novel – and the public soon grew passionate about this area of research and the 'treasures' uncovered. Fifty years later, Howard Carter and Lord Carnarvon's famous excavation of Tutankhamun's tomb in November 1922 produced a wave of 'Egyptomania' that spread throughout Europe. Evidence of this can be see in contemporary advertisements, particularly for luxury products (quality clothing, ornaments, perfumes), which associated the refinement of Egyptian civilization – as revealed by archaeological discoveries – with the tastes of an ever-expanding, urbanized, middle-class society. Textiles labelled as "a legacy from the reign of Tut-ankh-Amon", 'Pharaoh' blouses and 'Luxora' dresses are but a few examples of the numerous clothing lines inspired by Egypt, specifically the public's fascination with the discovery of the young pharaoh's intact tomb. The same theme also inspired a varied selection of perfume bottles, produced by the period's most prestigious crystal manufactures (Rice and MacDonald Chapter 1, this volume: Figure 1:4; Pantazzi 1994: 506–514).

Commercial exploitation of Ancient Egypt was particularly prevalent in France, Great Britain, Italy and Germany, the countries most heavily involved in Egypt's 'rediscovery'; the creative fields of these countries are particularly rich in references. Through the import of European fashions, products and various objects, the USA was also exposed to Egyptian styles and ideas which, in turn, influenced many architects and designers in the New World. Opera, cinema, literature and – more recently – cartoons have all contributed to the popularization of Ancient Egypt (Lupton Chapter 2, Sevilla Cueva Chapter 4, Serafy Chapter 5, all this volume), and to the development of ancient Egyptian 'clichés' which continue to affect western perceptions.

The conscious use of historical themes in advertising is based upon a set of reference points that are well anchored in the collective memory. Egypt constitutes one such inexhaustible reservoir, full of themes and images that were frequently exploited by commercial advertising during the 20th century. These include monuments (such as pyramids, obelisks or the Sphinx), historical or mythological figures (ancient Egyptian pharaohs or divinities), or references to world-famous works of art (such as the bust of Nefertiti or the statue of the 'seated scribe'). Each advertisement contains a core concept and a set of images that are selected to maximize impact on the intended consumer audience. The analysis of iconic images and the identification of underlying messages, and the values which the stereotype supposedly represents, open up a carefully maintained world of dreams and fantasy, references and images, "all feeding from visions from around the world and from cultural, social, ideological and mythic approaches" (Fresnault-Deruelle 1989: 11).

Such images function according to cleverly-weighted processes, where each product is associated with a specific symbolic value. Thus, the advertising world takes Egyptian themes and engineers them to portray such things as ambience, humour, self-image and technical arguments.

Pyramids are, without question, the monuments that have inspired the greatest number of designers (Humbert 2003). They evoke, through their enduring monumentality, resistance to time and an impenetrable aura of mythical eternity. The pyramids of Giza – particularly that of Kheops, the most imposing of the group – constitute one of the most powerful symbols of Egypt for the general public. They combine the mystery of lost civilizations, the fantasy of fabulous treasure and the dream of everlasting life (Adam 1988). Pyramids have served as a major advertising success. For example, in advertising 'Gestetner', the slogan "the unshakeable trust" was accompanied by an illustration in which a monumental pyramid served as the pedestal for a photocopier, with a thunderstorm in the background. This imagery therefore identifies the brand's strength and power with the pyramid's unalterable resistance to time. During the 1930s, Renault used the same concept with the "car that lasts" campaign, in which a Renault car appeared against a backdrop of three stylized pyramids. In 1984, Peugeot – another car manufacturer – employed a similar approach for the promotion of its 305 model. It used "all claws out" as its slogan, and presented the car in the famous avenue of ram-headed sphinxes in front of Karnak's temples. Peugeot also exploited its victory at the Rally of the Pharaohs by using "By Osiris! What a victory" as its advertising slogan, in which the car is represented in an Egyptian-like frieze. This concept of the 'hijacked' Egyptian fresco, in which a modern object is placed within an authentic antique setting, has often been used in advertisements that employ images of Ancient Egypt.

In addition to a touch of esotericism the image of the pyramid also carries connotations of the wisdom attained by the Egyptian civilization. The logo for the Editions Odile Jacob, for example, is a triangle/pyramid upon which the publishing house's name is elegantly inscribed. The pyramid, depicted under a starlit Egyptian sky, is a potent symbol of exoticism and the romantic. The advertisement for J&B whisky – "JB for the Night" – used this image, with a beautiful couple sitting on a rock, gazing at the moon over the Giza pyramids. 'Camel' cigarettes, 'The Nile' cigarette paper and 'Gauloises blondes' – with its use of an upturned pyramid resting on its apex and the slogan "Gauloises Blondes. Completely insane" – exploit Egypt's exoticism, lending consumers a sense of originality and non-conformity (Figure 12:2). The pyramid has also been used to market more commonplace products such as 'Brise Pyramide' deodorant or Nestlé's 'Les Pyramides' chocolate, the packaging for these items being visually prominent on supermarket shelving.

Egyptian mummies have also been used in advertising. Young and attractive mummies were awakened from their millennial sleep by the magic of 'Hollywood' chewing-gum or by drinking 'Perrier' sparkling water. Page's multipurpose wipes are used to wrap – like a mummy – a young and smiling Egyptian girl, the slogan announcing that "housewives are going to get all wrapped up about these new multipurpose cotton wipes". Such examples demonstrate how advertisers adapt history to their own ends, making it appeal to the 'typical' customer, whilst often attempting to win them over by making them laugh. The Carbel brand, which used to produce ink ribbons for typewriters, used a similar idea. Its very long 'Osiris Carbel' ribbon could be compared with the kilometres of bandaging used to wrap the mummies of Ancient Egypt.[1]

The sphinx of Giza is another monument that has attained universal status. Although it has appeared only rarely in advertisements, it too has been used to suggest longevity, mystery and exoticism. During the 1920s, 'Laurens' cigarettes employed a red sphinx as an advertising logo, their hoardings showing the sphinx within an oval frame backed by a starlit sky and three small pyramids in the distance. "Ramsès rice powder with its secret Sphinx flavour" (Figure 12:3) was a great success with elegant Parisian women at the beginning of the 20th century. Its success was such that, from 1927, the crystal manufacturer Baccarat created a receptacle for it, designed to resemble a canopic vase (Humbert et al. 1994: 548). The German steel pin manufacturer Heusch sold its products under the 'Sphinx' logo, which it displayed on small metal pin-boxes. In 1924, Neyret produced finely-worked gloves under the

Figure 12:2   Advertisement for the "Completely insane" Gauloises Blondes cigarettes (Archaeological Museum, Strasbourg).

brand 'Sphinx', probably in response to the wave of 'Egyptomania' following the discovery of Tutankhamun's tomb.

Despite its frequent presence in ancient Egyptian monumental and funerary contexts the obelisk has rarely been used in advertising. Its vertical shape is, like the pyramid, associated with notions of power and conquest. In 1928, the Saint-Louis Crystal Factory created the obelisk-shaped 'Bichara' perfume bottle. Embellished with

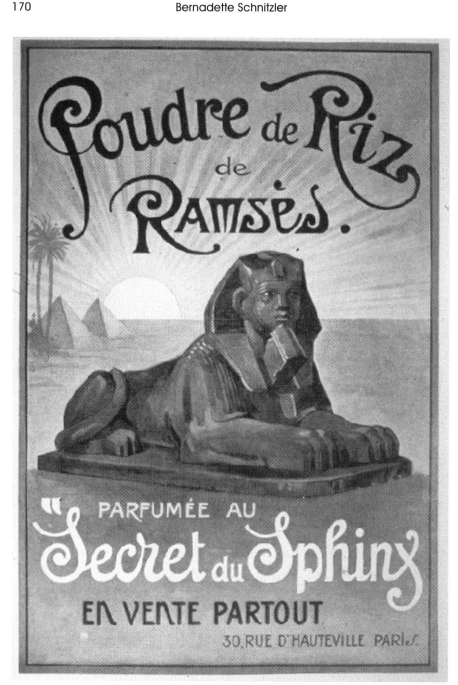

Figure 12:3   Poster for the "Ramsès rice powder with its secret Sphinx flavour" (Archaeological Museum, Strasbourg).

fine golden hieroglyphics, it was a scale model of the Place de la Concorde obelisk in Paris, and referred both to the mystery and power of Ancient Egypt, and to the elegance of 20th century Parisian life (Humbert *et al.* 1994: 550–551).

Powerful pharaohs and beautiful queens frequently feature in advertising, Queen Cleopatra being particularly favoured. Numerous ornaments and beauty products used the name of this queen – famous for her radiant beauty, artful seduction and taste for luxury – in order to achieve 'brand identification', a concept highly valued by commercial advertising. 'Cleopatra' soap is a good example of such a promotion; white in colour and pure as alabaster, the soap was branded as Egyptian with a deeply engraved cartouche, while the packaging was coloured blue and gold to denote pomp and splendour. 'Ellicor de Sinuhé' liqueur, which was produced in Barcelona, old Spain, also bore the name Cleopatra. 'Nefertiti and Cleopatra' cigarettes employed the same concept, and a 'Cleopatra' watch was described as being "of timeless beauty". Cleopatra Grains of Gold for "opulent and firm shapes" were advertised by the Lemaire pharmacy of Paris in 1934 (Figure 12:4). In 1923, a few months after the

Figure 12:4   Advertisement for "Cleopatra Grains of Gold" (Archaeological Museum, Strasbourg).

discovery of Tutankhamun's tomb, an advertisement for a laxative called 'Rectopanbiline' was published in the medical journal *Aesculape* (Figure 12:5). The report referred to the young king, and attempted to link the medical knowledge of Egyptian priests with modern medicine.

Some particularly famous Egyptian sculptures have been used in advertisements to suggest a subtle link between the intellectual achievements of Ancient Egypt and sophisticated modern technology. For example, the famous 'seated scribe' sculpture has been used to praise the merits of 'Algorel' – a software maintenance firm – and a low relief showing King Snofru using a computer has been used to promote IBM. The ancient Egyptian symbols of the sundisk and the winged vulture were displayed on ear-plug boxes, promising calm and protection to the wearer.

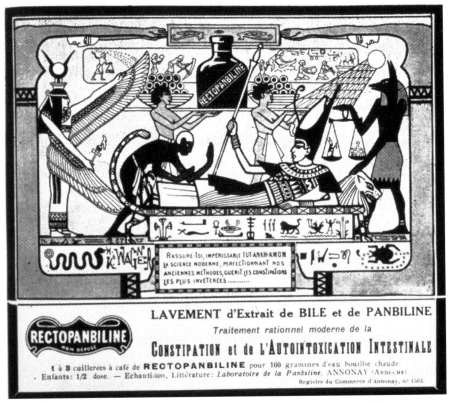

Figure 12:5   Advertisement for the medicine Rectopanbiline (Archaeological Museum, Strasbourg).

'Sheba' cat food represents another very interesting example. During the 1990s this firm launched a major advertising campaign based entirely on the theme of Ancient Egypt. The "Secrets of Sheba" campaign used images of the cat-goddess Bastet on its posters and tins. Through sophisticated, evocative and mysterious graphics Sheba attempted to attract potential customers by involving them in a virtual and elitist world designed especially for them.

Over the last few years the advertising industry has sought to expand its markets by increasingly focusing its efforts on young people. In 1997, the confectioner Kinder played on the public fascination with Egypt and created a collection of seven "Egypto-cat" figurines for 'Kinder Surprise' chocolate eggs. Children, already familiar with Ancient Egypt through the numerous cartoons located there (e.g. the French and Belgian adventure comic strips 'Papyrus' or 'Blake and Mortimer'), were immediately captivated by these small, amusing and collectable figurines.

Of all known ancient civilizations Egypt has undoubtedly achieved the most universal renown. In the eyes of advertisers at least it constitutes a 'sure bet' for most of western Europe and North America, and images derived from its culture provide points of intellectual reference in a world that is constantly evolving (Debbane 1987: 2). For the historical, political and economic reasons described above, Britain,

Germany and France were the most heavily affected by this phenomenon. Nonetheless, other European countries and later America have also experienced an enduring 'Egyptomania' (see e.g. Lupton Chapter 2, this volume). By evoking this ancient and glorious civilization – which now constitutes part of a common human heritage – there is reference to a reassuring immutability, a perfect and timeless beauty of a semi-sacred era. This return to the origins of civilization, with its nostalgic reminiscences of a distant and almost mythical past, affords the possibility to transcend today's world by conveying the reassuring illusion of a golden age. Egypt constitutes a unique case. No other civilization – whether it be the Celts, the Roman Empire, the formidable Vikings, the fabulous Incas or the warring Emperors of China – has held the fascination of so many people for so long.

Note

1   Most of the sources used in this chapter were originally gathered together in connection with the ArchéoPub exhibition, which was conceived and mounted by the Strasbourg Archaeological Museum in 1994.

CHAPTER 13

ALTERNATIVE EGYPTS

Lynn Picknett and Clive Prince

Ever since Egyptology emerged as an academic discipline in the 19th century it has coexisted with a corpus of theories and ideas about Ancient Egypt that are based less on conventional history and archaeology than on esoteric tradition and romantic visions. These non-academic views present an image of Ancient Egypt in sharp contrast to the one that emerged from 'mainstream' Egyptology, and until recently consisted of a loose body of competing theories about the nature and significance of Ancient Egypt that lacked a coherent identity and 'label'. However, in the 1990s, the current representatives of this school of thought began to use the term 'alternative Egypt' or 'alternative Egyptology'. (Academic Egyptologists were less kind: for example, Dr Zahi Hawass, the Egyptian official responsible for the Giza Plateau, bluntly called them 'pyramidiots'.)

The last decade of the 20th century saw a significant change. For the first time the new camp began to present a unified front, transforming itself effectively into a popular version of the academic discipline, with its own body of literature, periodicals and international conference circuit. This rode on the back of the explosion of popular interest in the mysteries of Ancient Egypt (as well as many other aspects of ancient history), undoubtedly due to the approach of the new millennium.

There were two noticeable results of this development. The first was the emergence of what almost amounted to an 'orthodoxy' within the alternative field, as one particular set of theories began to dominate the revisionist picture, particularly of the origins and early history of Ancient Egypt and its place in the development of human civilization. The second was that for the first time, the mainstream and alternative camps came into direct and open debate, albeit one still characterized by mutual mistrust and at times open hostility. This was largely the initiative of the alternative side, or at least a response to the demands of their audience, who wanted to test the reaction of Egyptologists to the new and exciting ideas. The increased interest among the general public also made Egyptologists and academics in other fields aware that there was a need to present the conventional side of the argument to a wider audience, although this was by and large the initiative of individuals – few academic institutions were inclined to take up the challenge. The 'pyramidiots' could no longer be ignored.

Another result of this popularist movement was that alternative Egyptologists, now lionized as international media stars, were able to take a more direct role in events in Egypt, particularly Giza, than had previously been possible – even to the point that on occasion they actually influenced decisions by the official bodies responsible for archaeological work at Giza.

Defining the alternatives

The broadest definition of 'alternative Egyptology' is that it is a collection of theories and interpretations of the origins, history and achievements of the ancient Egyptian civilization that are at variance with those accepted by 'mainstream' Egyptologists, historians and archaeologists. The literature is generally aimed at either a popular market or a specialized audience such as the New Age movement.

'Alternative Egyptology' is also characterized by the amateur status of its proponents, in the sense that they are seldom academically qualified and do not work within the protocols of academia. Many arrive at their theories because of their professional expertise in other fields (for example, in engineering, architecture or mathematics) and most are essentially self-taught in Egyptology. The alternative theorists argue that as they are independent of the scholastic world, particularly the constrictions of its funding mechanism, they are free to pursue lines of thought and inquiry that would not be permitted within academia. This is another reason for the disdain with which the alternative camp is treated by mainstream Egyptology: they are seen as ill-informed amateurs or impertinent outsiders.

The great majority of alternative theories focus on the earliest period of the ancient Egyptian civilization. This is in part because of its remoteness from our own time and therefore our incomplete knowledge about that era – many uncertainties still remain about the precise chronology and social structure of early dynastic Egypt. But undoubtedly the main reason is the awe-inspiring achievements of the Old Kingdom, as reflected most obviously in the pyramids and Great Sphinx of Giza.

A hallmark of alternative theories is the belief that the accepted chronology of Egyptian history is radically in error, and that the origins of Egyptian civilization, and in particular the dates for the building of the Giza pyramids and Sphinx, should be pushed back several thousand years into the past. (In some theories, the conventional dating of the Giza monuments is accepted, but it is argued that the builders were the heirs of the knowledge and techniques of a much older civilization.)

These views, of course, clash head-on with the teachings of mainstream Egyptology and the archaeological evidence of predynastic and early dynastic Egypt, and their proponents argue that mainstream Egyptologists are too conservative, incompetent or even engaged in a conspiracy to deceive the public.

A second characteristic feature of this world is the contention that not only were the Ancient Egyptians more scientifically and technologically advanced than Egyptologists acknowledge, but that their knowledge eclipses even that of our own day. Many theories take the view, in one form or another, that the ancient Egyptian priesthood possessed great scientific or magical secrets – which still remain beyond our grasp. Some claim that they were highly evolved technologically.

These ideas spring from the many unanswered questions about the technical achievements of the Ancient Egyptians, such as the building of the pyramids – particularly the Great Pyramid of Kheops. It is frequently argued that, for practical and logistical reasons, it is impossible to have constructed the Great Pyramid and its neighbours with the level of skill that the ancients were supposed to have possessed. Many of the blocks are too vast to have been moved by teams of workers with only ropes and wooden sleds, let alone raised to the level at which they were placed; the entire monument would require more labour than was available to the Old Kingdom rulers; the precision of the building is without parallel. Therefore the possession of some other form of technological skill – perhaps in a form unrecognized by our society, such as a mastery of acoustics – must have been involved.

Although the Great Pyramid is the favourite example of this line of reasoning, there are many others, large and small: the enormous limestone blocks or the granite blocks of Giza's Valley Temple and the Ancient Egyptians' skill in working and drilling granite without (if conventional thinking is correct) even iron tools, are two examples among many.

Because of these two cornerstones of alternative belief – the vast antiquity of the civilization and its access to advanced knowledge and technology – alternative theorists see Egypt in a much wider context that challenges accepted views of the origins, development and very nature of *all* human civilization. It is argued that Egypt is linked to an even older and even more advanced civilization, and its monumental achievements were either really those of that superior culture (did the Great Pyramid exist long before the rise of the ancient Egyptian civilization – and was it simply adopted by Kheops?), or the result of its legacy of knowledge.

Generally, proponents of this view – the most high profile in recent years being British journalist Graham Hancock (1995, 2001) – invoke the existence of a technologically advanced, global civilization that predated and influenced all others; a civilization that remains completely unrecognized by conventional historians (generally because it was destroyed in a great cataclysm). Many identify this civilization with Plato's Atlantis – the academics' much derided 'A-word'.

Other iconoclasts look to the stars for the civilization that shaped Ancient Egypt, proposing that extraterrestrial beings were responsible for building the pyramids and bringing civilization to the Nile Valley (and elsewhere on Earth) – a view advanced most prominently by Temple (1998) in *The Sirius Mystery*. The theme has also been used as the basis for popular movies such as *Stargate* and *The Fifth Element*.

Most alternative theories are not content with merely revising accepted history and understanding of Ancient Egypt, but take a prophetic line, suggesting that it has a direct relevance for our own time, usually in some mystical way linked with imminent changes on a worldwide scale. There are several variations of this concept, but broadly they fall into one of two categories. The first involves some impending world-shaking event – for example, some claim that the Egyptians left warnings about a catastrophe that was about to devastate the Earth in the near future, perhaps also kindly leaving advice on how to escape or avert it. The second relates to a shift in the collective consciousness that will be sparked off either as a consequence of the rediscovery of lost secrets or in the form of a spiritual reawakening triggered – somehow – by the monuments themselves.

Central to many of these heady concepts is the idea of a great discovery waiting beneath the sands of Egypt, perhaps locked within the Great Pyramid – a discovery that will vindicate certain theories or will prove to be linked to the prophetic material discussed above. This became a particularly prominent feature of the alternative Egypt scene in the 1990s, focusing on an alleged repository of ancient secrets known as the Hall of Records.

The Giza Plateau also acts like a beacon for certain factions of Christian fundamentalists: bizarrely, they see the great pagan monuments of Ancient Egypt as the focus for a prophecy of the Second Coming of Christ. This is found in Isaiah (chapters 19, 20):

> 19. In that day there shall be an altar to the Lord in the heart of Egypt, and a monument to the Lord at its border. 20. It will be a sign and witness to the Lord Almighty in the land of Egypt. When they cry out to the Lord because of their oppressors, he will send them a saviour and defender, and he will rescue them.

Somewhat unexpectedly, some Christian fundamentalists take the Great Pyramid as the promised 'altar to the Lord', and therefore take a keen interest in whatever happens at Giza. Although this group represents a minority within the alternative Egypt community, its messianic message has influenced certain high-profile authors in this genre (e.g. Bauval 1999: xxviii).

Finally, there are theories that do not attempt to rewrite the chronology of Ancient Egypt, or argue in favour of advanced technology or knowledge, but which challenge the consensus view about the cultural influences that shaped the Egyptian civilization. An example is Martin Bernal's (1991) *Black Athena*, which argues that the contribution of black African culture on Egypt (and many other aspects of western civilization) has been grossly undervalued. The early archaeologists discovered that Egypt had a large black population, and therefore did not consider the Ancient Egyptians' achievements to be on the same level as those of white cultures. Earlier versions of this approach took an opposing viewpoint, proposing that the Egyptian civilization was the product of European, and therefore white, colonization. Overall, however, this category of alternative Egypt theories accepts the prevailing academic view of the history, chronology and achievements of Egyptian civilization (Bernal 2003; North 2003).

The ancestry of alternative Egypt

On the above definition, today's alternative Egyptology is by no means a new phenomenon: indeed, today's most high-profile proponents of alternative theories are the direct descendants of a long, if not always particularly noble, tradition. Ironically, it is possible to argue that from a strictly historical viewpoint, it is *academic* Egyptology that is the newcomer – even, in a sense, the alternative to a view of Egypt that has prevailed for many centuries!

The fact is that ideas about Ancient Egypt, once regarded as the province of the occult, were enthusiastically adopted by the New Age movement and are now being presented to a more mainstream audience, albeit dressed in a more historical and scientific guise.

The view of Egypt as the land of mystery and lost secrets gave rise to the belief that somewhere in Egypt their key still lies hidden. This is by no means a new idea: even the later Egyptians themselves looked with something approaching superstitious awe at the products of their most distant ancestors. The Middle Kingdom P. Westcar (ca. 1650 BC) records a legend of Kheops' search for the "secret things of the house of Thoth" that he believed would help him in the construction of his pyramid. And later the Arabs had many tales of hidden texts or magical artefacts (El Daly 2003).

Egypt continued to fascinate successive generations of travellers. Its symbols – the pyramid, the sphinx and the enigmatic sacred writing of the hieroglyphs – powerfully stirred the imagination, becoming absorbed into many esoteric traditions. Freemasonry (Hamill and Mollier 2003), although tracing its legendary origins back to the Tribes of Israel and the building of the Temple of Solomon, also incorporated much Egyptian symbolism into its regalia and rituals – and, again, had traditions of hidden Egyptian knowledge.

However, one of the major elements in the re-evaluation of ancient Egyptian history was not the legacy of an occultist but that of a candidate for the role of one of the first alternative historians, the Minnesota Congressman Ignatius Donnelly (1831– 1901). Always questioning printed history (he was one of the first to argue that the works of Shakespeare were not penned by the Stratford actor), in 1882 he produced an extremely influential work in which he argued in favour of the existence of the fabled lost continent. Based on a comparison of the myths and artefacts of the Old and New Worlds, Donnelly argued that Plato's Atlantis was not only a reality, but it was the 'mother civilization' from which all others came – and its most direct heir was Ancient Egypt.

It can be argued that Donnelly's work is more central to today's view of Atlantis than Plato's original accounts. In this light, a writer such as Graham Hancock (e.g. 1995, 2001) may be viewed as the intellectual descendant of Donnelly. Donnelly's work was also seized upon by those intent on bringing an occult gloss to the reconstruction of the history of civilization and the evolution of the human race.

A characteristic of these emerging occult ideas was to push the dates of civilization back into immense antiquity, a trend that was to have a significant effect on ideas concerning the origins of the Egyptian civilization. An important figure in this development – hugely influential on modern occult ideas, although he is not widely known in the English-speaking world – was the French aristocrat Joseph-Alexandre Saint-Yves d'Alveydre (1842–1909). He was a prime mover in that peculiarly European, and predominantly French, school of thought that mixed esoteric and mystical ideas with politics, an explosive and often disturbing blend. Saint-Yves d'Alveydre (e.g. 1903) led the politico-occult philosophy that he termed Synarchy, which advocated rule by an 'enlightened' elite who were under the guidance of spiritually advanced beings (with which he himself claimed to be in psychic contact). He justified this retrospectively by inventing a pedigree for Synarchy – founded on 'revealed' information – based on a reconstruction of history in which a succession of races and civilizations each gave way to the next, superior, race. Atlantis played a prominent role in this version of history, and Saint-Yves d'Alveydre, like Donnelly, argued that civilizations such as Egypt owed their origins to survivors from the cataclysm that destroyed that continent. He placed the destruction of Atlantis, and thereby the origins of Egypt, at 12000 BC.

Similar ideas were also advanced by Helena Petrovna Blavatsky (1831–1891), who had a much greater influence on the English-speaking world through her new spiritual philosophy of Theosophy, which she synthesized from both western and eastern beliefs. Another godmother of the coming New Age was Alice A. Bailey (1880–1949), the British-born and naturalized American who began life as a disciple of the Theosophical Society, but she added the dimension of communication from extraterrestrials, claiming that humankind has been guided by spiritually advanced beings from the Sirius star system. In particular, they influenced the development of the Egyptian civilisation and the building of the pyramids.

Lost Egyptian knowledge is central to the traditions of the Ancient and Mystic Order Rosae Crucis (AMORC), the California-based modern-day Rosicrucian order founded by H. Spencer Lewis in the early 1920s. Lewis (1936) claimed to have inherited information concerning the existence of chambers and tunnels beneath the pyramids and Sphinx of Giza.

But undoubtedly the most influential figure on the modern alternative Egypt movement was the American psychic Edgar Cayce (1877–1945). Known as the 'Sleeping Prophet', the Kentucky native is today best known for his 'readings' (e.g. Cayce 1990) – information on the ancient past and the future gleaned while in a trance. These psychic communications fall into two categories: information about the ancient past, and prophecies for the immediate future – although the two are often intimately linked.

Cayce's reconstruction of ancient history aped Saint-Yves d'Alveydre's and Blavatsky's with its super-civilization of Atlantis and the awe-stuck prominence accorded to its colony, Pyramid-Age Egypt. This is perhaps not surprising, as Cayce was known to be familiar with Theosophical and similar literature before he began his series of readings (Bauval 1999: 166–169; Lawton and Ogilvie-Herald 2000: 247–248). He dated the demise of Atlantis, and the consequent building of the Great Pyramid and Sphinx, to around 10500 BC. More important, his readings stated that a repository of the Atlantean wisdom had been hidden at Giza, in the now-fabled Hall of Records allegedly beneath the Great Sphinx. Although Cayce was the first to use the term 'Hall of Records', the idea of a lost cache of ancient Egyptian secrets had a long pedigree. Cayce also predicted the immediate future, from just a few years ahead (in the mid-20th century) to the early years of the 21st.

The concept of the Hall of Records provides a bridge between Cayce's readings for the past and prophecies for the future. In trance readings in the 1930s, he stated that the Hall of Records would be rediscovered in 1998, and that its opening would be a trigger that would somehow propel the world into a New Age. And although he was not specific it is clear that he had the Millennium in mind.

In 1931 Cayce founded an organization to continue his work, the Association for Research and Enlightenment (ARE), based at Virginia Beach, which came to play an important role in events in Egypt from the 1970s onwards.

Another important figure in the development of alternative Egyptology was the Alsace-born esoteric philosopher R. A. Schwaller de Lubicz (1887–1961). After a complex career in occult circles in France and Switzerland, he settled in Egypt in 1938, where he remained for the next 14 years studying the religion and monuments of Ancient Egypt, in particular the Temple of Luxor (e.g. Schwaller de Lubicz 1998). He too believed that Egypt had a much greater antiquity than conventional history will allow.

Although his work is cited reverently by most of the current alternative Egyptologists, they invariably describe him inaccurately, for example as a 'philosopher' or 'mathematician'. However, Schwaller de Lubicz was first and foremost an occult scholar and philosopher, a student of both Theosophy and Saint-Yves d'Alveydre's Synarchy (see Vandenbroeck 1987). It is clear that his ideas concerning Egypt were very much shaped by his pre-existing belief and ideology (for example, with its god-kings and politically powerful priesthood, Ancient Egypt can be regarded as the supreme example of a Synarchist society), some of which were extremely disturbing. Sometimes described as a 'proto-Fascist', Schwaller de Lubicz espoused extreme right-wing views as well as being racist and vehemently anti-Semitic.

The 1990s

Although numerous books reinterpreting the history, meaning and mythology of Ancient Egypt have been published over the years, it was only in the 1990s that they began to find a wider audience – partly because alternative theories suddenly seemed to converge with new archaeological discoveries, seizing the popular imagination (Schadla-Hall and Morris Chapter 14, this volume).

Another important factor was the approach of the Millennium. An audience which was fascinated with the mysteries of the ancient past was much more receptive to a whole host of alternative books than in previous decades. The time was ripe for the plucking, and Edgar Cayce's prophecy of the discovery of the Hall of Records was perfect for the moment – and the market. Proving Cayce right in his readings about the ancient past would help to convince people that he was also likely to be right in his predictions for the immediate future – in particular about the opening of the Hall of Records in 1998. Indeed, there seems to have been a concerted effort either to find the Hall, or to exploit, for various reasons, the belief and expectancy invested in its imminent discovery.

The first development concerned the dating of the Great Sphinx of Giza, and was inspired by John Anthony West, an American maverick with a personal interest in the mysteries of Ancient Egypt, and an adherent of the philosophy of Schwaller de Lubicz. In 1979, he developed an observation of Schwaller de Lubicz's concerning the weathering on the body of the Sphinx and the walls of the Sphinx Enclosure, which he believed was characteristic of water-erosion rather than sand-blasting. Schwaller de

Lubicz's contention was that this was proof of a great flood – the flood that had destroyed Atlantis. West (1979: 198) realized that if Schwaller de Lubicz's observation could be shown to be correct it would help vindicate his own ideas concerning the antiquity of Egypt (and, by implication, also its religion). In 1990, he was able to persuade geologist Robert Schoch of Boston University to examine the erosion on the Sphinx and related places on the Giza Plateau. The involvement of Boston University also allowed West access to the site, as the Egyptian authorities would only allow work to be undertaken by projects that were backed by academic institutions (although there are many examples of this rule being ignored). The Sphinx Project, as it was called, was an interesting collection of individuals and organizations. Apart from West and the Boston University presence, it also consisted of television documentary-maker Boris Said and was partly funded by two American industrialist members of ARE, the Cayce organization. One of these, Joseph M. Schor, participated in the project as ARE's official observer.

Schoch (1992) published the results of his analysis, confirming that in his opinion it *was* water erosion, the result of long-term exposure to rain. Based on what is known of the climate of Egypt, there was insufficient rainfall to account for the depth of erosion in the 4,500 years that the Sphinx has existed according to the conventional dating; therefore it must be older. Schoch concluded that in order to have so much erosion the Sphinx would have had to have been carved between 7000 and 5000 BC – many millennia before the ancient Egyptian civilization is 'supposed' to have existed. These conclusions represented a major challenge to Egyptological orthodoxy, inspiring a debate that still rumbles on. But the most important effect of the Schoch affair was that, as an established university expert, for once Egyptologists could not just ignore his claim. The ball was in their court: now they had at least to attempt to keep it in play.

The continuing debate is now polarized between those who accept Schoch's dating – and all that it implies for the chronology of Ancient Egypt – and those who seek to explain the erosion by other factors, such as a form of rain-induced chemical reaction (weathering the stone more deeply than mere rain ever could).

Schoch's work, together with West's endorsement, for the first time effectively secured the alternative faction a platform. However, it is worth noting that while using Schoch's expertise to bolster support for his theories, West also rejected it when it suited him. Based on Schwaller de Lubicz's theories, which in turn derived from Saint-Yves d'Alveydre, West believed that the Sphinx dated from even before 7000 BC, arguing that Schoch's estimation had been conservative. He argued in favour of a date nearer to 10000 BC (Hancock 1995: 419).

Besides Schoch's study of the erosion, the Sphinx Project also carried out seismographic tests in order to establish if any chambers existed beneath the Sphinx Enclosure. Undoubtedly, this was prompted by the presence of ARE members in the team, who waited excitedly for the revelations of the Hall of Records. There were indications that a large void existed beneath the Sphinx's outstretched paws, but the results were not absolutely conclusive: it was possible that it was a natural cavity. The Sphinx Project, including Schoch's conclusions and the seismographic work, was the subject of a television documentary, produced by Boris Said and broadcast by NBC in

1993. Entitled *Mystery of the Sphinx*, this generated high ratings, a huge amount of public interest, and critical acclaim that led to it winning an Emmy award.

Shortly after Schoch published his results, another theory that challenged the orthodox view seized the popular imagination, based on another headline-grabbing discovery. Robert G. Bauval, who was born in Alexandria of Belgian parents, came from a background of management in the civil engineering industry, but had a long-standing passion for the antiquities of Egypt. In the late 1980s he had nurtured the theory – based on his observation that the three pyramids at Giza resembled the three stars of Orion's Belt – that the Giza pyramids were positioned deliberately to represent them. From this he developed the idea that the Great Pyramid's primary purpose was not to serve as a giant mausoleum but that it had a ritual function connected with the stellar religion of the fourth Dynasty, and in particular the association between the king and the god Osiris, who was represented by Orion in the Egyptian zodiac.

In March 1993, in circumstances that are still not entirely clear,[1] a team led by the German engineer Rudolf Gantenbrink used a small remote-controlled robot called 'Upuat 2' – fitted with a video camera – to explore the shafts leading from the Queen's Chamber in the Great Pyramid. It duly made a major discovery: what appears to be a slab or small door sealing off the southern shaft some distance inside the body of the Pyramid. A door normally leads somewhere: naturally speculation was rife about a possible chamber beyond, and of what it might contain.

Bauval became interested in Gantenbrink's discovery because, as the first person to explore the shaft to such an extent, the German was in a position to supply accurate data about its angle of inclination, data which Bauval needed to confirm or refute a particular aspect of his theory – namely that the southern shaft from the Queen's Chamber had been constructed to align with the sacred star Sirius when it culminated. The data supplied by Gantenbrink did indeed confirm this.

It was Bauval who took the lead in bringing Gantenbrink's discovery to the attention of the world's media, resulting in a front-page splash on 16 April 1993. He used the international media to promote his own theory of the Giza-Orion correlation, co-authoring *The Orion Mystery* (1994) with Adrian Gilbert. This became the first of the alternative Egypt blockbusters.

There is nothing inherently implausible in Bauval's 'Orion-Giza correlation' theory. The importance of the constellation of Orion to the Ancient Egyptians is well attested, and the notion that stellar alignments had guided the siting and construction of the Great Pyramid had been around for some years – in fact since the early 1960s, when it was discovered that the southern shaft from the King's Chamber was aligned with the stars of Orion's Belt. Therefore, in principle there is no Egyptological objection to Bauval's hypothesis: it is quite feasible that the architects may have sought to represent the stars in this way, and certainly they had the skill to do so. On the other hand, in the absence of any specific evidence – such as inscriptions – it is not possible to prove that this was the builders' intent, or to disprove the argument that the resemblance between the layout of the pyramid and the stars is coincidental.[2] A serious objection to the entire theory of a correlation between the stars of Orion's Belt and the three Giza pyramids was astronomical evidence that Mintaka (Delta Orionis), which was identified by the advocates of the theory as corresponding to the Menkaura pyramid, did not in fact correspond with it at all.

Despite all the furore, Bauval's hypothesis did not represent a major challenge to Egyptological orthodoxy, except that it disputed that the Great Pyramid was constructed simply as a tomb for Kheops, and argued that it had been used for rituals over an extended period of time. Indeed, his use of the shaft alignments to date the construction of the Great Pyramid (by determining the years in which Sirius and Al Nitak, the brightest star in Orion's belt, would have culminated in direct alignment with the southern shafts) tended to support the conventional dating.[3]

However, he did challenge the conventional chronology of the ancient Egyptian civilization as a whole, having observed that the orientation of the Giza pyramids to the north-south meridian did not match the orientation of the Belt stars to the celestial meridian at the period in which the pyramids were constructed. On looking at the change in orientation of the constellation due to the effects of precession, he claimed that the closest match between pyramids and stars occurred around 10500 BC. This was also the period in which Orion was at its lowest point in the precessional cycle.

Besides arguing that the Egypt of the Old Kingdom possessed the intellectual sophistication to understand precession (which is considered unlikely by conventional Egyptologists), Bauval concluded that, although built during the fourth Dynasty, the Giza complex had been purposely constructed in order to 'commemorate' the period of 10500 BC as a time of special significance. He further hypothesized that this showed that a sophisticated civilization had existed in the Nile Valley in that distant epoch, and that there was a direct continuation and transmission of culture between that civilization and the Old Kingdom. Bauval believes that the priesthood of Heliopolis, the religion that directly inspired the building of the Giza pyramids, was the repository of the wisdom of the earlier civilization. This notion of a civilization existing in Egypt in the 11th millennium BC is, of course, completely contrary to the accepted academic view.

Bauval's claim that the 'closest match' between monuments and stars occurred ca. 10500 BC has been hotly contested, the first person to do so being Cook (1996: 86), who had supplied the diagrams for *The Orion Mystery*. Similar criticisms are levelled by Ian Lawton and Chris Ogilvie-Herald (2000) and the present authors (Picknett and Prince 2000). Attempts to follow Bauval's reconstruction found that the most recent period that Belt stars had been in the 'Giza position' was in 12000 BC. So why did Bauval seem so set on 10500 BC? Had he simply made a miscalculation, and in doing so effectively pushed his hypothetical original Egyptian civilization back even further into antiquity? Bauval and Gilbert (1995) themselves noted that this date was the same as the one given by Edgar Cayce in his psychic readings. (However, Cayce had actually said that the Great Pyramid, as well as the Sphinx, was *built* at this time – something with which Bauval and Gilbert disagreed.)

The next major development was the publication, in April 1995, of former *Economist* correspondent Graham Hancock's phenomenal international bestseller *Fingerprints of the Gods*. Taking the non-academic world by storm in Britain and many other countries, this is a survey of the evidence for a lost, advanced civilization that predated and influenced the earliest known peoples, based on anomalies found at ancient sites throughout the world. Where Egypt was concerned, Hancock offered no new insights but drew together Robert Schoch's and Robert Bauval's theories, seeing them as mutually supportive. Hancock agreed with Bauval about the relationship of the Giza pyramids with the dateline of 10500 BC, but went further, suggesting that the pyramids may have been partly constructed at that time, and only finished in their present form in the fourth Dynasty. He also argued that Schoch's work on the water erosion of the Sphinx supported the same date. In this, Hancock followed West's contention that Schoch had erred on the conservative side, and that the Sphinx was, in reality, even older than Schoch had concluded. Hancock (1995: 413) argued more specifically for a date of 10500 BC for the Sphinx, justifying it by citing a period of torrential weather during the 11th millennium BC. However, as far as the conventional history of the climate of Egypt is concerned, there was no such wet period (Picknett and Prince 2000: 39–40). This notwithstanding, Hancock used West's interpretation of Schoch and Bauval's Orion-Giza correlation theory to support his major hypothesis, which was that a global, technologically advanced civilization, remembered as Atlantis, had existed in the remote past, and that this had come to an end in 10500 BC, as a result of the rise in sea levels caused by the end of the last Ice Age. The oldest civilizations, most notably Egypt but also those of Central and South America and the Far East, are the remnants of the lost civilization, whose monuments have been radically misdated by archaeologists and historians. Some of the wisdom and learning of the lost civilization was passed on to those cultures, which accounts for their achievements, such as the building of the Giza pyramids.

In 1995 a new team arrived at Giza to carry out a seismographic survey and ground scans in the area of the Sphinx. This was a joint project of Florida State University and the Schor Foundation, which was established by Joseph Schor, the multimillionaire life member of ARE and former participant in West's Sphinx Project. The Project's official purpose was to locate underground faults that might cause subsidence, but clearly, given Schor's involvement, its real objective was to try to locate the fabled Hall of Records. The team paid particular attention to a tunnel in the Sphinx's rump, which had been discovered but resealed in the 1920s, then reopened in 1980. However, any hopes that this might lead to an exciting new chamber beneath the Sphinx faded when it reached a dead end after a few feet. Rumours that the team had discovered something of great interest followed announcements by Graham Hancock and Robert Bauval that the Schor Foundation told them that they had discovered not one but *nine* chambers beneath the Sphinx.[4]

In 1996 Bauval and Hancock published their joint book *Keeper of Genesis* (entitled *Message of the Sphinx* in the USA), which extended the argument in favour of an original civilization in Egypt in 10500 BC. The date, as we have noted, was the same as that offered by Cayce for the origins of Egypt as a consequence of colonization by Atlantean survivors. In *Keeper of Genesis*, Bauval and Hancock set great store on the reality of the subterranean Hall of Records and its impending discovery (predicted by Cayce for 1998). Bauval and Hancock used further astronomical correlations to reinforce the idea of an intimate connection between the building of the Giza complex and the year 10500 BC. These have been much criticized – most prominently by American archaeoastronomer E. C. Krupp – for their selectivity. Briefly, Bauval and Hancock's theory involves a variety of relationships between the movements of the celestial bodies that they believe were of central importance to the Heliopolitan priests: the constellations of Orion and Leo (which they believe were represented by the Sphinx of Giza), the star Sirius and the sun. They argue that significant correlations between these bodies consistently occurred in 10500 BC, thereby establishing that date as being of particular importance. However, their argument is fatally flawed, if only on the grounds of extreme selectivity. Many of the astronomical events they cite are *not* unique to 10500 BC but occurred for several centuries either side of that year – and events that, according to Bauval and Hancock's logic, should be of equal significance also occurred in other periods.

The major claim of *Keeper of Genesis* was that it is possible to use these astronomical correlations to establish the existence of a chamber underneath the Sphinx (which they termed the 'Genesis Chamber'), thereby confirming Cayce's statements. However, the two authors also took on board Cayce's idea that its discovery would trigger some kind of new age. They linked this imminent global transformation with both the approaching Millennium and the advent of the Age of Aquarius, often using mutually contradictory arguments in an attempt to reinforce the significance of two dates: 10500 BC and 2000 AD.[5] Central to the working of the astrological ages is the Great Pyramid, which they see as a "device designed to trigger off messianic events" (Bauval and Hancock 1996: 282).

Together with researcher John Grigsby, Hancock and Bauval (1998) went on to add an extraterrestrial dimension to their developing reconstruction of the ancient past. The book used the 'Face on Mars' and other alleged 'monuments' on the red planet as evidence for the existence of a long-gone civilization that was destroyed by the impact of a comet or asteroid. They also went on to link this putative extraterrestrial civilization with Ancient Egypt – on very tenuous grounds. Hancock has since maintained his search for the lost civilization through underwater exploration.

Bauval continued with what some may see as an unashamed exploitation of the coming Millennium: "the Great Pyramid and the Giza necropolis as a whole have the innate energy to cause a powerful transcendental shift on a massive, even global scale" (Bauval 1999: xxix).

A curious phenomenon then reared its head: the alternative camp was beginning to produce an 'orthodoxy' of its own, coalescing around the figures and work of Hancock, Bauval and West, and based on the re-dating of the Sphinx and the Orion-Giza correlation, as well as the date of 10500 BC. For the first time, what appeared to be a coherent and consistent historical theory was promoted to the public, with new discoveries – real or rumoured – converging towards the same conclusion. As has been seen, this was only an outward appearance: the facts were often massaged to make them fit into the emerging scenario, one that ultimately owed its origin to Cayce's psychic pronouncements. Soon it became the case that any books that boldly advanced ideas that fell outside this enchanted ring found themselves without the same level of publicity or even debate. Authors who challenged the magic 10500 BC date were not given the same profile on the conference circuit, and in some cases found that they were virtually cold-shouldered among their peers. Ironically, the alternative camp began to produce its own dissenters and mavericks, who accused the Hancock-Bauval-West clique of stifling debate, refusing to acknowledge criticisms and suppressing or ignoring inconvenient facts – exactly the complaints levelled against academic Egyptology by the alternative camp, and particularly by Hancock, Bauval and West.

These developments also highlighted the strange and unexpected relationships within the world of Egyptology (both conventional and alternative), especially where events on the ground at Giza are concerned.

Essentially, there are three groups involved. There are the academic, professionally qualified Egyptologists and institutions, and the separate but interlinking group comprised of the Egyptian authorities with responsibility for sites such as Giza, represented most visibly by Zahi Hawass, currently the Secretary General of the Supreme Council of Antiquities. Together these form the 'Egyptological establishment' that was the prime target of 'Alternative' derision. Then there are the alternative theoreticians, such as Hancock and Bauval, who adopt a basically historical approach (or, their critics would say, a quasi-historical approach). Lastly there are individuals and organizations who may be labelled as the 'esotericists' – those whose interest in Ancient Egypt is primarily motivated by quasi-religious or mystical beliefs. These groups, which appear to be quite separate, in reality exist in a kind of symbiotic relationship, as events at Giza in the 1990s demonstrate.

The connection between the alternative writers and the esotericists is obvious enough. The popular authors draw inspiration from, say, Cayce's prophecies or the writings of Lewis: in return, the mystical groups use the alternative writers' work to add a more objective feel to their beliefs and traditions by, for example, 'proving' that the ancient Egyptian civilization is several millennia older that the history books recognize. For this reason, a close relationship grew up between West, Bauval and Hancock on the one side and ARE on the other, those writers being frequent speakers at ARE's headquarters at Virginia Beach.

More surprising is the cordial relationship between the pseudo-historians, the mystics and the Egyptological establishment: due to an unwritten understanding with esoteric organizations in Egypt, the authorities are happy to admit their members to the King's Chamber outside normal opening hours. In December 1997, when Hawass, then Director General of the Giza Plateau, announced that the Great Pyramid would be closed to the public for cleaning for a year from the following April, he made it clear that the nocturnal visits by what he termed 'metaphysical groups' would be allowed to continue during that period. He himself has a close relationship with the mystics, being a frequent speaker at ARE conferences at Virginia Beach – where he has announced archaeological discoveries in Egypt – and was a consultant to the modern-day Rosicrucian organization, AMORC, in California. It has also been stated that Hawass owed his Egyptological education in the US to a scholarship organized through ARE by Cayce's son, Hugh Lynn Cayce, although Hawass has strenuously denied this (Bauval 1999: xxi).

Mark Lehner is a leading American Egyptologist and author (Lehner 1997), yet he began as a passionate devotee of Cayce and owed his Egyptological qualifications to ARE. As a young student in 1973, Lehner was selected by Hugh Lynn Cayce to be the organization's 'inside man' in the Egyptological establishment. The following year Lehner (1974) tried to reconcile Cayce's statements about Ancient Egypt with current historical and archaeological understanding. Although he has since distanced himself from Cayce's readings – and is now one of the leading critics of the alternative scene – the relationship has continued. Curiously, however, Egyptology has benefited from this odd partnership: ARE has financed serious projects in the field. In 1978 it had funded the Sphinx Exploration Project (a survey of the Sphinx and its environs conducted by the American research institute SRI International) and, in the 1980s, Lehner's project to carbon date organic material taken from the mortar between the blocks of the Great Pyramid. Undoubtedly ARE contributed to these projects in the hope that they would prove Cayce right, but, although this did not happen, the discipline as a whole benefited.[6]

Other academic institutions have forged symbiotic partnerships with the mystics: for example the 1995 collaboration between the Schor Foundation and Florida State University. It seems incredible that this American institution was effectively engaged in an attempt to find the Hall of Records. Since the 1970s ARE had been collaborating with various institutions, most notably SRI International – one of the world's largest private research organizations – in and around Giza. Many of these projects have given rise to real benefits for Egyptology as a whole.

A very strange phenomenon began to manifest itself at Giza: although it might appear that these various groups and individuals were working very much to their own agendas, in fact it seemed more as if they were members of the same hive, working for mutual support and the furtherance of their apparently diverse ideas. For example, Hancock and Hawass, who began by being seen as representatives of opposite camps, soon appeared to be working together, and by the end of the 1990s, the likes of Hancock and Bauval almost seemed to be *in charge* at Giza. After years of portraying Hawass and Lehner as villains – either arrogant close-minded academics or actual conspirators – Hancock, Bauval and West suddenly issued endorsements of both of them in spring 1998, reassuring their audience that they were not part of a conspiracy and were truly professional Egyptologists whose integrity should be admired and respected. As far as the public was concerned, the qualified professionals now depended on the approval of the alternatives. This could happen only because they had achieved a position of real power: when, in the spring of 1996, Hancock and Bauval campaigned to get the Schor Foundation's license to dig at Giza revoked, they succeeded. Hancock and Bauval persuaded thousands of people to petition the Egyptian Supreme Council of Antiquities (their original objection being that they were suspicious that the Foundation was suppressing discoveries of chambers beneath the Sphinx). Two years later, Hancock and Bauval supported the reinstatement of the Schor Foundation's license, again successfully.

Such was the confused situation at Giza, with its complex and often apparently contradictory politicking (cf. Lawton and Ogilvie-Herald 2000; Picknett and Prince 2000). The claims that the Schor Foundation was suppressing certain discoveries was part of a wider phenomenon of the 1990s: rumours circulated about the finding of hidden chambers or of clandestine searches within the Great Pyramid or elsewhere on the Giza Plateau. In part, they were engineered to support the validity of the alternative theories by invoking the idea of a conspiracy: the powers that be knew that great secrets of world-changing importance were to be found in Egypt but sought to claim them for themselves; academic orthodoxy was therefore being used covertly to mislead the people. The leaders of the alternative field began to be seen – and to deliberately portray themselves – as crusaders for truth, standing up to the tyranny of orthodoxy whose attacks were rapidly turning them into martyrs.

The rumours centred on a number of locations: not one but nine chambers had been found and clandestinely opened beneath the Sphinx; a secret tunnel was being dug from the uppermost of the relieving chambers above the King's Chamber, presumably in an attempt to discover what lay behind 'Gantenbrink's door'; the Great Pyramid had been closed not for cleaning but to keep the public away while covert excavations were carried out, and so on. On further investigation, however, all of these rumours have been demonstrated to be false: sinister motives had been eagerly attributed to quite innocent work. The final focus of pre-Millennium expectancy demonstrates not only how mysteries were conjured out of nothing, but also the odd way in which the camps present at Giza often worked in a kind of weird collusion. As all other claims of suppressed finds at Giza turned to dust, attention shifted to a feature known as the Water Shaft. This shaft, descending through three levels to a chamber some 120 feet beneath the Giza Plateau, is entered through an 'underpass' under the main causeway linking the pyramids to the Sphinx and its associated temples. First explored in the 1930s, rising water levels rendered it inaccessible, and its presence was not widely known. In the late 1990s it began to be touted as a new discovery that may be – or may lead to – the fabled Hall of Records.

The Water Shaft was reopened as the result of pumping work organized by Hawass, which for the first time allowed the chamber at the bottom to be reached. It contains a sarcophagus that has been dated to the sixth or seventh centuries BC. In early 1997, members of the Schor Foundation team, including filmmaker Boris Said, were allowed access to the Water Shaft chamber. A film was widely promoted on the alternative circuit: might it finally reveal the entrance to the Hall of Records? Excitingly, there were suggestions that a tunnel led off from the chamber in the direction of the Sphinx. Bauval (1999: 300) was also allowed access to the chamber, and he described this tunnel and speculated that it might connect to chambers beneath the Sphinx. Perhaps more surprisingly, Hawass also seemed to take part in the active campaign of mythmaking about the chamber. He theorized publicly that the sarcophagus might actually be the tomb of the god Osiris – in a symbolic sense only, but even so, unsurprisingly it caused ripples of excitement among the 'alternative' followers. He also drew attention to the putative tunnel on camera for a Fox TV special (*Opening the Lost Tomb – Live*), describing his 'discovery' of the Water Shaft chamber as his "greatest adventure ever" and saying "you never know what the sands and tunnels of Egypt may hide" (March 1999).

The story rumbled on, gaining momentum: the Water Shaft chamber was further promoted by James Hurtak, who preaches a mystical philosophy allegedly derived from highly evolved universal intelligences and which incorporates many elements of Bailey's (1957) teachings. Hurtak has been active at Giza since the 1970s, and also achieved prominence in the 'Face on Mars' controversy. He was with Boris Said and the Schor Foundation team when they were given permission to enter the Water Shaft chamber in 1997, and was also photographed in it. But in lectures Hurtak depicted the small (30 square feet) chamber as part of an immense subterranean complex of colonnaded halls, vast temples and underground watercourses. However, according to Lawton and Ogilvie-Herald (2000: 476–477), who also entered the chamber in 1999, there is no way out of it at all: the much-vaunted 'tunnel' (which actually leads towards the Great Pyramid, not the Sphinx) is simply a natural geological feature that ends after a few feet – in fact, everyone who has ever seen it is aware of this, despite what they might say to the contrary.

Face to face

The other major result of events in the 1990s was that the 'alternatives' could no longer be ignored – and to rub salt into the wound, the alternative camp was getting the better of the argument, at least as far as the public was concerned

Several conferences were organized in which leading figures from both sides of the great divide were invited to air their respective positions.[7] However, the orthodox camp invariably found itself on the defensive, being expected to justify its opposition to the alternative ideas such as the Giza-Orion correlation and the antiquity of the Sphinx. As far as most people were concerned, it seemed that the 'alternatives' leaders were regarded as the authorities in matters concerning Ancient Egypt, and academic Egyptologists as narrow-minded, conservative rationalists. The Egyptological community was slow to respond to the challenge. Throughout the 1990s a plethora of television documentaries featured the alternative theories in which (with the exception of Zahi Hawass, who delighted in playing up to the audience) academic Egyptologists, if they were included at all, were presented as hidebound and reactionary. Such programmes did very well worldwide. Indeed, it was not until the end of 1999 that the opposition found a voice, with the BBC's prestigious science series *Horizon* producing two programmes: *Atlantis Uncovered* and *Atlantis Reborn*, written and produced by Jacqueline Smith and Chris Hale respectively. The second was particularly devoted to heavy criticism of Hancock and Bauval's theories about Ancient Egypt. Unsurprisingly, those authors, along with their many followers, cried foul and claimed that the programme was not only biased (a claim that could equally well be made of the Channel 4 series based on Hancock's books), but also edited specifically to show the authors in a bad light. The pair took a complaint to the Broadcasting Standards Commission, claiming 10 points of unfair treatment. The BSC rejected all but one (concerning the omission of Bauval's rebuttal of counter-arguments to his Orion-Giza correlation theory, to which the BBC agreed to broadcast a re-edited version including his comments).

In Britain, the *Horizon* programme was astonishingly successful: virtually overnight the whole subject of alternative Egyptology came to be viewed with suspicion. Certainly, after the Millennium interest in the subject has greatly declined, but whether this is due to disillusionment with the esoteric promises of Egypt (most palpably the failure to find the Hall of Records in time) or the *Horizon* programme is unclear.

Exploiting Egypt

The Stargate Conspiracy explored another aspect of the alternative history field: the deliberate exploitation and manipulation of popular interest in alternative ideas for a variety of ends. The title and subtitle (Picknett and Prince 2000) were designed to be provocative and appeal to the usual 'alternative' readers, who we wanted to make aware of some of the information that is carefully kept out of the popular books of the genre.

A more recent example of the dangers of uncritically accepting alternative ideas concerning ancient history can be found in the tragic story of the Order of the Solar Temple, whose mass deaths in 1994 in Switzerland and Canada and in 1995 in France provoked public outrage and a continuing controversy. The doctrines of this cult incorporated a number of esoteric, New Age and alternative ideas. An explicitly Synarchist organization, it was allied to the extreme right-wing underworld of Europe and adopted ideas derived from Bailey, such as the influence of extraterrestrials from the Sirius system on the blossoming of human civilization – especially that of Egypt.[8] Following the mass suicides (or perhaps murder) of 53 members on the night of 4/5 October 1994, the Swiss authorities received letters explaining their radical action, which stated that the membership had chosen suicide because their task on Earth was completed, and that after death their souls would be transferred 'home' to Sirius, an event in some way signalled by the opening of a chamber in the Great Pyramid in March of the previous year.

The reference to the discovery of a chamber is clearly the discovery of the 'doorway' in the Queen's Chamber's southern shaft by Gantenbrink's team in 1993. To this they had added Bauval's theory of 1994, to the effect that the southern shaft was built to align with Sirius in the belief that the pharaoh's soul would be symbolically projected to that star. These two concepts had been twisted by the leaders of the Solar Temple and used as a justification for mass death. Undoubtedly, without Gantenbrink's discovery and Bauval and Gilbert's book, they would have found some other justification for their determination to die, but it does demonstrate how tragic consequences can follow from uncritical acceptance of alternative ideas.

The more serious ramifications of such ideas did not end there: in the lead-up to the Millennium, Synarchist organizations in Britain used the widespread interest in alternative Egypt in an attempt to recruit new members. Their literature promised that the questions raised by popular books on the subject would be answered by the Synarchist doctrines, but failed to mention its more disturbing elitist and political aspects.

Conclusions

The positive side is that the events of the 1990s did at least get the two sides talking, albeit through gritted teeth. Egyptology does itself no favours by ignoring alternative ideas about Ancient Egypt, especially where the public is concerned. A large and receptive audience still hungers for information about Egypt, which is widely perceived as evocative and profoundly fascinating – perhaps, ironically, what inspired most Egyptologists to study the subject in the first place. However, it must be said that the public's need is met more satisfactorily by the alternative market because it stirs the imagination more immediately and profoundly than the dry and erudite books on the subject.

There is also the fact that the alternative ideas are not in themselves necessarily devoid of merit. Many focus on genuine mysteries that need to be addressed – for example, there *are* uncertainties about the chronology of Ancient Egypt. Schoch's analysis of the erosion on the Sphinx and Sphinx Enclosure is a case in point. Apart from the spin invested in his work by certain authors, Schoch's findings cannot simply be ignored: he *is* a specialist in his field. While it cannot be said (but often is) that Schoch's redating of the Sphinx has been proven, there will have to be a serious alternative explanation for the erosion (or perhaps of the history of the climate of Egypt). Either way, something valuable will have been learned.

Despite the assurances of Egyptologists, it is not really certain how the Great Pyramid was built – or how the ancients learned how to construct such an astonishing monument after having made so few previous examples. It is probable that the scientific, mathematical and even philosophical sophistication of the ancient Egyptians is seriously undervalued. Because of the lack of conclusive evidence for the Giza pyramids having been *only* built as tombs, the alternatives have every right to challenge the academics' certainty about such matters.

Some of the less extreme alternative views are worthy of serious consideration, such as Bernal's (1991, 2003) claim that the traditional dismissal of ancient Egyptian sophistication is a side effect of 18th and 19th century racism. And although the modern Egyptologist is no more racist than the next academic, this traditional distaste for Egyptian religion, philosophy and even masterpieces of engineering is still paramount and continues to infect the whole subject.

After the excesses of the late 1990s, it will be a pity if matters revert to the two camps ignoring each other and occasionally spitting across the fence. The whole alternative scene has diminished to some degree, but quite how much remains to be seen. Apart from big names like Graham Hancock, publishers are now reluctant to invest in the alternative history genre in general on the grounds that it was only a Millennial phenomenon – but this is probably self-fulfilling: if they refuse to publish the books in the first place, no one can buy them. The mass hunger for Egyptological excitement seems to be satisfied, at least in part, by the hugely successful *Mummy* movies (Lupton Chapter 2, this volume) – misleading the public even further about the ancient culture, although enlivening the image of librarians considerably.

Like it or not, alternative Egypt is here to stay (indeed, as has been seen, it was around before Egyptology) and, rightly or wrongly, this will always be the case. Far better not to sneer or condescend, but to accept that this whizz-bang approach has something to offer, and in return provide the checks and balances. Between the two camps something very valuable may well emerge.

Notes

1   Gantenbrink's discovery was officially made on 22 March 1993, but Bauval (1999) writes of indications that the video was shown to Egyptian officials a week or two before this date.

2   Bauval (1994) advanced a wider theory, that outlying pyramids were laid out to represent the entire constellation of Orion, but he subsequently abandoned this suggestion.

3   In fact, Bauval's date was about a century *after* the usual date.

4   Hancock made the claim on the Art Bell radio show in July 1996, and Bauval at 'The Incident' conference in London in October of that year.

5   To Hancock and Bauval, 10500 BC was important because it marked the beginning of the Age of Leo, and they also claim that 2000 AD is the end of the Age of Pisces/beginning of Aquarius. However, because astrological ages are 2,160 years long, if Leo began in 10500 BC, the end of Pisces will not occur until 2460 AD. Conversely, if 2000 AD marked the end of Pisces, Leo must have started in 10960 BC.

6   The carbon dating did suggest that the Great Pyramid was about 400 years older than it is supposed to be, but this fell short of the 8,000 years hoped for by ARÉ.

7   For example, the Giza Debate, organized by *Quest for Knowledge* magazine in London in March 1998, which brought together John Anthony West, Adrian Gilbert and Ali Hassan, the former Secretary General of the Supreme Council of Antiquities. A conference held aboard a cruise ship off Alaska in May 1998 included Graham Hancock, Zahi Hawass and astronomer Ed Krupp. Several similar conferences were held in Egypt.

8   The Order of the Solar Temple's doctrines, beliefs and statutes were published in 'Perronik' 1975.

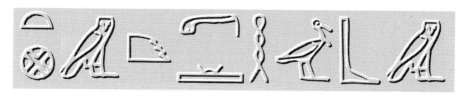

CHAPTER 14

ANCIENT EGYPT ON THE SMALL SCREEN – FROM FACT TO FACTION IN THE UK

Tim Schadla-Hall and Genny Morris

The popularity of Ancient Egypt lies in a paradox, for it is both unusual and mysterious as well as reassuringly familiar; this, combined with the spectacular visual imagery of Ancient Egypt, made it a civilization and subject tailor-made for television when it appeared as the mass communication medium from the second half of the last century. Archaeologists have been accused in the past of ignoring or failing to recognize "the role of popular representations" (Moser 2001: 263) in terms of the wider understanding (or frequently misunderstanding) of the past. Visual culture has become increasingly important, especially since the advent of television as a means of both presenting and explaining the past. One suspects that nowhere has this new 'language' vehicle had more impact than in the area of displaying and presenting Ancient Egypt.

Television is capable of showing 'real' Ancient Egypt, stripped of the film star element, for what it was, or might have been. Like cinema, first in monochrome, but by the late 1960s in colour, it undoubtedly had a profound effect on the appreciation of the nature and appearance of Ancient Egypt and made it more accessible to a wider audience. In the same period, despite the publication of more lavishly produced, competitively priced, colour illustrated books and magazines, print media was hard pushed to compete with the moving images and wide sweep of the small screen when it came to showing the potential breadth of the Egyptian experience.

Ancient Egypt was an obvious choice for any historically based documentaries from the outset of television development, simply because of the relative familiarity of the population with things Egyptian – the pyramids, Tutankhamun, and early civilization were all ideal subjects. In the UK, the first television documentaries on Egyptian subjects were provided with a niche in early archaeological programmes. However, since the 1980s, the number of programmes has burgeoned, and has been transformed. Nowadays, documentaries and programmes on Ancient Egypt are widespread, though they are generally confined to BBC2 and Channels 4 and 5. So prevalent now are these programmes that recently the ITV Director of Channels, David Liddiment, attacked what he described as "overkill" of mysterious, apocalyptic histories of all things ancient on BBC2 and Channel 4, listing such programmes as: *Secrets of the Dead*; *Mysteries of Lost Empires*; *Ancient Secrets*; *Secrets of the Ancients*;

Ancient Voices; Private Lives of the Pharaohs; Mystery of the Pharaoh's Obelisk, etc. Liddiment (2001: www.media.co.uk) was led to conclude:

… there are others, but as Private Eye would say – that's enough spooky pyramids – Ed

This comment reflects the current extent of the public's seemingly insatiable appetite for all things ancient and Egyptian. Moreover, the preponderance of such phrases as 'Lost Empires', 'mysteries', 'secrets', etc. exposes the essence of all these documentaries: the exploitation of Ancient Egypt, not only as a historical fact but also as a mystical, spiritual and enigmatic entity with a wealth of cultural capital that may be drawn upon to appeal to a wide spectrum of society. The result of this glamourizing of Ancient Egypt is that it has become almost impossible for anyone except a dedicated specialist to distinguish between *bone fide* academic documentaries on Ancient Egypt and 'alternative archaeology', fantasy and even science fiction programmes involving Egypt. Constantly, 'respectable' documentaries are jumping on the 'mysteries and secrets' bandwagon in order to gain airtime. Conversely, 'alternative archaeology' programmes are adopting the 'talking head' style of filming that was traditionally reserved for more didactic documentaries. Thus, the boundaries are blurred through techniques of filming and it becomes increasing difficult to separate the wheat from the chaff when it comes to television programmes on Ancient Egypt.

Additionally, the images created for cinema and the big screen are now endlessly recycled on the small screen as the number and range of channels that now exist, as well as the 24-hour nature of programming, have created an insatiable need for recycled films. Indeed, since the advent of the video cassette recorder (VCR) it is possible to capture images of Ancient Egypt almost continuously should one so desire. The inconvenience of visiting the cinema or waiting to watch a programme at a specific time is long gone – Ancient Egypt is now available in more forms, or rather transforms, than ever before.

The small screen has been adapted in other ways in the last half-century. How Ancient Egypt is portrayed on television is mirrored in the world of computer games. People's familiarity with Ancient Egypt provides an invaluable component in historic/strategic games, yet the images of splendour, treasure and mystery make Egypt an ideal backdrop to the science fiction/fantasy style of game. Finally, the small screen in the age of the internet and the increasing sophistication of image reproduction has seen the explosion of ancient Egyptian images in a myriad of websites, releasing a stream of ever more imaginative and unlikely views on Ancient Egypt.

This chapter is restricted to examining television images of Ancient Egypt in the UK because the early production of television documentaries was directly affected by the structure of governance in the country concerned, and the UK was the original home of the quality documentary. However, the products available today, in the era of so-called beneficial globalization, are accessible in all parts of the English-speaking world. The trend towards global Ancient Egypt marches hand in hand with increasing uniformity created by the economics and market-led basis of global television. Most of the products commissioned or made in the UK today will be sold simultaneously in the US and to satellite television companies, and vice versa. Programmes are an economic product (Abercrombie 1996).

Background to the development of TV

Despite an uncertain start in 1936, after the war, television in the UK was rapidly taken up as the preferred leisure and entertainment medium. Its success can be illustrated by the speed with which household ownership of television increased: ca. 130,000 sets in 1948, to 340,000 in 1950, to 10.5 million in 1959, to over 90 per cent of households by the mid-1970s (Currie 2000). The era of mass media had arrived; today the overwhelming majority of households now have television; at least 95 per cent of homes have at least one television, and there are now 19.3 million licenses (Werndly and Marshall 2002). The growth in ownership was matched by the growth in terrestrial channels – one in 1950, two in 1955, three in 1964, four in 1982, and five in 1997. This growth was overtaken by the development of satellite TV in the 1990s to such a degree that there are now more than 100 channels available for viewing. The explosion in broadcast hours of available TV to UK viewers rose from 42 hours per day in 1977 to 3,000 hours per day in 2002 (*Observer Review*, 2 June 2002). This amount of broadcast hours has led to the rise of specialist channels of varying types (for example the Discovery Channel, which specializes in archaeology-related programmes). This proliferation has also led to an overall decline in viewer numbers for the main channels as minority interests have been able to pursue their own specialist areas. Thus, in just over half a century the whole nature of the television product has evolved out of all recognition from the way in which it was originally perceived by its earlier controllers. Television started as an adjunct to the BBC (British Broadcasting Corporation), and was initially very much a poor relation of radio. After the war its popularity was rapidly recognized, and in any case the success of television in the US, where broadcasting was not regulated, in contrast with the UK, made clear its likely long term impact. Initially the BBC was controlled in line with the Reithian principles that had been laid down for radio (Abercrombie 1996), but early on attempts were made to create more broadcasting channels by the introduction of commercial television.

Television was becoming a matter of concern for government, especially how it should be controlled, regulated and presented. As early as 1949 the Beveridge Report came out clearly against 'sponsored' – i.e. commercial – television because it feared that advertisers would be able to dictate the content of programmes (Currie 2000: 14). The continuing pressure for commercial television combined with a change in government resulted in the establishment of ITV (Independent Television) in 1955. ITV was a commercial broadcasting operation, which rapidly produced a more popular product as it attempted to capture a larger slice of the audience. From the early 1950s the controllers of television, essentially drawn from the middle classes and keen to see the population 'improved' and 'cultured', quickly demonstrated the higher educational value of television. The development, from the mid-1950s, of commercial television, with regional output and advertising, saw an increasing emphasis on popular and entertaining programmes. These companies needed to demonstrate to advertisers that they could attract impressive numbers to their channel (Abercrombie 1996). They were highly successful, but this success did not radically alter the approach of the BBC. Soon after that there were numerous attacks claiming that ITV was sending the medium downmarket. The government at the time was concerned that television should still be widely educational, and in 1962 the Pilkington Committee, set up by the government, produced an anti-market-led report on the management, and to a lesser degree the product, of ITV (Currie 2000: 18). This report was largely ignored by the government, but the debate expressing the concerns about control, regulation and content has dogged television in the UK until relatively recently. It is after all still the dominant information medium. For historical reasons there had always been concerns about its effect on the population. One could easily argue that survival of the high quality documentary for example owes its continuity and development to the continuing need for all channels to demonstrate the improving, educational and informative role of the medium. As a result, in the third quarter of the last century, Reithian principles still dominated in what was an essentially three-channel television operation which – whilst not under state control, still tended to be essentially conservative in approach.

Early encounters with Ancient Egypt: discovering the small screen, 1960s–1980s

Ancient Egypt has captured the public's imagination for centuries. This increased markedly in the 19th and early 20th centuries when there was an explosion of Egyptian themes in books, in fashion, in the arts and eventually on the cinema screen (Lupton Chapter 2, Serafy Chapter 5, both this volume). The development of television after World War II, together with increasingly sophisticated camera equipment, meant that for the first time Egypt was captured at the touch of a button. What had been available to the few through travel, through museums (often displaying mummies and Egyptian artefacts), and to many more through illustrated books and magazines, was now widely available for the first time. The role of cinema in the pre-war period, when most productions were seen in black and white, was restricted to the reconstruction of ancient Egyptian buildings to create a backdrop for the actors. The sets were often highly speculative and wildly exaggerated, and whilst they might well have increased interest in the nature of Ancient Egypt, they lacked authenticity (see Humbert Chapter 3: 53–54, this volume, for 'authenticity' in opera scenery). Post-war cinema saw the advent of colour technology, and to some extent a slightly more realistic approach to the sets, but the tradition of costumed dramas continued.

From the late 1960s the worldwide growth in mass tourism and the advent of increasingly adventurous package holidays, as well as more and more specialist holiday packages from the 1980s, made Egypt accessible not only in the home but even more so in reality (El Daly Chapter 10, this volume). The wealth and rising incomes in the west as well as the (relatively) decreasing costs of air transport have resulted in the increased importance of tourism as an element of all national economies (in the case of Egypt, there are 5.5 million tourists, and the industry contributes over 20 per cent of the GDP). With a tourist publicity strategy based on the wealth of its archaeological remains and long history, it is hardly surprising that the vast majority go to look at the pyramids. This burgeoning group of 'been there, seen that' viewers also increased the audience potential for looking at Ancient Egypt on TV.

The appearance of BBC2 in 1964, at a time when the BBC still held the moral high ground in television output, was meant to (and did) open up a golden age for cultural and highbrow programmes that might be considered as being of minority interest, but 'improving' in their nature. These included a whole series of well-crafted and highly visual, expertly narrated documentary programmes, best exemplified in the UK by series of stunning programmes, such as *Chronicle* (see below). Previously, the only medium that had quenched the thirst for the mysteries of Ancient Egypt had been through the big screen epics that are dealt with elsewhere in this volume (Serafy Chapter 5). The opening up of the reality of Ancient Egypt to a mass audience, with a 'talking head' presenter, allowed access to a far wider audience than previously.

Television had therefore rapidly created a mass communication medium that was able to deliver to a wider audience what had previously only been available in books. The commercial potential of this was slowly realized in the post-war euphoria of a steadily improving and increasingly wealthy world. The initial reaction by the television controllers was to use it as a civilizing tool, promoting new knowledge for all.

It was now that programmes such as *Animal, Vegetable, Mineral?* awoke a public interest in archaeology, and "was an instant and spectacular success. Libraries found that neglected shelves of archaeological books were suddenly empty" (Daniel 1978: 7). This success saw Paul Johnstone, who had produced the *AVM?* series, go on to make archaeological documentaries. The first full length series to be broadcast on British television – under the title *Buried Treasure* – ran on BBC from 1954 until the early 1960s. These programmes not only introduced a post-war British public to archaeology outside the UK, but also took advantage of the increasingly scientific developments of post-war archaeology. The advent of C14 dating for example, and subsequent developments such as TL dating and a battery of laboratory driven techniques that became available to archaeological activity, all meant that archaeology could combine the excitingly old with new knowledge and ideas.

This approach had all sorts of appeal for post-war Britain. It suggested new discoveries in the new Elizabethan age, and also the onward and upward progress of science in a world recovering from the deprivations of post-war Europe. It also allowed a form of armchair tourism that was subsequently to be made real. The BBC was not alone, for alongside its popular programme production, ITV was also developing documentaries about the past as one-off programmes and occasional series. For example, in the early 1960s Kenneth (later Lord) Clark fronted a short series of programmes on ancient Egyptian civilization, in the days when the independent television companies were anxious to match the quality and educational content of early mass television that had been developed by the BBC. At least initially the style of documentaries was similar to that of the BBC, not surprisingly because of the initial move of BBC staff across to ITV, or indeed the fact that ITV had high ideals and often followed tried and tested successful formulae. Thus, only four years on from *The Tutankhamun Post-Mortem*, Professor R. G. Harrison was the main figure and expert on ITV's *Tutankhamun Kinship*, in a programme that effectively built on the *Chronicle* documentary (see below).

In 1966, the BBC created the 'Archaeological and Historical Unit' with Paul Johnstone at its head, and *Chronicle* was launched, based on the experience of these earlier programmes and using the wealth of contacts and knowledge that had been developed by Johnstone and his team over previous years. It had as its *raison d'être* the need to show the nature of the past in all its aspects. Of course *Chronicle* was by no means the only programme dedicated to the presentation of the past, but it was in many ways the high point in the early television documentary genre, and created a standard and subsequently an almost mythical memory of a golden age of television archaeology – a standard against which subsequent work would be judged.

Out of the original series of *Chronicle* programmes shown between 1966 and 1977, at least seven dealt with Egypt. At that time viewing figures were in the region of three million, although those for Egyptian subject programmes were always significantly higher (Roy Sutcliffe, pers. comm.). The programmes dealt with the then state of knowledge of Egypt and brought together high quality images along with informed thoughtful analysis, using acknowledged experts, scientific techniques and the sense of discovery.

Taking one *Chronicle* programme and providing an analysis gives an insight into the nature of the presentation of Ancient Egypt which had now emerged. *The Tutankhamun Post-Mortem*, which was first screened in 1969, had started to be planned in 1967, and was largely funded by the BBC. Geoffrey Harrison, Professor of Anatomy at Liverpool University, had begun to work on mummification as a process from the late 1950s (Harrison 1978), and after initial research, became involved with attempts to relate Tutankhamun with Akhenaten, as a result of earlier suggestions that there was no relationship between the two. The investigative work was, like the filming and crew size involved, costly in terms of time, travel and equipment, but Paul Johnstone offered "financial aid on a substantial scale" (Harrison 1978: 44). This documentary had:

- A familiar and central figure – Tutankhamun, who because of the original Carnarvon/Carter excavations of the 1920s, and countless books and museum exhibitions, was well known to a significant section of the public.

- A familiar myth – 'the curse of King Tut' (which was discussed in the programme).

- A clear scientific angle – in this case forensic anatomy (bringing the past together with the present), and scientists in white coats!

- Discovery – opening the sarcophagus in Tutankhamun's tomb and looking at human remains (not ours and very old!).

- The whole of Ancient Egypt to film as a backdrop.

The programme itself was divided into setting the scene and showing spectacular shots of the original discoveries and discussing the 'mystery of King Tut', followed by the scientific examination of the mummified bodies and the subsequent results. There were a number of 'talking head' shots and pieces to camera, without an interviewer present. The whole film was interspersed with high quality general views (GVs) of Egyptian landscape and archaeology.

Overall, it was visual images and discovery through science that distinguished this, and the rest of the early *Chronicle*-type productions. There was a lack of props and reconstructions, and the presentation involved lofty and relatively remote experts talking to an audience. It was about the handing down of information on a new discovery, delivered as fact and instruction, in line with the somewhat remote and authoritarian stance that the BBC adopted in those days. In addition, there was not a great deal of background music to add atmosphere to the programmes – and what there was was used sparingly and very much derived from classical music. This approach was very different from the next generation of television documentaries; it was not accompanied by filming gimmicks or 'high tech' interpretation using computer enhanced images. Reconstruction drawings did make an occasional appearance, as did maps, but only sparingly, although it is worth noting that in the *Chronicle* programme on the reconstruction of Akhenaten's temple in 1971 computer aided reconstruction was used for the first time (P. Jordan, pers. comm.). The subject clearly assumed some knowledge of Ancient Egypt, but built very much on the known – Tutankhamun. There were clear differences between this approach and that used in the 2001 BBC2-screened mini series, *Ancient Apocalypse* (see below).

In 1972, the BBC also produced 13 programmes, each lasting less than half an hour, on the world of Tutankhamun. This series, which was introduced by Cyril Aldred of the National Museum of Scotland, was almost an entirely voice-over production, with superlative visuals. It had huge appeal and was broadcast to coincide with and illuminate the 'Treasures of Tutankhamun' exhibition, the British Museum's first post-war blockbuster exhibition and part of a worldwide tour. This exhibition had queues for weeks, stretching for hundreds of yards from the main entrance of the museum.

The success of *Chronicle* in the field of Ancient Egypt was nothing new. It is important to note that in these early days the quality of filming was of a remarkably high standard – this had much to do with the tradition, derived from making big screen movies and the then requirement for perfectly composed shots, in which clarity and visual effect were seen as critical to the final product and where the quality of the camera work was paramount. Time was not a great constraint on these productions that were made by company employees who were concerned to demonstrate craftsmanship and perfection, and who were supported by acknowledged experts. It is unlikely that anyone today would have the time or the budget to emulate these early programmes.

Jordan (1981: 211), looking back on this period of documentary work, commented about archaeology programming in general:

> Since the beginning, archaeology programs have been popular on television. Curiously enough, they are often difficult to make. The difficulty depends upon the sort of subject involved, for there are several sorts of television archaeology programs. There are programs that tell an established story, whether of discovery in the past or of some aspect of a site or ancient culture; and there are programs which follow the course of a current discovery or investigation ... At this level, any good archaeological program also helps in some way to dispel the *misapprehension and mistaken assumptions of the lunatic fringe* [emphasis added].

Jordan, who was intimately involved with many of the early documentaries about Egypt, enthused about the power of television to develop the public's interest in archaeology; his almost patrician and didactic approach is clear, and undoubtedly reflects the views of many involved in documentary productions, for

> programmes which set out to tell an established story have some advantages over the ones that follow the course of discoveries … At their grandest, in the form of a many part series, they can set out to present the audience with comprehensive views of whole cultures, with comprehensive views of whole ancient cultures … Such series are *terrifically educative* and, as they go on being made and extended in scope, *their power to enlighten the public as to the best thinking of the archaeological specialists must prove to be not only a valuable source of entertainment and information but also a needed antidote to the slapdash irrationalism of the 'ancient gods and spacemen' school. The very popularity of the latter indicates the desirability of some more missionary work in that direction.*

(Jordan 1981: 212; emphasis added)

How these hopes have been dashed in subsequent years!

As the subjects that could be covered were exhausted and as television became an increasingly acceptable medium, the range of matters that could be dealt with concerning Ancient Egypt expanded – for example, it was possible to combine medicine (always a popular theme on television) with Ancient Egypt by carrying out autopsies on mummies from the Manchester museum using modern techniques to unravel and operate on Ancient Egyptians – a series that echoed both the fascination for (then) current medical work, which was being shown live on TV at the time, with the image of Ancient Egypt. Increasingly, more and more angles on Egypt were being brought into play. The documentary genre had already become hybridized with elements of drama and detection.

Thus, by the end of the mid-1980s the BBC, and to a lesser degree ITV, had exploited Ancient Egypt in an educational and authoritative series of programmes which used expertise, had possibly become a little formulaic but which had made Ancient Egypt more widely known than ever before in terms of image, achievement and history. It seems reasonable to describe this period as one in which the visual language of Ancient Egypt was established for a wider audience – one in which encountering and discovering Ancient Egypt became a familiar experience for millions of people, including the next generation of television programmers. This visual and factual 'beginners textbook' of Egypt with its 'language' in place could now be further developed. The Egyptian Civilization documentary genre had been established.

Familiarity to fantasy – and beyond: transforming the image of Ancient Egypt, the late 1980s onwards

The authoritative documentary described above had certainly not run its course by the 1980s, but a series of changes in the television world were having an increasing impact on the output and direction of television itself. It had become the universal preferred medium of communication in the UK. Television has been constantly evolving since its appearance; in a sense this constant change is reflected in all aspects of output and activity. The personnel controlling television were changing; a second generation of managers and editors was beginning to appear, who had the advantage of being trained in 'creative media skills'. The technology had developed in all areas from camera through to film, from enhancement of images through to techniques of presentation. The size and complexity of what had become a huge and financially profitable leisure and entertainment industry meant that quality was not necessarily what drove development and programmes. It was more a matter of growing viewer numbers and holding market share to satisfy advertisers and thus to maximize profits.

At the same time the BBC had been increasingly scrutinized in terms of costs and output. The era of measurement and cost accountancy had reached the leisured world of publicly funded television, which had inevitably been drawn into competition on the basis of audience ratings rather than quality of product, although the term 'quality' is still stressed in most television companies. The BBC was examined as never before, and 'outsourced' much of its production facilities (another term for making redundancies). This approach was similar to the regime of the independent television companies, and as it developed, more programme makers no longer worked for the BBC itself but were independent and had to sell their ideas and wares through commissioning editors. Independent production companies increasingly made decisions about the nature, content and form that programmes would take. Money, time and approval (from commissioning editors) were now critical. Investment required returns and competition, as usual, was cost sensitive.

In an increasingly diverse and wealthy post-modern society, public tastes had changed, as had the nature of demand. A new generation of viewers would no longer be satisfied by output that emphasized quality and fact. The universality of the medium, the competitive nature of the industry and the increasing fissiparity of public demand as the choice of channels multiplied meant that not only the range of product increased, but also that there was a relentless search for the 'new', the latest, and the trendy.

In encountering Ancient Egypt there was a need to 'update' the product, to make the presenter more familiar and viewer-friendly, and to craft an image that resonated with evolving taste and the demands for the preferred medium of communication. Specialists and academics could be replaced by professional presenters who provided a bridge to a wider audience and who, it was believed, would relate better to an audience than a dry-as-dust academic who was trained to communicate to an educated elite through the medium of the lecture room. (Curiously enough, increasingly the academic world has begun to respond to this trend by creating a whole new type of media-friendly persona, especially in the field of presenting the past!) Ancient Egypt needed to be recreated into an image of the wider television world, to pursue the trendy and the new and to involve and establish contact with the audience. The establishment in the minds of many viewers of a basic Egyptian dictionary/language meant that Ancient Egypt could now be developed as a reference point into new areas of entertainment that did not require back referencing and that could be used to develop a further ('new' and alternative) series of understandings and images of Egypt.

An apparent cohesiveness and certainty had been replaced by a pluralist, multi-cultural, more questioning and uncertain approach to the past – and the future. A search for the new and the mysterious, the bizarre and the uncertain replaced the certainty of the western Christian imperialist philosophy. There were no longer answers, only possibilities as post-war relief was replaced by doubts about what was going to happen. This was reflected in the approach to Ancient Egypt and its civilization as portrayed on the small screen.

The trend towards the production of television documentary programmes changed from the late 1980s; new programmes concentrated less on the achievements of Ancient Egypt and more on wider and less explained aspects of Egypt. A series of shows (e.g. *Pharaohs and Kings*, Channel 4, 3 September 1995) fronted and conceived by David Rohl exemplifies this shift. It concentrated upon, for example, ritual and speculation, curiously mirroring the early cinema efforts to create a mysterious past full of sinister overtones, cataclysmic events and sacrifice. Egypt again became mysterious and sinister, with music creating an eerie environment, and whilst the 'talking head' presenter and expert still appeared as the interpreter of Egypt, he or she might not necessarily be a recognized authority with a university background, but someone who had made a lifelong study of the subject, offering an alternative to accepted wisdom. This reflected the requirements of a pluralist society in which the (academic) elite could increasingly be questioned, and doubted for its promulgation of the 'official view'.

This demonstrates the democratizing properties of the mass medium where the past becomes the possession of the many rather than the few, and also clearly panders to the professed inclusiveness of television. These and similar programmes were accompanied by a series of stunning visuals, whilst the factual and authoritative content was increasingly replaced by speculation, overt and unlikely interpretation and a questioning approach. It was almost as if, having completed showings of the achievement of Egypt, the point had been reached when television could begin to create a new market that had hitherto been exploited by the larger screen fiction of *The Mummy's Curse*, and earlier films that were now beginning to make a comeback after their relative demise in the 1940s and 1950s (Lupton Chapter 2, this volume). This development also fitted in well with the way that western society has been prepared to take on increasingly 'mystical' explanations of the past as accepted explanations have been repeatedly questioned (Picknett and Prince Chapter 13, this volume). The appetite for Ancient Egypt remained, but it was being spread across a wider span of programmes. The existing lexicon of established images could be translated into fiction and be used as the foundation for allied and yet unrelated (at least in terms of reality) projects. The development of the old themes became even more potent, popular and recognizable in the market place for mystery and entertainment. Now iconographic images derived from factual documentaries could be transferred, incorporating the developing images of mystery and intrigue into a series of fictional programmes. These programmes, such as *Stargate*, could borrow and transform the imagery of Ancient Egypt, now a more widely accepted currency as a result of their availability on the small screen. Thus, fiction now uses an increasingly acceptable background language about Ancient Egypt to create a fantasy world, reflected in costume and architectural statements. Ancient Egypt has become in this case a starting point for new fantasies.

At the same time Egypt's familiar images are used to construct reference points for a series of increasingly alternative archaeological explanations in which the known images/understanding of Egypt can be used as a base upon which to build further ideas. The *Mystery of the Mummies* series developed by Channel 4 in the late 1990s used the already recognizable image of mummies to speculate about the possibility of hyperdiffusion from Egypt. This approach harks back to the work of Grafton Elliot Smith (1923) and W. J. Perry (1923), which has been largely dismissed by archaeologists and was certainly not acceptable to the vast majority of the academic world even by the 1950s (Champion 2003; Daniel 1992: 74–76). However, many of the hypotheses in such programmes were based upon the assumed familiarity (of the audience) with Ancient Egypt = mummies = civilization. For example, in the programme dealing with the Azores, the reed boats so beloved of Thor Heyerdahl in the Ra Expedition (Heyerdahl 1970) are used to explain migration, and are supported with a series of images of Ancient Egypt and by a group of 'experts', who appear on programmes often linked to ancient Egyptian mummies (anatomists, not archaeologists).

There are no answers, but a series of questions in this format. The trend towards having 'talking head' 'experts' with no necessarily archaeological qualifications develops and is an inevitable corollary of the move towards pluralist interpretations of the past. The Egyptian reed boat was used to explain hyperdiffusionism by Heyerdahl and then subsequently used by Graham Hancock as an indicator of an even earlier civilization that he postulates to have given the idea of the reed boat to the world!

The element of fantasy and decreasing certainty has been continued in other mini-series; one that has attracted considerable discussion and aroused the ire of archaeologists is the Graham Hancock series *Heaven's Mirror*, a Channel 4 series with an accompanying book that sold millions of copies worldwide (Hancock and Faia 1998). Hancock dealt with the well-rehearsed myth of a lost and early civilization, using Egypt as an anchor for other images and speculation. Although Ancient Egypt was not the central focus of the series, which speculated on a pre-Egyptian civilization, it formed a recognizable and major reference point for both the argument and evidence offered. The steady growth of alternative archaeology, aided by the appetite for mystery and the proliferation of accessible and cheap media platforms, ranging from television, with its increasing need to fill the ever-expanding broadcast hours, to the internet with its limitless sites and size, has found an ideal focus in Ancient Egypt.

Developing encounters with Ancient Egypt – the small screen enhances its product

Ancient Egypt, as a place with archaeological remains and discoveries, continued from the 1980s to attract the programme makers. The continuous research and discovery of archaeological remains, as well as the continuing public appetite for programmes on Egypt, made the subject more and more familiar, so that hardly a month went by without some programme examining some facet of Egyptian archaeology. The steady improvements in technology – lighter cameras and smaller crews – all had an impact in keeping Egypt at the forefront of the television documentary. But other fashions and influences were at work that would also affect the product. Television had become big business, with an increasing emphasis on the new and the different, and increasing competition between television channels was also a factor. The 'talking head' became less fashionable and the drive towards entertainment more pronounced.

Whilst many modern documentaries on Ancient Egypt aim to portray an accurate image of the civilization, there is a trend for the majority to turn towards hyperbole and grandiose concepts in order to attract audiences. Nowhere is this more apparent than in the titles of programmes such as *Ancient Apocalypse*, *Mysteries of Lost Empires*, *Mystery of the Mummies* and *Ancient Secrets*. It seems that a documentary on Ancient Egypt is of no value unless it reveals some new secret or uncovers some hitherto unheard of mystery. However, the actual content of these documentaries varies very little and groundbreaking revelations are few and far between. Thus, Ancient Egypt by its very nature is viewed as synonymous with mystery. Take, for example, the following two excerpts from documentaries on Ancient Egypt:

> … over three thousand years a story has been hidden under the sands of Egypt … told in stone, papyrus and gold. An epic tale.
>
> (*Egypt's Golden Empire*, Lion Television, BBC, 2001)

> … To this day, Tutankhamun and the end of his family remain mysterious … Many of the exquisite pieces [of his funerary goods] show the tantalising life of the boy-king.
>
> (*Private Lives of the Pharaohs*, Channel 4, 1999)

The scripts for documentaries on Ancient Egypt involve superlatives and hyperbole and they succeed in drawing viewers; *Mysteries of Lost Empires* (Channel 4), for example, ranked ninth in the ratings when it was aired in June 2000, and received over seven million viewers (www.rogerhopkins.com). The mysteries of Ancient Egypt are a powerful commodity. To enhance the claims of secrets the producers of documentaries on Ancient Egypt have at their disposal many tried and tested techniques such as use of language, as well as popular images of Egypt, reconstructions and background music.

The most famous image of Ancient Egypt is undoubtedly the pyramid (Humbert 2003). Even when the documentary series *Egypt's Golden Empire* focused on a period of Egyptian history that took place over 1,000 years after the pyramids had been built, images of the pyramids featured prominently in the opening and closing shots. The series started life as *Egypt: The New Kingdom*, but the American co-producing company asked for the word "Empire" to be included (because it had a strand of 'Empire' programmes already). Subsequently the co-producer wanted to create a sense of 'wonder', and "Golden" was added. The appearance of the pyramids was also at the request of the co-producer despite the chronological gap between them (Justin Pollard, pers. comm.). It is highly unlikely that a producer of a historical documentary on, say, the English Civil War would find it necessary to include myriad shots of Stonehenge. Yet the image of the pyramid is inextricably linked to that of Ancient Egypt, it is a touchstone with which everyone is familiar and is a powerful image. In *Egypt's Golden Empire* the closing shot is of clouds and their shadows fleeting over the pyramids of Giza – there is no better image that could so simply portray the notion of time passing in aeons.

Another popular shot in documentaries is one of fixing on the eyes of a statue so that it seems that it is the *eyes* rather than the face or body of the statue that is the focus. This may be partly because, to the inexperienced eye, most Egyptian sculpture can seem very similar due to the artistic canons of Ancient Egypt. However, the thousands of statues seem, as with the pyramids, to be staring into eternity. Indeed, the Ancient Egyptians themselves carved such monuments and statues with immortality in mind and the television producers have certainly picked up on this theme and made it their own. The Sphinx in particular is the embodiment of mystery and the passage of time, and has been correspondingly exploited in documentaries.

Reconstructions are also popular, not only of the time of the pharaohs but also of 19th and 20th century archaeological excavations. It is easy to understand the popularity of reconstructions of archaeological excavations. These bring the viewer closer to the point of discovery; the audience is, for example, able to witness the opening of Tutankhamun's tomb and see 'everywhere the glint of gold'. The monuments of Ancient Egypt are difficult to reconstruct; they are often subject to speculation and may in consequence be inaccurate. Some documentaries deal with the problem of reconstruction by showing only vague aspects of the scene or building concerned; in *Egypt's Golden Empire*, for example, all reconstructions are shown at ground level and all that is seen are the feet of soldiers, children or priests. However, other documentaries, such as *Private Lives of the Pharaohs*, are audacious enough to act out a scene of early courtship between Tutankhamun and his half-sister. The possibilities for misleading the viewer are endless but the aim is not archaeological or historical pedantry but entertainment, and if it means resorting to movie-making techniques, the producers will say 'so be it'.

Private Lives of the Pharaohs, a Channel 4 mini-series in 1999, had, as an increasing number of documentary series do, an accompanying publication (Tyldesley 2000) illustrated with stills from the original series. It stretched the ancient Egyptian documentary into medical, thriller and scientific discovery. DNA has become another vital part of the genre and has provided the potential for even more 'scientist and laboratory' shots as well as ancient mystery. It combined many of the older documentary elements, authoritative, respectably academic, with high technology, ancient mystery and uncertainty.

Music increasingly plays an important role in creating an atmosphere of mystery. The style of music used in documentaries varies little from programme to programme. The general trend is towards chanting and slow drumbeats, no doubt meant to instil images of religious orders partaking of rituals. It is either that or 'snake-charmer' pipe music that emanates from western ideas of a mysterious orient. It is true that there is evidence that the Ancient Egyptians played pipes of some kind, though the subtext of such background music is more redolent of the mysteries which the snake charmer invokes. Thus, again, the programmes exploit and pander to current/western preconceptions of Ancient Egypt.

The techniques mentioned above are now all used in documentaries with an academic historical/scientific basis, for it is deemed necessary in this day and age to market Ancient Egypt in a package of mystery and secrecy if anyone is to take an interest. Unfortunately, due to this phenomenon, it has become almost impossible to distinguish between *bona fide* academic programmes and the 'lunatic fringe' which have imitated the way in which such documentaries have been presented and exploited this style to great success.

One recent documentary was shown as part of a mini-series in autumn 2001. *Ancient Apocalypse* featured a number of mysteries. The programme entitled *Death on the Nile* (which automatically assumes a resonance with the Agatha Christie thriller and the well known, star-studded cinema film which is constantly recycled on television, this providing another example of an assumed familiarity with a basic Ancient Egyptian 'language') dealt with the apparent catastrophic end of the Old Kingdom. It had:

- A mystery – the end of the Old Kingdom, which it established through a series of GVs of the pyramids, and voice-over as being about 4,000 years ago.

- The current and fashionable post-1980s concern of disaster and global climate change.

- A combination of several scientific angles.

- Discovery in several different forms (with no less than seven reputable scientists and archaeologists performing).

- The backdrop of Ancient Egypt.

There are similarities and echoes here which reach back to earlier documentaries (see above), but there are also significant differences. In terms of its ambitions, this programme was far more wide-ranging in the way it was framed. It offered a single but far more complex subject in which there were fewer certainties and in which the viewer could participate and consider the way in which the archaeologist was working. There was disagreement between Professor Fekri Hassan, who was developing an explanation for the end of the Old Kingdom based on a climatic catastrophe, and Dr Gaballah Ali Gaballah, then of the Egyptian Supreme Council of Antiquities. Some of the attempts to gather evidence failed to provide the answers that would have fitted into the programme's hypothesis, so that it was shown that scientists did not have all the answers, with archaeologists appearing as searchers for, but not necessarily finders of, the truth. In addition, several different forms of scholarly evidence were used, from archaeological material to geological work with deep-sea cores, from botany, charcoal and woodland species analysis to the analysis of stalagmites.

All of this involved clips from several different locations around the world, and the participants often only partly explained the techniques that were being used. A great deal was left to the assumption that the viewer would be able to follow the jumps that were being made. There were 'talking heads', but only in short bursts, and other devices were supplied through the voice-over, so that for example whenever a translation of the disaster at the end of the Old Kingdom was being described from contemporary accounts, the voice became strangulated and whispered, thus adding to the mystery of the past. The filming was largely done with hand-held cameras which did not always produce perfectly stable shots of the past. The shots themselves were often produced from bizarre angles – another much loved device of the modern documentary which demonstrated the changing art of the cameraman. This is intended both to nod in the direction of current techniques that make things different, and also to increase the distance of the past from the viewer. This film, which was shot on video as opposed to the 16 mm film of 30 years earlier, could also be easily manipulated in terms of colour. The editor was able to change the colour composition to purple trees and sepia colours at the flick of a button. This was intended to add to the air of mystery, and other-world-ness, as well as the menace of the past. Images were projected across the screen that were intended to take the place of words; for example sandstorms and grainy indistinct figures represented desiccation.

The whole production was breathless in its pace, and relentless in introducing new elements into the storyline. Although the film came to a conclusion, viewers were really invited to look at the evidence for themselves, and allowed to form their own views. Computer generated models of the pyramids, the sphinx and surrounding landscape, which included figures and was meant to represent the Old Kingdom, were remarkable in their detail and showed the power of this technique to the full. In addition, the film was accompanied throughout by specially commissioned electronic music (another benefit of technological change). This dominated the film and was used to create a mood of mystery, uncertainty and danger throughout, whilst at the same time hinting at traditions of Arab music, and clearly owing much to pop video production and technique.

The final product used a series of technological innovations: from the power and flexibility of the editing machinery through to availability of electronic mood music; from virtual reality computer enhancement to recreate the past to a series of camera angle techniques which added nothing to the story but added to the air of mystery. These same techniques created a resonance with many of the fictional uses of Ancient Egypt and allowed the viewer to relate to such series as *Stargate*, for example, and blurred the relationship between fact and fiction. At the same time the pace of the film echoed the detective thriller and the idea of the scientist as searcher after truth and as hero, derived from the big screen epics of the 1980s and 1990s such as *Indiana Jones and the Raiders of the Lost Ark*. The experts and the 'talking heads' are still in evidence, as is the sense of discovery, but the end product is closer to a detective thriller than the patient scientific analysis of the past, and is far less certain in its conclusions.

At the end of the screening of the programme, the audience was invited to discuss it with Professor Fekri Hassan live on the internet. The new technology really does allow audience participation and emphasizes the importance of the small screen.

Egypt – the impact of the small screen

Television is a democratizing and popularizing medium; there is no doubt that access to television has changed the whole of society's understanding of all the dimensions of its environment. It has had unimagined effects on interpreting the nature of the world; it has made the unfamiliar and the exotic everyday and almost normal. In the case of Ancient Egypt, it has made it ubiquitous and commonplace, over a period of around 50 years.

- In its early days, television provided authoritative and clear presentations of Ancient Egypt; and *Chronicle* typifies the type of programme that characterized presentation of the subject: clear, composed camera work, drawing on expertise, 'talking heads', and utilizing well known images and 'mainstream' topics. The subject was allowed to speak for itself. There was an element of certainty and unhurried steadiness in the texts. Most of the readily accessible subjects were covered, and Tutankhamun proved to be a major point of departure. Programmes tended to be didactic and educational.

- The 1980s saw the progressive use of science, and the development of the genre; the thriller/detective mode became more common as the discourse with Ancient Egypt developed. A greater degree of uncertainty was introduced, and programmes began to examine more general problems that created an air of increasing mystery and discovery. The coverage tended to be faster, more 'breathless' in treatment and far less authoritative. Familiar images were used, but the past became more mysterious and complex. Camera techniques began to change, and 'talking heads' were less in evidence.

- By the 1990s Ancient Egypt had begun to spill over into fictional images in television drama series such as *Stargate*, and computer games became more widespread, using the 'language' of Ancient Egypt. Archaeology in general was more and more widely portrayed on television and old, already transmitted topics were being repackaged and recycled to fill increasing broadcast hours. The mystery/apocalyptic elements of Egypt had been emphasized and texts took increasing advantage of new scientific techniques to explain or re-mystify the uncertain past. The presenter was often a generalist rather than academic and often created questioning and open-ended texts that left the audience to make up their own minds, using data on a worldwide scale (for example *Mystery of the Mummies*, or, even more speculatively, *Quest for Civilizations*). The emphasis had changed – programmes began to reflect current fears of worldwide catastrophe (for example in *Ancient Apocalypse*) – which clearly resonated with concerns of ecological disaster and uncertainty for the future. Equally, the interest in individuals and individual lives was reflected in such series as *Private Lives of the Pharaohs*, in which the past is portrayed in the 'people like us' genre, as the past becomes more human. It can be argued that by then the lunatic fringe had arrived. However, despite the alternative, mysterious and uncertain, much of the traditional approach of the 1970s documentary has survived, albeit in a form that has been affected by fashion and technological change.

- The importance and impact of television's technological advances and industrial changes on the unfolding image of Egypt on the small screen are critical. The television world has changed. Most programmes are now made to be sold around the world, and cater for a bewildering range of audiences. The demands of the audience is ever changing and is constantly monitored. Egypt remains a steady seller, and a safe, saleable product within the industry; nevertheless, even in this case, the nature of the medium has changed the message (to adapt McLuhan's (McLuhan and Zingrone 1997: 212) words, "the medium is the message").

There can, therefore, be no doubt that television has become a major vehicle for disseminating information concerning Ancient Egypt. Archaeologists have been slow to consider the effect of the media on the understanding and images of the past, and few television workers and producers have bothered to enunciate their approaches or views to a wider readership. James (2001: 46) commented that "in assessing the impact and usage of historical ideas we cannot afford to ignore these [film and novels] aspects of popular discourse". He could have added television as well. The most sinister development from an archaeological point of view is the rise of the 'factoid' (as James (1999: 145) defines it): "an unproved idea or assumption that is repeated so often that it becomes accepted as factual truth."

Undoubtedly, an increasing number of factoids are being presented about Ancient Egypt, but the question is whether this should be a cause for concern. The answer is probably yes; because "Archaeology, the most visual of the historical disciplines, is inherently didactic" (Silberman 1995: 261), and factoids will, therefore, be powerful. It is undeniable that "Archaeological narratives cannot help but be constructed in contemporary idiom, with emphasis on each society's specific hopes and fears" (Silberman 1995: 261); this holds true for Ancient Egypt on the small screen. Christine Finn's (2001) recent analysis of archaeology and the media refers specifically to the ways in which Ancient Egypt is portrayed, when she discusses Silberman's (1999) critique of two programmes: *Opening the Lost Tombs: live from Egypt* (Fox) and *Cleopatra's Palace: in search of a legend* (Discovery). Both have subsequently been screened on UK terrestrial channels. Silberman opined that "It is archaeologists, not scriptwriters, who are not ready for prime time" in the case of *Opening the Lost Tombs*, describing it as "a magician's show of opened tombs, buried skeletons and scary stories about fearsome curses", concluding that "accuracy and scholarly standards had nothing to do with it".

In the case of *Cleopatra's Palace*, which was a mixture of archaeological diving scenes and clips from old films about Cleopatra, it was never clear that Cleopatra had anything to do with the results except by implication. Silberman argued that it "was a program of conjecture" (Finn 2001: 266). That seems generous; even inserting the term 'extreme' would be generous. Nevertheless, conjecture is halfway to 'factoid' in terms of documentary text.

Ancient Egypt has always been subject to changing perspectives and interpretations whatever the archaeologist would wish; as Frayling (1992: xii) commented in his foreword to the book that accompanied the BBC2 five-part TV series *The Face of Tutankhamun* (and was advertised as "as seen on TV") screened in 1992, the aim was to "present a series of perspectives on the discovery of the tomb of Tutankhamun as *a social and cultural phenomenon, and as an aspect of popular culture from the 1920s to the present day. They mix fact and fiction*, as did popular reactions to the news of the finding of the treasure" (emphasis added) (see Lupton Chapter 2, this volume).

The idea that "television works to … promote serious programmes about real archaeology and keep out too much in the way of the lunatic preoccupations of fringe archaeology" (Jordan 1981: 208) seems doomed to relate to a short period from the late 1960s to the late 1970s. Plenty of lunatic preoccupations now dominate the texts of television screens, and they are on the increase! Maybe there is no reason to worry:

> Over a century of increasing scholarly light in dark places has completely failed to destroy the myth of Egyptian hermetic wisdom. A remarkable succession of occultists, numerologists, Pythagoreans and the like … continues to promote any number of arcane theories … What is more, these fantasies command a large and apparently insatiable market.
>
> (Green 1989, quoted in Frayling 1992: 272)

How true, and yet the traditional documentary still survives … just.

There has been a steady hybridization of the pure documentary genre, with elements of detection, and drama, and subsequently science fiction – the dominant discourse has nearly always been Ancient Egypt and the Egyptian civilization, but the generic text has always been subject to change; the dominant theme of Egypt and discovery has been constantly changed and altered by elements of science fiction, drama, thriller/mystery approaches, current social and political trends, and the never-ending development of the technical aspects of the medium. Maybe one should rejoice at the continuing reinvention of Ancient Egypt, rather than worry about scholarly truth. After all, Ancient Egypt always benefits, and so do the scholarly minority!

Endgames

There can be no doubting Ancient Egypt's place in the public's consciousness, and it is for this reason that Egypt invariably appears in 'historical' computer strategy games as a touchstone to the past. Ancient Egypt is known to all; it is mysterious; it is visually pleasing. About Egypt's profile in 'Civilization' (Sid Meier, Firaxis Games) it is said:

> Few civilizations have left such an indelible mark on history as the Egyptians. They built the pyramids of Giza and the Sphinx, and were among the first civilizations to brew beer. And let's not forget the mummy … think where modern horror cinema would be if they had not invented it! Throughout history, continuing to the present day, the Egyptians' craftiness, mysticism and sense of fashion have fascinated and puzzled us.
>
> (www.civ3.com)

It is little wonder, then, that in 'Age of Empires I' and 'II' (Ensemble Studios), Egypt should be the first and easiest level to play, as opposed to more esoteric civilizations such as the Hittites or the Choson. It is noticeable when listing the different empires that several are thought to require further explanation – for example Shang, Choson and Yamoto are amended parenthetically with China, Korea and Japan respectively (www.ensemblestudios.com.); no such elucidation would ever be required for the Ancient Egyptians. Both 'Civilization' and 'The Age of Empires' endeavour to maintain historical accuracy; in 'The Age of Empires' there is a 40,000 word encyclopaedia that provides historical notes on the empires, including the rise of civilization and the rise of warfare (www.microsoft.com/games/empires). 'Civilization III' provides a profile of all the empires in the game and gives a brief but accurate history of the Egyptian empire, from its unification by Menes to the Islamic invasion (www.civ3.com).

Other 'historical' games are concerned less with warfare and more on economic progression, such as 'Pharaoh', in which the aim is to develop a civilization on the Nile by building homes, religious monuments, business infrastructures and towns. Pitfalls include failing to hold enough religious festivals to appease the gods or drought due to a low Nile flood (www.gamesdomain.com). However, 'Pharaoh' does not focus as much on ancient Egyptian history as the games mentioned above, though it nonetheless attempts to be fairly accurate in its portrayal of Egypt.

The same is also true of 'A Tale in the Desert', in which the central concept is that the player must try to recreate the perfection of Ancient Egypt. This is measured through the Seven Tests of Perfection – Leadership; Thought; the Human Body; Worship; Architecture; Art & Music; and Conflict (http://rpgvault.ign.com/features/interviews/taledesert). The notion that the Ancient Egyptians had achieved human perfection is not a new one; many cults from the Rosicrucians to the modern Fellowship of Isis have looked towards Ancient Egypt for spiritual guidance (and see Picknett and Prince Chapter 13, this volume). 'A Tale in the Desert' is simply taking a popular time-held image of Egypt and transferring it to the modern medium of the computer game.

The alternative to the historical/strategic games are the 'fantasy' games that exploit the images, mythology and mystery of Egypt without any deference to historical accuracy. The new game 'The Age of Mythology' (Ensemble Studios) can perhaps be seen as the turning point between history and fantasy. It emanates from the same studio as 'The Age of Empires' and, again, it is a strategy-based game. However, it is not based on historical reality but on Egyptian, Greek and Norse mythology. The advert for 'The Age of Mythology' depicts an image of a humanoid Minotaur and a sickle-wielding Anubis standing before several Egyptian temples, pyramids, palm trees and obelisks (www.ensemblestudios.com). It is clear that the emphasis is on image; a blurb for the new game reads:

The Age of Mythology takes stunning advantage of its all-new 3D technology to present realistic worlds, eye-popping special effects and in-game cinematics that seamlessly drive the ambitious single player campaign.

(www.ensemblestudios.com)

What better showcase could there be for this new technology than a re-creation of Ancient Egypt?

A trend that has become obvious is the parallel between elements of computer games and recent Hollywood movies featuring Ancient Egypt. In 'The Age of Mythology', for example, the Anubis-warriors strike a chord with the armies of Anubis seen in *The Mummy Returns* (Universal Studios, May 2001). Likewise, the new 'Tomb Raider' game, 'The Last Revelation', has many similarities with the blockbusting movie *The Mummy* (see Lupton Chapter 2, this volume), the plot of which revolves around Lara Croft as she tries to counter the evil god Seth, whom she unwittingly released from his sleep of death, and re-entomb him inside the pyramids. She must also discover the burial place of Cleopatra and her temples in order to find the treasures that made her Queen of the Nile and goddess of light. The critics were quick to link the plot of 'The Last Revelation' to *The Mummy* (Chi Kong Lui in www.gamescritics.com/review_tomb-raider4.html), with Seth in place of Imhotep and Cleopatra's city a substitute for the legend of Hamunaptra. The plot of 'Tomb Raider' also encompasses details such as the alignment of the stars at the turn of the Millennium (www.hotgames.com), quite regardless of the fact that the Millennium is a Christian event that would have had no bearing on Ancient Egypt whatsoever. So it seems that 'The Last Revelation' sought, unashamedly, to incorporate every aspect of 'Egyptomania' currently in fashion. All, that is, except for aliens from outer space.

That concept has been reserved by the game 'Serious Sam' (Croteam Games: www.croteam.com).

Again, Hollywood and computer games have their parallels with 'Serious Sam' and the 1995 blockbuster *Stargate*. 'Serious Sam' has the following plot: at some time in the near future a galaxy-roaming alien named Mental decides to mass-murder earthlings for fun. Fortunately, the humans have a secret weapon left to them by an extinct civilization from Sirius that had been to Ancient Egypt and whose pictograms are very similar to ancient Egyptian hieroglyphs. The weapon – the Timelock – enables special forces agent Sam 'Serious' Stone to return to the time of Ancient Egypt to assassinate Mental before he has developed too much power. The notion that aliens from outer space had been present in Ancient Egypt has been a very popular one since von Daniken published *Chariots of the Gods?* in 1971. That a computer game should adopt this idea is of little surprise, for it has all the elements required for such entertainment: a familiar yet entertaining plot, aliens to destroy and a perfect environment in which to set it all:

> cyberpunk meets fantasy fiction and the beautiful world of Ancient Egypt.

> (www.croteam.com)

Meanwhile, the persevering 'Age of Empires I' player who activates the 'pyramid level' (Figure 14:1) is proclaimed on the screen as '*VICTORIOUS!*'.

Enough said.

Acknowledgments

Grateful thanks to Andrew Gardner, John Tait, Justin Pollard, Paul Jordan, Ray Sutcliffe and Peter Ucko for many attempts to improve this chapter, but all the faults remain ours.

Figure 14:1 A scene from 'Age of Empires I': the victorious player has battled through, and has successfully constructed a pyramid (© Microsoft/Ensemble Studios).

References

Note: references to chapters and books in the *Encounters with Ancient Egypt* series are denoted in bold type.

Abbas, J. 1992, *Athar Misr al-qadimah fi Kitabat al-rahalah al-'arab wa al-ajanib*. Cairo: Al-Dar Al-Masriah Al-Lubnaniah

Abdel Qader, A-M. 1996, *Hekayaat al Om Tuffaha*. Cairo: Il Hay at il 'Aamat lil Kitaab

Abdoun, S. 1971, *Genesi dell'Aida*. Parma: La Nazionale

Abercrombie, N. 1996, *Television and Society*. Cambridge: Polity

Adam, J-P. 1988, L'archéologie travestie, dans l'archéologie et son image, VIIIe rencontres internationales d'archéologie et d'histoire d'Antibes, 29–31 octobre 1987, Association pour la Promotion et la Diffusion des Connaissances Archéologiques, 185–199

Addy, S. M. 1998, *Rider Haggard and Egypt*. Accrington: AL Publications

Adkins, L. and R. Adkins 2000, *The Keys of Egypt*. London: HarperCollins

Aida 1976, Paris: L'Avant-Scène Opéra, 4 (1st edition)

Aida 1993, Paris: L'Avant-Scène Opéra, 4 (2nd edition revised)

Aida 1998, Programa. Madrid: Teatro Real de Madrid, 98

Aird, C. 2000, *Little Knell*. London: Macmillan

Albertson, E. 2000, *The Mummy's Curse*. San José, Cal: Writer's Showcase

Alcott, L. M. 1869, Lost in a Pyramid; or the Mummy's Curse. *The New World* 1

Alier, R. 1985, *La Corte de Faraón*. Madrid: Daimon

Allen, G. 1880, My New Year's Eve Among the Mummies. *Belgravia Magazine*

Allison, J. 1997, Dramatic and Double Vision. *The Times*, 23 September

Allison, J. 1998, Sicily's Grand Theatre Reopens. *The Times*, 13 May

Amal-Naguib, S. 1990, Egyptian Collections: Myth-makers and Generators of Culture. *Göttinger Miszellen* 114, 81–89

Anderson, C. 1994, *Hollywood TV: The Studio System in the Fifties*. Austin: University of Texas Press

Arthur, R. 1965, *The Three Investigators and the Mystery of the Whispering Mummy*. New York: Random House

Auerbach, J. A. 1999, *The Great Exhibition of 1851, A Nation on Display*. New Haven: Yale UP

Babcock, E. A. and A. C. Krey (trans.) 1943, *William of Tyre: A History of Deeds Done Beyond the Sea*. New York: Records of Civilization and Studies

Baikie, J. 1911, *Peeps at the Heavens*. London: A&C Black

Baikie, J. 1913, *Peeps at the Royal Navy*. London: A&C Black

Baikie, J. 1924, *A Century of Excavation in the Land of the Pharaohs*. London: Religious Tract Society

Baikie, J. 1932, *Egyptian Antiquities in the Nile Valley: A Descriptive Handbook*. London: Methuen

Bailey, F. 1957, *The Spirit of Masonry*. Tunbridge Wells: Lucis

Bailey, H. S. 1990, *The Art and Science of Book Publishing*. 3rd edition, Athens, Ohio: Ohio UP

Bakathir, A. A. 1940, *Akhenaton wa Nefertiti*. Cairo: Maktabat Misr

Ball, J. 1942, *Egypt in the Classical Geographers*. Cairo: Government Press

Baqader, A. 1997, Sociologia al-siaha. *Al-Fikr Al-Arabi* 89, 133–147

Barthes, R. 1984, *Camera Lucida*. London: Vintage

Bauder, D. 2000, ABC Strikes Gold with 'Ten Commandments'. *The Detroit News,* 20 April

Bauval, R. 1999, *Secret Chamber: The Quest for the Hall of Records*. London: Century

Bauval, R. and A. Gilbert 1994, *The Orion Mystery: Unlocking the Secrets of the Pyramids*. London: William Heinemann

Bauval, R. and A. Gilbert 1995, *The Orion Mystery*. London: Mandarin

Bauval, R. and G. Hancock 1996, *Keeper of Genesis*. London: William Heinemann

Beard, M. 1992, Souvenirs of Culture: Deciphering (in) the Museum. *Art History* 15, 505–332

Beard, M. and J. Henderson 1999, Rule(d) Britannia: Displaying Roman Britain in the Museum, in N. Merriman (ed.), *Making Early Histories in Museums*, 344–372. Leicester: Leicester UP

Beck, K. K. 1986, *Murder in a Mummy Case*. New York: Walker

Benavente, J. 1942, De Sobremesa-crónicas. *Obras Completas* 7

Benjamin of Tudela 1783, *Travels of Rabbi Benjamin, son of Jonah, of Tudela* (trans. Rev B. Gerrans). London: Messrs Robson, J. Murray, T. Davis, W. Law

Benjamin, W. 1992, *Illuminations*. London: Fontana

Bernal, M. 1991, *Black Athena: The Afro-Asiatic Roots of Classical Civilization Vol. 2, The Documentary and Archaeological Evidence*. London: Free Association Press

Bernal, M. 2003, Afrocentrism and Historical Models for the Foundation of Ancient Greece, in D. O'Connor and A. Reid (eds), *Ancient Egypt in Africa*, 23–30. London: UCL Press

Bernard, W. Bayle. 1833, *The Mummy, A Farce in One Act*. London: Duncombe and Moon

Boothby, G. 1894, A Professor of Egyptology. *The Graphic,* 10 December

Boothby, G. 1898, *Pharos the Egyptian*. London: Ward, Lock and Co

Bourdieu, P. 1996, *Photography*. Cambridge: Polity

Brier, B. 1994, *Egyptian Mummies*. New York: William Morrow

Brier, B. 1998, *The Encyclopedia of Mummies*. New York: Facts on File

British Museum 2001, *Shopping in the British Museum*. London: British Museum Press

Brown, E. 1739, *The Travels and Adventures of Edward Brown*. London: Bettesworth and Hitch

Brunas, M., J. Brunas and T. Weaver 1990, *Universal Horrors*. Jefferson, NC: McFarland

Budge, Sir E. A. Wallis 1893, *The Mummy: Chapters on Egyptian Funereal Archaeology*. Cambridge: CUP

Budge, Sir E. A. Wallis 1897, *The Nile: Notes for Travellers in Egypt*. London: Thos. Cook and Sons

Budge, Sir E. A. Wallis 1898, *The Book of the Dead*. London: Kegan Paul

Budge, Sir E. A. Wallis 1950, *The Rosetta Stone*. London: British Museum Press

Burnett, C. 2003, Images of Ancient Egypt in the Latin Middle Ages, in P. J. Ucko and T. C. Champion (eds), *The Wisdom of Egypt: changing visions through the ages*, 65–100. London: UCL Press

Butler, B. 2003, 'Egyptianizing' the Alexandrina: The Contemporary Revival of the Ancient Mouseion/Library, in J-M. Humbert and C. A. Price (eds), *Imhotep Today: Egyptianizing architecture*, 257–282. London: UCL Press

Butler, St John 1999, *Registering the Difference: Reading Literature through Register*. Manchester: Manchester UP

Cannuyer, C. 1984a, Les Pyramides d'Egypte dans la littérature médio-latine. *La Revue Belge de philologie et d'histoire* 62, 673–681

Cannuyer, C. 1984b, Une Desription Mecinnue de l'Egypte au XIIe siècle. *Göttinger Miszeuen* 70, 13–18

Carruthers, J. and L. Harris 1997, *African World History Project: The Preliminary Challenge*. Los Angeles: Association for the Study of Classical African Civilizations

Carter, H. and A. C. Mace 1954, *The Tomb of Tutenkhamun, Discovered by the Late Earl of Carnarvon and Howard Carter*. London: Cassell

Case, D. 1981, *The Third Grave*. Sauk City, Wisconsin: Arkham House

Cayce, E. 1990, *Edgar Cayce: Modern Prophet*. London: Outlet

Caygill, M. L. and M. N. Leese 1993, A Survey of Visitors to the British Museum 1992–3. London: British Museum Occasional Paper 101

Champion, T. C. 2003, Egypt and the Diffusion of Culture, in D. Jeffreys (ed.), *Views of Ancient Egypt since Napoleon Bonaparte: imperialism, colonialism and modern appropriations*, 127–146. London: UCL Press

Champollion, J-F. [1822] 1989, Lettre a Monsieur Dacier, secrétaire perpetuel de l'Académie Royale des inscriptions et belles-lettres relative a l'alphabet des hieroglyphs phonétiques employés par les Egyptiens pour inscrire sur leurs monuments les titres, les noms et les surnoms des souverains grecs et romains, in *Journal des Savants*. Paris: Fata Morgana

Champollion, J-F. 1824, *Précis du système hiéroglyphique des anciens Egyptiens, ou, Recherches sur les éléments premiers de cette écriture sacrée, sur leurs diverses combinaisons, et sur les rapports de ce système avec les autres méthodes graphiques Egyptiennes*. Paris: Imprimerie Royale

Chapaz, J. L. 1990, Mettre en scène Aida, in *L'Egitto fuori dell'Egitto, Dalla riscoperta all'Egittologia*, 83–87. Bologna: Acte du Congrès International tenu à Bologna

Clayton, P. 1982, *The Rediscovery of Ancient Egypt: Artists and Travellers in the Nineteenth Century*. London: Thames and Hudson

Cohen, E. 1984, Sociology of Tourism. *Annual Review of Sociology* 10, 373–392

Cohen, M. 1965, *Rudyard Kipling to Rider Haggard: The Record of a Friendship*. Rutherford, NJ: Fairleigh Dickinson UP

Cohn, L. 1993, All-Time Film Rental Champs, by Decade. *Variety* 345: A86–A106

Conner, P. 1979, *The Oriental Architecture of the West*. London: Thames and Hudson

Conner, P. 1983, *The Inspiration of Egypt. Its Influence on British Artists, Travellers and Designers, 1700–1900*. Brighton: Brighton Borough Council

Cook, R. 1979, *Sphinx*. New York: G. P. Putnam's Sons

Cook, R. J. 1996, *The Horizon of Khufu*. London: Seven Islands

Corriere della Sera 1996, Elefanti, laser e un serpente: *Aida* 'matala' nella Plaza de toros, 28 June

Corteggiani, J-P. 1990, Mariette invente Aïda. *Mémoires d'Egypte*, 226–247

Cox, D. R. 1985, *Arthur Conan Doyle*. New York: Frederick Ungar

Crick, M. 1989, Representations of International Tourism in the Social Sciences: Sun, Sex, Sights, Savings, Servility. *Annual Review of Anthropology* 18, 307–344

Curl, J. S. 1994, *Egyptomania: The Egyptian Revival*. Manchester: Manchester UP

Curran, B. A. 2003, The Renaissance Afterlife of Ancient Egypt (1400–1650), in P. J. Ucko and T. C. Champion (eds), *The Wisdom of Egypt: changing visions through the ages*, 101–132. London: UCL Press

Currie, T. 2000, *A Concise History of British Television 1930–2000*, Devon: Kelly

Daly, N. 1994, That Obscure Object of Desire: Victorian Commodity Culture and Fictions of the Mummy. *NOVEL* 28, 24–51

Danby, M. 1995, *Moorish Style*. London: Phaidon

Daniel, G. 1978, Introduction, in R. Sutcliffe (ed.), *Chronicle: Essays from Ten Years of Television Archaeology*, 7–9. London: BBC

Daniel, G. 1981, *A Short History of Archaeology*. London: Thames and Hudson

Daniel, G. 1992, *Writing for Antiquity*. London: Thames and Hudson

Daniken, E. 1971, *Chariots of the Gods?* New York: Bantam

Dannenfeldt, K. 1959, Egypt and Egyptian Antiquities in the Renaissance. *Studies in the Renaissance* 6, 7–27

Daumas, F. 1984, L'origine égyptienne de la tripartition de l'âme chez Platon, in *Mélanges Adolphe Gutbub*, 41–54. Montpellier: Montpellier University

David, R. and R. Archbold 2000, *Conversations With Mummies*. New York: William Morrow

Davies, N. de G. 1901, *The Mastaba of Ptahhetep and Akhethetep at Saqqarah*. London: Egypt Exploration Fund

Davis, W. 1979, Plato on Egyptian Art. *Journal of Egyptian Archaeology* 65, 121–127

Dawson, W. R. and E. P. Uphill 1995, *Who was Who in Egyptology*. 3rd edition, revised M. L. Bierbrier, London: Egypt Exploration Society

Debbane, J-P. 1987, *L'Histoire de France illustrée par la publicité – de Vercingétorix au paquebot Normandie*. Grenoble: J-P. Debbane

Del Vecchio, D. and T. Johnson 1992, *Peter Cushing: The Gentle Man of Horror and His 91 Films*. Jefferson, NC: McFarland

Delamaire, M-S. 2003, Searching for Egypt: Egypt in 19th Century American World Exhibitions, in J-M. Humbert and C. A. Price (eds), *Imhotep Today: Egyptianizing architecture*, 123–134. London: UCL Press

Denon, V. [1802] 1990, *Voyage dans la basse et la haute Égypte: pendant les campagnes du Général Bonaparte*. Cairo: Institut Français d'Archéologie Orientale

Description 1809–1828, *Description de l'Égypte, ou Recueil des observations et des recherches qui ont été faites en Égypte pendant l'expédition de l'Armée française*. 1st edition, Paris: Imprimerie Impériale

Diab, A. 1994, *Al-siaha fi misr fi al-qarn al-tasi' 'ashar*. Cairo: National Book Organization

Donnelly, I. 1882, *Atlantis, or the Antediluvian World*. New York: Harper

Douglas, C. N. 1999, The Mummy Case, in E. Gorman and M. H. Geenberg (eds), *Cat Crimes Through Time*, 319–335. New York: Carroll and Graf

Downey, M. T. 1992, *The Twentieth Century: Postwar Posterity and the Cold War*. New York: Macmillan

Doyle, A. C. 1890, The Ring of Thoth. *The Cornhill Magazine* 61, 46–61

Doyle, A. C. 1892, Lot No 249, *Harper's Monthly Magazine* 24, 525–544

Dreadstone, C. 1976, *The Mummy*. New York: Berkley

DuQuesne, T. 1999, Egypt's image in the European Enlightenment. *SESHAT* 3, 32–51

Eden, F. 1871, *The Nile without a Dragoman*. London: Henry King

Edwards, A. B. 1877, *A Thousand Miles up the Nile*. London: Longman

Edwards, A. B. 1891, *Pharaohs, Fellahs and Explorers*. New York: Harper

Edwards, I. E. S. 1947, *The Pyramids of Egypt*. Middlesex: Pelican

Edwards, L. 1923, *Jerry Todd and the Whispering Mummy*. Detroit: Sprague

El Daly, O. 1998, The People of Cairo as seen by Medieval Arab Travellers. *Bulletin of the Association for the Study of Travel in Egypt and the Near East* 6, 3–4

El Daly, O. 2000, Egyptian Deserts in Early Medieval Arabic Travel Writing, in J. Starkey and O. El Daly (eds), *Desert Travellers from Herodotus to D. H. Lawrence*, 21–32. Durham: Durham UP

El Daly, O. 2003, Ancient Egypt in Medieval Arabic Writings, in P. J. Ucko and T. C. Champion (eds), *The Wisdom of Egypt: changing visions through the ages*, 39–64. London: UCL Press

El Ghitani, G. 1992, *Moutoun il Ahram*. Cairo: Dar Sharqeyaat lil tawzi' wal nashr

El Hakim, T. 1933, *'Awdat il Rooh*. Cairo: Maktabat Misr

El Hakim, T. 1939, *Raqesas il ma 'bad*. Cairo: Maktabat Misr

El Hakim, T. 1955, *Isis*. Cairo: Maktabat Misr

El Khayat, M. 1997, *'Arsh Osoriis*. Cairo: Il Hay at il 'Aamat lil Kitaab

El Mahdy, C. 1989, *Mummies, Myth and Magic*. London: Thames and Hudson

Elbert, W. 2000, Cultural Treasures, Religious Monuments and Mass Tourism, in *Proceedings of Saint Catherine Foundation Symposium, 'Religious Heritage and Mass Culture in the Third Millennium'*. London

Elkins, A. 1994, *Dead Men's Hearts*. New York: Mysterious

Elliott, C., K. Griffis-Greenberg and R. Lunn 2003, Egypt in London – Entertainment and Commerce in the 20th Century Metropolis, in J-M. Humbert and C. A. Price (eds), *Imhotep Today: Egyptianizing architecture*, 105–122. London: UCL Press

Everett, H. D. 1896, *Iras, a Mystery*. New York: Harper

Fahim, H. 1998, European Travellers in Egypt: The Representation of the Host Culture, in P. Starkey and J. Starkey (eds), *Travellers in Egypt*, 7–12. London: Tauris

Fazzini, R. 1995, Presenting Egyptian Objects: Concepts and Approaches. *Museum International* 47, 38–43

Ferrante, I. 2001, www.opera.it

Findlater, J. 1996, 100 Years of Leighton House. *Apollo* February, 4–9

Finn, C. 2001, Mixed Messages – Archaeology and the Media. *Public Archaeology* 1, 261–268

Fisher, S. 2000a, What is the Appeal of Ancient Egypt? Qualitative Research with the Public. Susie Fisher Group: unpublished report for the Petrie Museum of Egyptian Archaeology, University College London

Fisher, S. 2000b, Exploring Peoples' Relationships with Egypt: Qualitative Research for the Petrie Museum. Susie Fisher Group: unpublished report for the Petrie Museum, University College London

Frank, K. 1994, *Lucie Duff Gordon: A Passage to Egypt*. London: Hamish Hamilton

Frayling, C. (ed.) 1992, *The Face of Tutankhamun*. London: Faber and Faber

Freeman, R. A. 1911, *The Eye of Osiris*. London: Hodder and Stoughton

Fresnault-Deruelle, P. 1989, *Les Images prises au mot (rhétorique de l'image fixe)*. Paris: Médiathèque Edilig

Gabra, G. 1993, *Cairo: The Coptic Museum, Old Churches*. Cairo: Egyptian International Publishing Co (Longman)

Game, A. 1993, *Undoing the Social*. Buckingham: Open UP

Gaunt, M. 1925, *The Mummy Moves*. New York: Edward T. Clode

Gautier, T. 1840, The Mummy's Foot. *Le Moniteur Universal*

Gautier, T. 1856, *Romance of a Mummy*. Philadelphia: J. B. Lippincott

Gedge, P. 1990, *The Scroll of Saqqara*. Toronto: Viking

Gellens, S. 1990, The Search for Knowledge in Medieval Muslim Societies: A Comparative Approach, in D. Eickelman and J. Piscatori (eds), *Muslim Travellers*, 50–65. London: Routledge

Genette, G. 1997, *Paratexts: Thresholds of Interpretation* (trans. J. E. Lewin). Cambridge: CUP

Ghidalia, V. 1971, *The Mummy Walks Among Us*. Middletown, CT: Xerox

Gillespie C. C. and M. Dewachter (eds) 1987, Monuments of Egypt, in *The Napoleonic Expedition: The Complete Archaeological Plates from La Description de l'Égypte*. Princeton: Princeton Architectural Press

Glover, D. 1996, *Vampires, Mummies and Liberals: Bram Stoker and the Politics of Popular Fiction*. Durham, NC: Duke UP

Glut, D. 1978, *Classic Movie Monsters*. Metuchen, NJ: Scarecrow

Gordon, L. D. [1865] 1997, *Letters from Egypt*. London: Virago

Grafton, A. 1991, *Defenders of the Text. The Traditions of Scholarship in Age 1450–1800*. Cambridge, Mass: Harvard UP

Grant, L. 1986, *The Long Night of the Grave*. West Kingston, Rhode Island: Donald M. Grant

Green, L. 1992, Mummymania. *KMT* 3, 34–37

Green, P. 1989, *Classical Bearings: Interpreting Ancient History and Culture*. London: Thames and Hudson

Greenberg, M. H. 1990, *Mummy Stories*. New York: Ballantine

Griffith, F. L. 1893, Preface, in P. E Newberry, *Beni Hasan Part 1*, vii–viii. London: Kegan Paul, Trench, Trübner and Co

Griffith, G. 1906, *The Mummy and Miss Nitocris*. London: T. W. Laurie

Haarmann, U. 1976, Eviliya _elebis bericht über die Altertümer von Gize. *TURICIA, Revue d'Etudes Turques* 8/9, 157–229

Haarmann, U. 1991, In Quest of the Spectacular: Noble and Learned Visitors to the Pyramids around 1200 AD, in W. Hallaq and D. Little (eds), *Islamic Studies Presented to Charles J. Adams*, 56–67. Leiden: Brill

Haarmann, U. 1996, Medieval Muslim Perceptions of Pharaonic Egypt, in A. Loprieno (ed.), *Ancient Egyptian Literature: History and Forms*, 605–627. Leiden: Brill

Haekal, M. H. 1930, Pharaonic Tomb from Saad. *Al Sayassa al Yawmeya*, 23 January

Haekal, M. H. 1933. Thawrat 'al-'adab. Cairo: Matba 'at 'al-Siyasah

Haggard, H. R. 1887, *She*. London: Longmans, Green and Co

Haggard, H. R. 1904, The Trade in the Dead. *Daily Mail*, 22 July

Haggard, H. R. 1912–1913, Smith and the Pharaohs. *The Strand Magazine* 264–266

Haikal, F. 1994, L'Eau dans les metaphores de l'Egypte ancienne, *Bulletin de l'Institut Français d'Archéologie Orientale du Caire*, 205–211

Haikal, F. 2003, How Does Egypt View Her Past? Paper presented to the American Research Center, Egypt, Annual Meeting, Atlanta, April

Haikal. F. 1997, A Gesture of Thanksgiving in Ancient Egypt, in H. Guksch and D. Polz (eds), *Stationen Beitrage zur Kulturegeschichte Ägyptens*, 291–292. Mainz: Philipp von Zabern

Haining, P. 1988, *The Mummy: Stories of the Living Corpse*. London: Severn House

Halberstam, D. 1993, *The Fifties*. New York: Villard

Halliwell, L. 1986, *The Dead That Walk*. London: Grafton

Hamill, J. and P. Mollier 2003, Rebuilding the Sanctuaries of Memphis: Egypt in Masonic Iconography and Architecture, in J-M. Humbert and C. A. Price (eds), *Imhotep Today: Egyptianizing architecture*, 207–220. London: UCL Press

Hancock, G. 1995, *Fingerprints of the Gods*. London: William Heinemann

Hancock, G. 2001, *Fingerprints of the Gods* (revised edition). London: Century

Hancock, G., R. Bauval and J. Grigsby 1998, *The Mars Mystery*. London: Michael Joseph

Hancock, G. and S. Faia 1998, *Heaven's Mirror. Quest for the Lost Civilization*. London: Michael Joseph

Hankey, J. 2001, *A Passion for Egypt: Arthur Weigall, Tutankhamun and the 'Curse of the Pharaohs'*. London: Tauris

Hard, T. W. 1979, *Sum VII*. New York: Harper and Row

Harris, E. and J. Harris 1965, *The Oriental Cults in Roman Britain*. Leiden: Brill

Harrison, R. G. 1978, The Tutankhamun Post-Mortem, in R. Sutcliffe (ed.), *Chronicle: Essays from Ten Years of Television Archaeology*, 41–52. London: BBC

Harrison, T. 2003, Upside Down and Back to Front: Herodotus and the Greek Encounter with Egypt, in R. Matthews and C. Roemer (eds), *Ancient Perspectives on Egypt*, 145–156. London: UCL Press

Hassan, F. 2003, Imperialist Appropriations of Egyptian Obelisks, in D. Jeffreys (ed.), *Views of Ancient Egypt since Napoleon Bonaparte: imperialism, colonialism and modern appropriations*, 19–68. London: UCL Press

Hawass, Z. 2000, *Valley of the Golden Mummies*. New York: Harry N. Abrams

Hawthorne, J. 1893, The Unseen Man's Story, in J. Hawthorne (ed.), *Six Cent Sam's*, 218–253. St Paul: Price-McGill

Hayes, W. C. 1941, Daily Life in Egypt. *National Geographic* 80, 419–514

Hermans, J. 2002, L'Esthétique du geste polyphonique. *Magazine de La Monnaie de Bruxelles* 51, February–March, 8

Heyerdahl, T. 1970, *The Ra Expeditions*. London: George Allen and Unwin

Higgins, D. S. 1980, *The Private Diaries of Sir H. Rider Haggard, 1914–1925*. New York: Stein and Day

Higham, C. 1976, *The Adventures of Conan Doyle*. New York: W. W. Norton

Holt, P. 1998, Pietro Della Valle in Ottoman Egypt, 1615–1616, in P. Starkey and J. Starkey (eds), *Travellers in Egypt*, 15–23. London: Tauris

Holt, V. 1973, *Curse of the Kings*. New York: Doubleday

Hopwood, D. 1989, *Tales of Empire: The British in the Middle East*. London: Tauris

Hopwood, D. 1999, *Sexual Encounters in the Middle East*. Reading: Garnet

Horbury, M. 2003, The British and the Copts, in D. Jeffreys (ed.), *Views of Ancient Egypt since Napoleon Bonaparte: imperialism, colonialism and modern appropriations*, 153–170. London: UCL Press

Hornung, E. 2001, *The Secret Lore of Egypt: its impact on the West*. Ithaca: Cornell UP

Hugo, V. 1831, *Notre Dame de Paris*. Paris: Charles Gosselin

Humbert, J-M. 1976, A propos de l'égyptomanie dans l'oeuvre de Verdi: attribution à Auguste Mariette d'un scénario anonyme de l'opéra *Aïda*. *Revue de Musicologie* 62, 229–256

Humbert, J-M. 1985, Mariette Pacha and Verdi's *Aida*. *Antiquity* 59, 101–104

Humbert, J-M. 1989, *L'Egyptomanie dans l'art occidentale*. Paris: ACR

Humbert, J-M. 2003, The Egyptianizing Pyramid, from the 18th to the 20th Century, in J-M. Humbert and C. A. Price (eds), *Imhotep Today: Egyptianizing architecture*, 25–40. London: UCL Press

Humbert, J-M., M. Pantazzi and Ch. Ziegler (eds) 1994, *Egyptomania. L'Egypte dans l'art occidental 1730–1930*, Catalogue d'exposition, Paris, 20 janvier–18 avril 1994. Paris: Réunion des Musées Nationaux

Hume, F. 1908, *The Green Mummy*. New York: G. W. Dillingham

Hunke, S. [1960] 2001, *Allahs Sonne über dem Abendland. Unser arabisches Erbe*. Stuttgart: Fischer Taschenbuch

Ibn Zahirah 1969, *Mahasin Misr wa Al-Qahirah* (attributed also to Abu Hamid Al-Qudisi). Cairo: Dar Al-Kutub

Iversen, E. 1961, *The Myth of Egypt and its Hieroglyphs in European Tradition*. Copenhagen: Gad

Jakeman, J. 1997, *The Egyptian Coffin*. London: Headline

James, S. 1999, *The Atlantic Celts. Ancient People or Modern Invention?* London: British Museum Press

James, S. 2001, The Roman Galley-Slave: Ben Hur and the Birth of a Factoid. *Public Archaeology* 2, 35–49

James, T. G. H. 1992, *Howard Carter: The Path to Tutankhamun.* London: Kegan Paul

James, T. G. H. 1997, *Egypt Revealed. Artist-Travellers in an Antique Land.* London: Folio Society

Jeffreys, D. 2003, Introduction – Two Hundred Years of Ancient Egypt: Modern History and Ancient Archaeology, in D. Jeffreys (ed.), *Views of Ancient Egypt since Napoleon Bonaparte: imperialism, colonialism and modern appropriations*, 1–18. London: UCL Press

Jensen, P. M. 1996, Excavating the Mummy. *Midnight Marquee* 52, 5–13

Johnson, C. S. 1991, The Limbs of Osiris: Reed's *Mumbo Jumbo* and Hollywood's *The Mummy. MELUS* 17, 105–115

Johnson, T. and S. D. Cowie 2001, *The Mummy in Fact, Fiction, and Film.* Jefferson, NC: McFarland

Jordan, P. 1981, Archaeology and Television, in J. D. Evans, B. Cunclifffe and C. Renfrew (eds), *Antiquity and Man. Essays in honour of Glyn Daniel*, 207–213. London: Thames and Hudson

Jung, C. G. 1956/1967, *The Collected Works, vol. 5: Symbols of Transformation.* London: Routledge and Kegan Paul

Jung, C. G. 1959, *The Collected Works, vol. 9 Pt. 1: The Archetypes and the Collective Unconscious.* London: Routledge and Kegan Paul

Kákosy, L. 1993, Plato and Egypt: The Egyptian Tradition, in I. Hahn (ed.), *Gedenkschrift Herausgegeben von György Németh*, 25–28. Budapest: Budapest UP

Karnouk, L. 1988, *Modern Egyptian Art: The Emergence of a National Style.* Cairo: American University in Cairo

Karnouk, L. 1995, *Contemporary Egyptian Art.* Cairo: American University in Cairo

Khadry, A., A. Abdel-Hamid and A. Safwat Al-Alfy 1985, *Our National Heritage: challenge and response.* Cairo: Egyptian Antiquities Organization

Kinnard, R. 1995, *Horror in Silent Films.* Jefferson, NC: McFarland

Kircher, A. 1650, *Obeliscus Pamphilias.* Rome: Grigorius

Kircher, A. 1652–1654, *Oedipus Aegyptiacus.* Rome: Vitalis Mascardi

Lafon, F. 1984, A l'assaut d'Aïda. *Le Monde de la Musique* 66, April, 23

Lane, E. W. 1860, *An Account of the Manners and Customs of the Modern Egyptians.* London: John Murray

Lant, A. 1992, The Curse of the Pharaoh, or How Cinema Contracted Egyptomania. *October* 59, 87–112

Lawton, I. and C. Ogilvie-Herald 2000, *Giza: The Truth.* London: Virgin

Leatherdale, C. 1996, Introduction, in C. Leatherdale (ed.), *The Annotated Jewel of Seven Stars*, 7–16. Westcliff-on-Sea: Desert Island Books

Lehner, M. 1974, *The Egyptian Heritage, based on Edgar Cayce.* Virginian Beach: ARE

Lehner, M. 1997, *The Complete Pyramids.* London: Thames and Hudson

Leiper, N. 1979, The Framework of Tourism: Towards a Definition of Tourism, Tourist and the Tourist Industry. *Annual Tourism Research* 6, 390–407

Lewis, H. Spencer 1936, *The Symbolic Prophecy of the Great Pyramid.* San José: Ancient and Mystic Order Rosae Crucis

Lichtheim, M. 1973, *Ancient Egyptian Literature I.* Berkeley: University of California Press

Lichtheim, M. 1980, *Ancient Egyptian Literature III.* Berkeley: University of California Press

Lindsay, J. 1970, *The Origins of Alchemy in Graeco-Roman Egypt*. London: Frederick Muller

Loprieno, A. 2003, Travel and Fiction in Egyptian Literature, in D. O'Connor and S. Quirke (eds), *Mysterious Lands*, 31–52. London: UCL Press

Loudon, J. W. 1827, *The Mummy – a Tale of the 22nd Century*. London: Henry Colburn

Luckert, K. W. 1991, *Egyptian Light and Hebrew Fire*. Albany: SUNY

MacDonald, K. C. 2003, Cheikh Anta Diop and Ancient Egypt in Africa, in D. O'Connor and A. Reid (eds), *Ancient Egypt in Africa*, 93–106. London: UCL Press

MacDonald, S. 2002, An Experiment in Access. *Museologia* 2, 101–108

Madison, A. 1980, *Mummies in Fact and Fiction*. New York: Franklin Watts

Maehler, H. 1992, Visitors to Elephantine: Who Were They?, in J. Johnson (ed.), *Life in a Multi-Cultural Society: Egypt from Cambysés to Constantine and Beyond*, 209–215. Chicago: Oriental Institute

Maehler, H. 2003, Roman Poets on Egypt, in R. Matthews and C. Roemer (eds), *Ancient Perspectives on Egypt*, 203–216. London: UCL Press

Mahfouz, N. 1939, *'Abath il aqdaar*. Cairo: Maktabat Misr

Mahfouz, N. 1943, *Radopis*. Cairo: Maktabat Misr

Mahfouz, N. 1944, *kifah Tiba*. Cairo: Maktabat Misr

Mahfouz, N. 1983, *Amam al 'Arsh*. Cairo: Maktabat Misr

Mahfouz, N. 1985, *Il 'Aayesh fi il haqiqa*. Cairo: Maktabat Misr

Mahfouz, N. 2002, *Views from the Other World: Ancient Egyptian Tales*. Cairo: American University in Cairo

Mank, G. W. 1989, Production Background, in P. J. Riley (ed.), *The Mummy*, 21–34. Absecon, NJ: MagicImage Filmbooks

Manley, D. 1991, *The Nile: A Traveller's Anthology*. London: Cassell

Mann, J. 1939, *The Ninth Life*. London: Wright and Brown

Marlowe, J. 1974, *Spoiling the Egyptians*. London: Andre Deutsch

Maspero, G. 1894, *The Dawn of Civilization: Egypt and Chaldaea*. London: SPCK

Maspero, G. 1904, *Notice biographique de Mariette*. Paris: Bibliothèque Égyptologique XVIII

McLuhan, E. and F. Zingrone (eds) 1997, *Marshall McLuhan 1911–1980: Essential McLuhan*. London: Routledge

Merriman, N. (ed.) 1999, *Making Early Histories in Museums*. Leicester: Leicester UP

Meunier, P. 1983, L'air plouc d'Aïda. *Télérama*, 27 July

Milnes, R. 1996, Abstract but Absorbing Night by the Nile. *The Times*, 25 January

Milnes, R. 1999, Silly Bit of Pyramid Setting. *The Times*, 7 May

Mitchell, G. 1998, Winning a Battle but Losing the War Over the Blacklist. *New York Times*, 25 January

Montserrat, D. 1998, Louisa May Alcott and the Mummy's Curse. *KMT* 9, 70

Morales Lezcano, V. 1988, *Africanísmo y orientalísmo español en el siglo XIX*. Madrid: UNED

Morales Lezcano, V. 1993, *España y el mundo Árabe. Imágenes cruzadas*. Madrid: Agencia Española de Cooperacion Internacional

Morrah, D. 1933, *The Mummy Case*. New York: Harper

Moser, S. 1999, The Dilemma of Didactic Displays: Habitat Dioramas, Life Groups and Reconstructions of the Past, in N. Merriman (ed.), *Making Early Histories in Museums*, 95–116. Leicester: Leicester UP

Moser, S. 2001, Archaeological Representation. The Visual Conventions for Constructing Knowledge about the Past, in I. Hodder (ed.), *Archaeological Theory Today*, 262–283. Cambridge: Polity

Motawi, S. and N. Merriman 2000, Ancient and Modern Egypt in the British Museum, paper given at *Encounters with Ancient Egypt* conference, Institute of Archaeology, UCL, 16–18 December 2000

Moukhtar, G. M. 1964/1965, Ahmad Kamal il 'aalim il athary il awal fi misr. *English Historical Review* 12, 43–57

Murray, M. A. 1905, *Saqqara Mastabas I–II*. London: British School of Archaeology in Egypt/B. Quaritch

Naguib, S-A. 1993, Miroirs du passé. *Cahiers de la Société d'Egyptologie de Genève* 2

Naud, Y. 1977, *The Curse of the Pharaohs*. Geneva: Editions Ferni

Netton, I. 1996, *Seek Knowledge: Thought and Travel in the House of Islam*. Surrey: Curzon

Neumann, E. 1954, *The Origins and History of Consciousness*. Princeton: Princeton UP

North, J. 2003, Attributing Colour to the Ancient Egyptians: Reflections on *Black Athena*, in D. O'Connor and A. Reid (eds), *Ancient Egypt in Africa*, 31–38. London: UCL Press

Notman, D. 1986, Ancient Scannings, in R. David (ed.), *Science in Egyptology*, 251–320. Manchester: Manchester UP

O'Connor, D. and A. Reid (eds) 2003a, *Ancient Egypt in Africa*. London: UCL Press

O'Connor, D. and A. Reid 2003b, Introduction – Locating Ancient Egypt in Africa: Modern Theories, Past Realities, in D. O'Connor and A. Reid (eds), *Ancient Egypt in Africa*, 1–22. London: UCL Press

Oakley, J. R. 1990, *In God's Country: America in the Fifties*. New York: Dembner

Paine, M. 1988, *Cities of the Dead*. New York: Charter

Panckoucke, C. L. F. 1821–1830, *Description de l'Égypte, ou Recueil des observations et des recherches qui ont été faites en Égypte pendant l'expédition de l'Armée française*. 2nd edition, Paris: Imprimerie de C. L. F. Panckoucke

Pantazzi, M. 1994, Les années Toutankhamon, in J-M. Humbert, M. Pantazzi and Ch. Ziegler 1994, *Egyptomania. L'Egypte dans l'art occidental 1730–1930*, Catalogue d'exposition, Paris, 20 janvier–18 avril 1994. Paris: Réunion des Musées Nationaux

Parker, R. B. and R. Sabin 1974, *Practical Guide to Islamic Monuments in Cairo*. Cairo: AUC

Patterson, J. T. 1996, *Grand Expectations: The United States, 1945–1974*. Oxford: OUP

Pearce, S. 1994, Collecting Reconsidered, in S. Pearce (ed.), *Interpreting Objects and Collections*, 193–204. London: Routledge

Pearce, S. 1995, *On Collecting*. London: Routledge

'Perronik' 1975, *Pourquoi la résurgence de l'Ordre du Temple?* Monte Carlo: Editions de la Pensée Solaire

Perry, W. J. 1923, *The Children of the Sun: A Study in the Early History of Civilization*. London: Methuen

Petrie, W. M. F. 1901, *Diospolis Parva. The Cemeteries of Abadiyeh and Hu 1898–9*. London: Egyptian Exploration Fund

Pettigrew, T. J. 1834, *History of Egyptian Mummies*. London: Longman, Rees, Orme, Brown, Green and Longman

Phillips, D. 1997, *Exhibiting Authenticity*. Manchester: Manchester UP

Pick, C. 1991, *Egypt: A Traveller's Anthology*. London: John Murray

Picknett, L. and C. Prince 1997, *The Templar Revelation*. London: Bantam

Picknett, L. and C. Prince 1999, *The Stargate Conspiracy*. London: Little, Brown

Picknett, L. and C. Prince 2000, *The Stargate Conspiracy: Revealing the Truth Behind Extraterrestrial Contact, Military Intelligence and the Mysteries of Ancient Egypt*. London: Warner

Poe, Edgar Allan 1845, Some Words with a Mummy. *The American Whig Review* 1

Poore, D. A. 1995, *The Mummy's Mirror*. New York: Zebra

Pousaz, E. 1999, Représenter Aida aujourd'hui, in *Programme des representations d'Aïda*, 25–31. Geneva: Grand Théâtre de Genève

Pratt, A. 1910, *The Living Mummy*. New York: Frederick A. Stokes

Price, C. and J-M. Humbert 2003, Introduction – An Architecture Between Dream and Meaning, in J-M. Humbert and C. A. Price (eds), *Imhotep Today: Egyptianizing architecture*, 1–24. London: UCL Press

Pringle, H. 2001, *The Mummy Congress*. New York: Hyperion

Pronzini, B. 1980, *Mummy! A Chrestomathy of Crypt-ology*. New York: Arbor House

Quirke, S. 2003, Measuring the Underworld, in D. O'Connor and S. Quirke (eds), *Mysterious Lands*, 161–182. London: UCL Press

Radwan, A. 1993, *Catalogue of the Faculty of Archaeology*, Cairo University

Rauch, A. 1994, Introduction, in A. Rauch (ed.), *The Mummy*. Ann Arbor: University of Michigan Press

Rayner, E. 1991, *The Independent Mind in British Psychoanalysis*. London: Free Association Press

Rees, J. 1995, *Writings on the Nile*. London: Rubicon

Reeves, N. 1990, *The Complete Tutankhamun*. London: Thames and Hudson

Reid, D. M. 1985, Indigenous Egyptology: The Decolonization of a Profession? *Journal of the American Oriental Society* 105, 233–246

Reid, D. M. 2002, *Whose Pharaohs? Archaeology, Museums and Egyptian National Identity from Napoleon to World War I*. Berkeley: University of California Press

Reilly, C. P. 1974, *Athanasius Kircher, S. J. Master of a Hundred Arts 1602–1680*, Rome and Wiesbaden: Edizioni del Mondo

Reisner, G. A. 1942–1955, *A History of the Giza Necropolis I, II*. Cambridge, Mass: Harvard UP

Rice, A. 1989, *The Mummy, or Ramses the Damned*. New York: Ballantine

Rice, M. 1984, *Search for the Paradise Land*. Harlow: Longman

Rice, M. 1997, *Egypt's Legacy. The Archetypes of Western Civilization 3000–30 BC*. London: Routledge

Rickels, L. A. 1992, Mummy's Curse. *American Journal of Semiotics* 9, 47–58

Ridley, M. 1998, *The Tutankhamun Exhibition: Souvenir Guide*. Dorchester: World Heritage

Riley, P. J. (ed.) 1989, *The Mummy*. Absecon, NJ: MagicImage Filmbooks

Robinson, L. W. 1972, *Edgar Cayce's Story of the Origin and Destiny of Man*. London: Neville Spearman

Rohmer, S. 1903, The Mysterious Mummy. *Pearson's Weekly Magazine*, Christmas extra issue

Rohmer, S. 1904, The Leopard-Couch. *Chambers' Journal*, 30 January

Rohmer, S. 1913, The Headless Mummies. *The New Magazine* 56

Rohmer, S. 1914–1915, Brood of the Witch Queen. *The Premier Magazine*, May–January

Rohmer, S. 1916, In The Valley of the Sorceress. *The Premier Magazine*, January

Rohmer, S. 1917, Death-Ring of Sneferu. *The Premier Magazine*, November

Rohmer, S. 1918, The Whispering Mummy. *The Premier Magazine*, March

Rohmer, S. 1920, *The Green Eyes Of Bast*. New York: McBride

Rohmer, S. 1923, It Came Out of Egypt. *Munsey's Magazine*, September–November

Rohmer, S. 1925, The Treasure of Taia. *Munsey's Magazine*, 17 November

Rohmer, S. 1928, *She Who Sleeps*. New York: Doubleday, Doran and Co

Rohmer, S. 1931, *The Daughter of Fu Manchu*. New York: Doubleday, Doran and Co

Rohmer, S. 1933, The Witch's Son Mystery. *Illustrated Detective Magazine*, March–October

Rohmer, S. 1938, The Mummy That Walked. *Collier's Weekly*, 15 January

Rohmer, S. 1939, The Mummy of Cleopatra, in S. Rohmer (ed.), *Salute to Bazarada*, 130–157. London: Cassell

Rohmer, S. 1944, The Mark of Maat. *Collier's Magazine*, 15 January

Roman, S. 1990, *The Development of Islamic Library Collections in Western Europe and North America*. London and New York: Mansell

Romer, J. 1981, *Valley of the Kings*. New York: Henry Holt

Romer, J. 1982, *Romer's Egypt*. London: Michael Joseph

Romer, J. 1993, *The Rape of Tutankhamun*. London: Michael O'Mara

Rosenthal, F. 1997, The Stranger in Medieval Islam. *Arabica* 44, 35–75

Roullet, A. 1972, *The Egyptian and Egyptianizing Monuments of Imperial Rome*. Leiden: Brill

Roux, M-A. 2001, in *Le Monde*, 14 September

Rubincam, E. R. 2001, John Balderston. *Filmfax*, 87/88, 86–89

Rutherford, I. 2003, Pilgrimage in Greco-Roman Egypt: New Perspectives on Graffiti from the Memnonion at Abydos, in R. Matthews and C. Roemer (eds), *Ancient Perspectives on Egypt*, 171–190. London: UCL Press

Saad el Din, M. and J. Cromer 1991, *Under Egypt's Spell: the influence of Egypt on writers in English from the 18th century*. London: Bellew

Sadgrove, P. 1998, Travellers' Rendezvous and Cultural Institutions in Muhammad 'Ali's Egypt, in P. Starkey and J. Starkey (eds), *Travellers in Egypt*, 257–266. London: Tauris

Saint-Yves d'Alveydre, A. 1903, *L'Archéomètre*. Paris

Saleh, M. and H. Sourouzian 1987, *Official Catalogue of the Cairo Museum*. Cairo: Organization of Egyptian Antiquities

Schoch, R. M. 1992, Redating the Great Sphinx of Giza. *KMT* 3

Schwaller de Lubicz, R. A. 1998, *The Temple of Man: Apet of the South at Luxor* (trans. D. Lawlor and R. Lawlor). Rochester, VT: Inner Traditions

Sheikholeslami, C. 1996, in *Cairo Today*, March and April

Shelley, M. W. 1818, *Frankenstein*. London: Lackington, Hughes, Harding, Mavor and Jones

Silberman, N. A. 1995, Promised Lands and Chosen Peoples: The Politics and Poetics of Archaeological Narrative, in P. L. Kohl and C. Fawcett (eds), *Nationalism, Politics and the Practice of Archaeology*, 249–262. Cambridge: CUP

Silberman, N. A. 1999, Is Archaeology Ready for Prime Time? Digging and Discovery as Mass Entertainment. *Archaeology* May/June, 79–82

Silverman, D. P. 1987, The Curse of the Curse of the Pharaohs. *Expedition* 29:2, 56–63

Silverman, D. P. (ed.) 1997, *Ancient Egypt*. Oxford: OUP

Sirvin, R. 1987, Le mariage d'Aïda et de l'ordinateur. *Le Figaro*, 3 August

Skal, D. J. 1993, *The Monster Show: A Cultural History of Horror*. New York: W. W. Norton

Smith, G. E. 1923, *The Ancient Egyptians and the Origins of Civilization*. London: Harper

Smith, H. S. 1983, in H. S. Smith and R. M. Hall (eds), *Ancient Centres of Egyptian Civilization*, 5–6. London: Egyptian Education Bureau

Sontag, S. 1980, *On Photography.* Harmondsworth: Penguin

Starkey, P. and J. Starkey (eds) 1998, *Travellers in Egypt.* London: Tauris

Stephens, J. R. 2001, *Into the Mummy's Tomb.* New York: Berkley

Stevenson, B. 1917, *A King in Babylon.* Boston: Small, Maynard

Stewart, S. 1993, *On Longing.* Durham, NC: Duke UP

Stoker, B. 1897, *Dracula.* London: Constable

Stoker, B. 1903, *The Jewel of the Seven Stars.* London: Heinemann

Sullerot, E. 1966, *La Presse féminine.* Paris: Armand Colin

Sutcliffe, R. (ed.) 1978, *Chronicle: Essays from Ten Years of Television Archaeology.* London: BBC

Sweetman, J. 1988, *The Oriental Obsession.* Cambridge: CUP

Tait, J. 2003, The Wisdom of Egypt: Classical Views, in P. J. Ucko and T. C. Champion (eds), *The Wisdom of Egypt: changing visions through the ages*, 23–38. London: UCL Press

Temple, R. K. G. 1998, *The Sirius Mystery: New Scientific Evidence of Alien Contact 5,000 years ago.* Revised edition, London: Sidgwick and Jackson

Thompson, J. 2003, "Purveyor-General to the Hieroglyphics": Sir William Gell and the Development of Egyptology, in D. Jeffreys (ed.), *Views of Ancient Egypt since Napoleon Bonaparte: imperialism, colonialism and modern appropriations*, 77–86. London: UCL Press

Thurston, C. 2000, *The Eye of Horus.* New York: William Morrow

Thurston, E. T. 1926, *Mr Bottleby Does Something.* New York: George H. Doran

Tuñón de Lara, M. (ed.) 1993, *Revolución burguesa, oligarquía y constitucionalísmo 1834–1923, Vol. VII de Historia de España.* Barcelona: Labor

Tuska, J. 1984, *Dark Cinema: American Film Noir in Cultural Perspective.* Westport: Greenwood

Tyldesley, J. 2000, *The Private Lives of the Pharaohs.* London: Channel 4 Books

Ucko, P. J. and T. C. Champion (eds) 2003, *The Wisdom of Egypt: changing visions through the ages*. London: UCL Press

Unwin, S. 1960, *The Truth About Publishing.* 7th edition, London: Allen and Unwin

Unwin, S. 1976, *The Truth About Publishing.* 8th edition, revised and partly rewritten by Philip Unwin, London: Allen and Unwin

Usick, P. 2002, *Adventures in Egypt and Nubia. The Travels of William John Bankes (1786–1855).* London: British Museum Press

Van Dine, S. S. 1930, *The Scarab Murder Case.* New York: Charles Scribner's Sons

Van't Dack, E. 1983, Les Relations entre l'Égypte ptolémaïque et l'Italie, in E. Van't Dack, P. van Dessel and W. van Gucht (eds), *Egypt and the Hellenistic World*, 383–406. Proceedings of the International Colloquium, Leuven, 24–26 May 1982, Lovanii: Studia Hellenistica 27

Vandenberg, P. 1975, *The Curse of the Pharaohs.* New York: J. B. Lippincott

VandenBroeck, A. 1987, *Al-Kemi: Hermetic, Occult, Political and Private Aspects of R. A. Schwaller de Lubicz.* Hudson: Lindisfarne

Vantini, G. 1975, *Oriental Sources Concerning Nubia.* Warsaw: Polish Academy of Sciences

Venturi, C. 1995, Che Luxor quell'Aida! *Lyrica, Opera e dintorni*, 21 September, 50–52

Vercoutter, J. 1986, *A la recherche de l'Égypte oubliée.* Paris: Gallimard

Vercoutter, J. 1992, *The Search for Ancient Egypt.* London: Thames and Hudson

Verdino-Süllword, C. M. 1991, in *Opera International,* July–August, 29

Vespa, B. (ed.) 2001, *Verdi e l'Arena.* Rome: Edizioni Fotogramma

Viale Ferrero, M. 1996, Aida à Milan. L'image de l'Egypte auz archives Ricordi, in J-M. Humbert (ed.), *L'Egyptomanie à l'Epreuve de l'Archéologie,* 531–550. Brussels: Gramm

Volkoff, O. 1970, *A la recherche de manuscrits en Egypte.* Cairo: Institut Français d'Archéologie Orientale

Wakeling, T. 1912, *Forged Egyptian Antiquities.* London: A&C Black

Walker, J. 1996, The Real Thing. *Museological Review* 2

Walker, J. 1997, Acquisition, Envy and the Museum Visitor, in S. Pearce (ed.), *Experiencing Material Culture in the Western World,* 255–263. Leicester: Leicester UP

Waltari, M. 1949, *The Egyptian.* New York: G. P. Putnam's Sons

Watt, W. M. 1972, *The Influence of Islam on Medieval Europe.* Edinburgh: Edinburgh UP

Weigall, A. 1923, The Malevolence of Ancient Egyptian Spirits, in A. Weigall, *Tutankhamen and Other Essays,* 110–126. London: Thornton Butterworth

Wells, M. 2001, Travel Shows 'portray paradise and hide reality'. *The Guardian,* 28 August

Werndly, A. and L. Marshall 2002, *The Language of Television.* London: Routledge

Werner, A. 2003, Egypt in London – Public and Private Displays in the 19th Century Metropolis, in J-M. Humbert and C. A. Price (eds), *Imhotep Today: Egyptianizing architecture,* 75–104. London: UCL Press

West, J. A. 1979, *Serpent in the Sky.* London: Wildwood House

Whitlatch, J. 1933, The Mummy. *The Mystery Magazine,* January

Wild, N. 1996, Eugène Lacoste et la première d'Aida à l'Opéra de Paris, in J-M. Humbert (ed.), *L'Egyptomanie à l'Epreuve de l'Archéologie,* 507–529. Brussels: Gramm

Wildung, D. 1995, What Visitors Want To See. *Museum International* 47, 4–9

Willingham, B. 1997, *The Lady's Mummy.* New York: Zebra

Wilson-Smith, T. 1996, *Napoleon and his Artists.* London: Constable

Winstone, H. V. F. 1991, *Howard Carter and the Discovery of the Tomb of Tutankhamun.* London: Constable

Witt, R. 1971, *Isis in the Ancient World.* Baltimore: Johns Hopkins UP

Wortham, J. D. 1971a, *British Egyptology.* Newton Abbot: David and Charles

Wortham, J. D. 1971b, *The Genesis of British Egyptology 1549–1906,* Norman: University of Oklahoma Press

Yapp, P. (ed.) 1983, *The Traveller's Dictionary of Quotation.* London: Routledge

Zaki, Abdel-Rahman 1943, *Al-Qahira* (in Arabic). Cairo: Dar El-Mustakbal

Ziegler, Ch. 1994, Tutankhamun and Art Deco, in J-M. Humbert, M. Pantazzi and Ch. Ziegler (eds) 1994, *Egyptomania. L'Egypte dans l'art occidental 1730–1930,* Catalogue d'exposition. Paris, 20 janvier–18 avril 1994. Paris: Réunion des Musées Nationaux

Index